AUSTRALIA
LBC Information Services
Brisbane ● Sydney ● Melbourne ● Perth

CANADA
Carswell
Ottawa ● Toronto ● Calgary ● Montreal ● Vancouver

AGENTS:
Steimatzky's Agency Ltd., Tel Aviv;
N. M. Tripathi (Private) Ltd., Bombay;
Eastern Law House (Private) Ltd., Calcutta;
M.P.P. House, Bangalore;
Universal Book Traders, Delhi;
Aditya Books, Delhi;
MacMillan Shuppan KK, Tokyo;
Pakistan Law House, Karachi

The New Law on
Disability Discrimination

The New Law on Disability Discrimination

with annotations by

Gareth Thomas

(LL.B., B.C.L., Senior Lecturer in Law,
University of East Anglia)

LONDON
SWEET & MAXWELL
1997

Published in 1997 by
Sweet & Maxwell Limited of
100 Avenue Road
London NW3 3PF
Typeset by MFK Information Services Ltd,
Hitchin, Herts
Printed and bound in Great Britain by
Butler & Tanner Ltd, Frome and London

A CIP catalogue record for this book is available
from The British Library

ISBN 0–421–57880–7

CONTENTS

Preface

The passage of the Disability Discrimination Act 1995 marks a significant watershed in the legal response to disability discrimination in the U.K. For the first time, the 6.5 million disabled people in the U.K. are to enjoy a legally enforceable right not to be discriminated against in relation to employment, the provision of goods, facilities and services, and the sale and letting of premises. The Act also imposes a duty on employers and service providers to make reasonable adjustments to policies, practices and physical facilities in order to enable disabled people to overcome barriers which place them at a substantial disadvantage in relation to employment, or which make it impossible or unreasonably difficult for them to gain access to goods, facilities or services. In addition, the Act makes detailed provision for the accessibility of public transport vehicles, requires schools, colleges, universities and LEAs to provide information on their arrangements and facilities for disabled people, and establishes the National Disability Council to advise the Government on discrimination against disabled people.

Hailed by the Minister for Disabled People, Alistair Burt, as a fundamental advance for the rights of disabled people, the Disability Discrimination Act has nevertheless been given a lukewarm reception by the disability movement, and has not halted the campaign for comprehensive civil rights legislation for disabled people. Some of the most serious objections to the Act are structural, for example, the exclusion of small employers from the employment provisions, the exclusion of education and transport from the right of access to goods, facilities and services, the absence of any express prohibition against indirect discrimination, and the failure to establish a Commission with powers to investigate complaints and to support those seeking to enforce their rights under the Act. Other criticisms focus on the inherent vagueness of many of the Act's key provisions, in particular the definition of disability, the scope of the justification defence and the extent of the duty to make reasonable adjustments. The meaning of these key provisions has to some extent been clarified by the regulations, guidance and Codes of Practice issued under the Act, but there is still considerable uncertainty over the scope of the Act's provisions, and it is likely to be some time before its full implications can be assessed.

In this book I have attempted to analyse and explain the new provisions, and to offer a critical assessment of their practical implications. The full text of the regulations, guidance and Codes of Practice issued under the Act to date are included, with annotations highlighting significant features and cross-referring to the relevant provisions of the Act. The annotations to the Act itself are reproduced here as they first appeared in Current Law Statutes 1995, c.50. It has not been possible to amend them to take account of the subsequently-issued regulations, guidance and Codes of Practice, but readers may care to note that many of the examples given by Ministers in debates on the Bill and quoted in the original annotations subsequently found their way into the guidance and Codes of Practice.

The provisions on protection against discrimination in the field of employment came into force on December 2, 1996, along with the duties on service

Preface

providers not to refuse goods, facilities and services, and the provisions concerning education. At the time of writing, the implementation dates for the duties on service providers to change policies, practices and procedures, to provide auxiliary aids and services and to remove physical barriers are yet to be announced, although it is widely expected that the first of these will be introduced in 1998.

I would like to record my thanks to Clare Farleigh, Jane Letts, Helen Weldon and David Wilson for their help in the early stages of my research into the Act, and to the School of Law at the University of East Anglia for granting me study leave, part of which was spent working on the book. As always, my personal thanks go to Cathie, Sam, Ffion and Eleri for their support and encouragement.

Gareth Thomas
February 1997

TABLE OF CASES

References are to the Introduction or the General Note to the specified section of the 1995 Act.

TABLE OF STATUTES

References are to the Introduction or the General Note to the specified section of the 1995 Act or to an Appendix.

xiii

TABLE OF STATUTORY INSTRUMENTS

References are to the General Note to the specified section of the 1995 Act or to an Appendix.

DISABILITY DISCRIMINATION ACT 1995*

(1995 C. 50)

---

* Annotations by Gareth Thomas, LL.B., B.C.L., Senior Lecturer in Law, University of East Anglia.

PART VII

SUPPLEMENTAL

PART VIII

MISCELLANEOUS

An Act to make it unlawful to discriminate against disabled persons in connection with employment, the provision of goods, facilities and services or the disposal or management of premises; to make provision about the employment of disabled persons; and to establish a National Disability Council. [8th November 1995]

PARLIAMENTARY DEBATES
Hansard, H.C. Vol. 253, col. 147; Vol. 257, cols. 697, 840. H.L. Vol. 564, cols. 800, 830, 1182, 1640, 1723, 1895, 1975; Vol. 565, cols. 608, 686, 1839; Vol. 566, cols. 114, 168, 205, 386, 434, 969.

INTRODUCTION AND GENERAL NOTE

The Disability Discrimination Act 1995 (c. 50) is the first piece of legislation in the U.K. to tackle discrimination against disabled people. It outlaws discrimination against disabled people in relation to employment, the provision of goods, facilities and services, and the sale and letting of property; it requires schools, colleges, universities and local education authorities to provide fuller information concerning their arrangements and facilities for disabled people; and it allows the Government to issue regulations setting minimum standards for the accessibility of land-based public transport for disabled people. It also establishes the National Disability Council and the Northern Ireland Disability Council to advise the Government on discrimination against disabled people. The Act, a Government-sponsored measure, was the culmination of a lengthy period of intense pressure for anti-discrimination legislation by disability rights campaigners, during which no fewer than 14 abortive Private Members' Bills were introduced. Until recently, the Government had consistently argued that discrimination against disabled people was a matter best tackled by education and persuasion, rather than by legislative means. However, in the aftermath of the furore surrounding the "talking-out" of the Civil Rights (Disabled

Persons) Bill in 1994, the Government published a Consultation Document on *Government Measures to Tackle Discrimination Against Disabled People* (July 1994), which invited views on the enactment of statutory anti-discrimination rights for disabled people. The Disability Discrimination Bill was published in early 1995, at the same time as the White Paper, *Ending discrimination against disabled people*, Cm. 2729.

As originally published, the Disability Discrimination Bill fell some way short of meeting the aspirations of disabled rights campaigners. The principal areas of concern were: the scope of the definition of disability in s.1, and in particular the exclusion of those with a history or reputation of disability, and those with a genetic predisposition to a disability; the exclusion of small firms from the employment provisions in Pt. II; the ability of employers and service providers to justify discrimination against disabled people in certain circumstances; the exclusion of education and transport from the right of access to goods and services under Pt. III; and the absence of a Commission with powers to investigate complaints of discrimination, to provide assistance to individuals in enforcing their rights, and to take enforcement action on its own account. The Bill was heavily amended during its passage through Parliament, more than doubling in length from 32 to 80 pages, and a number of these concerns were addressed in the process; for example, the definition of disability was extended to cover those with a history of disability, and measures were introduced in the areas of employment and transport, although falling some way short of the right not to be discriminated against advocated by many campaigners. Notwithstanding these amendments, the Disability Discrimination Act still fails to meet the aspirations of many disabled rights campaigners for comprehensive civil rights legislation, and is therefore unlikely to represent the last word of Parliament in this area.

A notable feature of the Act is the extent to which it allows for the issue of regulations, Guidance and Codes of Practice to expand upon and clarify a number of its most fundamental aspects, for example, the definition of disability, and the duty of employers and service providers to make reasonable adjustments.

Part I of the Act defines disability as a physical or mental impairment which has, or has had, a substantial and long-term adverse effect on a person's ability to carry out normal day-to-day activities. This definition is supplemented by Scheds. 1 and 2, which allow for regulations to be made clarifying the definition, and s.3, which empowers the Secretary of State to issue guidance about the matters to be taken into account in determining whether an impairment has the necessary substantial or long-term adverse effect.

Part II makes it unlawful for an employer who has 20 or more employees to discriminate against a disabled employee or job applicant in relation to employment by treating that person less favourably, for a reason which relates to his or her disability, than the employer treats or would treat others. Unlike the legislation prohibiting discrimination on grounds of sex or race however, discrimination by an employer against a disabled person may be justified if the reason for it is both material to the circumstances of the particular case and substantial. There is no specific prohibition on indirect discrimination, but the Act places a duty on employers to make reasonable adjustments to working practices and the physical environment where these would place a disabled job applicant or employee at a substantial disadvantage in comparison with people who are not disabled. An unjustified failure to make a reasonable adjustment will amount to unlawful discrimination. Where an employer leases premises, the Act provides that the landlord must not unreasonably withhold consent to alterations which the employer needs to make in order to comply with the duty to make reasonable adjustments. Enforcement is by complaint to an industrial tribunal, and the remedies available are similar to those which apply in cases of sex and race discrimination, *i.e.* a declaration of rights, compensation and a recommendation that the employer take steps to remove or reduce the effect of the discrimination on the complainant. The Act does not set a maximum award of compensation. This part of the Act also outlaws discrimination in trade organisations and against contract workers.

Part III makes it unlawful for a service provider (*i.e.* a provider of goods, facilities or services) to discriminate against a disabled person by treating that person less favourably, for a reason which relates to his or her disability, than he treats or would treat others. It also places a duty on service providers to make reasonable adjustments in relation to the provision of services to disabled people. So, a service provider must take reasonable steps (i) to change any practice, policy or procedure which makes it impossible or unreasonably difficult for a disabled person to make use of a service which is provided to other members of the public, (ii) to remove or alter any physical barrier which makes it impossible or unreasonably difficult for a disabled person to make use of such a service, or to provide some alternative means of making the service accessible and (iii) to provide auxiliary aids or services which would make it easier for disabled people to use their services. As in the case of employment, discrimination by a service provider may be justified in certain circumstances, for example, where the treatment is necessary in order to ensure that health and safety is not endangered, or to enable the service provider to continue providing the service to other members of the public. The Government has indicated its intention to use its powers under the Act to set a financial limit on the duty to make adjustments. The provisions in Pt. III apply to all goods, facilities and services, with the exception of education and transport vehicles. Part III also makes it unlawful to discriminate against a disabled person in connection with the sale, letting and management of premises, for example, by refusing to sell or rent property to a disabled person, or by offering the property on worse terms than would be offered to anyone else. Enforcement under Pt. III is by way of complaint in the county court, and the remedies available are those available in the High Court. As with employment, there is no upper limit on compensation, although there is a power to set an upper limit on the damages which may be awarded for injury to feelings.

Part IV concerns education. As originally published, the Bill did not apply to education. The Government were however persuaded during the passage of the Bill through Parliament to strengthen the provisions of the Education Acts of 1993 (c. 35) and 1994 (c. 30) and the Further and Higher Education Act 1992 (c. 13) relating to the provision of information by schools, colleges, universities and local education authorities on arrangements and facilities for disabled pupils and students.

Part V contains a series of provisions empowering the Secretary of State for Transport to issue regulations setting a timetable for the achievement of a fully accessible public transport system by introducing minimum access standards for buses, trains, taxis and other public service vehicles. As originally published, the Bill was heavily criticised for making no provision for access to public transport. Indeed, during the debates on the Bill it was pointed out that, as a consequence of the exclusion of transport vehicles from the provisions on access to goods and services in Pt. III, a disabled person would have a right of access to a railway station, but no right to get onto a train. The Government were persuaded to use the opportunity presented by the Bill to set minimum access standards for taxis, public service vehicles and rail vehicles, with a timetable for implementation. The new requirements are likely to apply only to new vehicles, and do not extend to travel by air or sea.

Part VI provides for the establishment of a National Disability Council ("NDC") to advise the Government on general issues relating to discrimination against disabled people. The NDC also has a duty to draw up codes of practice at the request of the Secretary of State. Unlike the Equal Opportunities Commission and the Commission for Racial Equality, the NDC is not empowered to investigate complaints, to provide assistance to individuals in enforcing their rights before the courts and tribunals, or to take strategic enforcement action of its own accord. Nor will it have responsibility for advising the Government on employment matters, the giving of advice in that area remaining for the time being the preserve of the National Advisory Council on Employment of People with Disabilities. Separate provision is made in Sched. 8 for a Northern Ireland Disability Council.

Parts VII and VIII contain supplemental and miscellaneous provisions. In particular, s. 61 repeals the provisions of the Disabled Persons (Employment) Act 1944 (c. 10) relating to the register of disabled persons, the quota system which obliges employers with more than 20 employees to employ a three per cent quota of registered disabled persons, and the designated employment scheme whereby certain types of employment are reserved for disabled employees.

The Government's intention is that the Act will be implemented in a number of stages. At the time of writing the likely timing for commencement of various parts of the Act was as follows:
—the education provisions—from July 1996;
—protection in the field of employment—around the end of 1996;
—protection from being refused goods, facilities and services—around the end of 1996;
—the duty of service providers to make adjustments to practices, policies or procedures—1998;
—the duty of service providers to provide auxiliary aids and services—2000;
—the duty of service providers to remove physical barriers—2005.

ABBREVIATIONS

ACAS	:	Advisory, Conciliation and Arbitration Service.
A.D.A.	:	Americans with Disabilities Act 1990.
CEPDs	:	Committees for the Employment of People with Disabilities.
CORAD	:	Committee on Restrictions Against Disabled People.
CRE	:	Commission for Racial Equality.
DIAL	:	Disability Information and Advice Line Service.
DPTAC	:	Disabled Persons Transport Advisory Committee.
E.A.T.	:	Employment Appeal Tribunal.
EOC	:	Equal Opportunities Commission.
E.P.(C.)A. 1978	:	Employment Protection (Consolidation) Act 1978 (c.44).
NACEDP	:	National Advisory Council on Employment of People with Disabilities.
NDC	:	National Disability Council.
PACTs	:	Employment Service's Placing, Assessment and Counselling Teams.
PSVs	:	public service vehicles.
RADAR	:	Royal Association for Disability and Rehabilitation.
R.N.I.D.	:	Royal National Institute for the Deaf.
R.R.A.	:	Race Relations Act 1976 (c. 74).
S.D.A.	:	Sex Discrimination Act 1975 (c. 65).
T.U.L.R.A.	:	Trade Union and Labour Relations (Consolidation) Act 1992 (c. 51).
1847 Act	:	Town Police Clauses Act 1847.
1869 Act	:	Metropolitan Public Carriage Act 1869.

PART I

DISABILITY

Meaning of "disability" and "disabled person"

1.—(1) Subject to the provisions of Schedule 1, a person has a disability for the purposes of this Act if he has a physical or mental impairment which has a substantial and long-term adverse effect on his ability to carry out normal day-to-day activities.

(2) In this Act "disabled person" means a person who has a disability.

GENERAL NOTE

At the heart of the Act is the definition of "disability" in subs. (1). This definition proved to be a major source of controversy during the Act's passage through Parliament. It is based on a predominantly medical model of disability, in that it defines disability in terms of impairments and their effect on a person's ability to carry out "normal day-to-day activities". In contrast, the social model of disability favoured by many commentators views disability as a social construct whereby disabled people are handicapped by the organisation and structure of the society in which they live and work. This was acknowledged in the report of the Committee on Restrictions against Disabled People (CORAD, 1982), which stated:

"There is no direct relationship between the degree of disability and the degree of handicap; adverse social and environmental factors can place the mildly disabled at a severe disadvantage and an enabling environment can reduce any disadvantage experienced by a severely disabled individual .... The frustrating experience of almost all disabled people is that not only are they often restricted by their own physical limitations, but they have imposed on them additional restrictions by the structure of the society in which they live." (paras. 2.2 and 2.3).

The definition adopted for the purposes of the Act was however defended by the Government as a "commonsense" definition based on the general perception of the population as to the meaning of disability. In the words of the Minister for Social Security and Disabled People, William Hague, the definition of disability;

"... must fit a generally acceptable perception of what disability means to employers, to service providers, to disabled people and to the nation at large. It must also give as much certainty as possible to courts and tribunals .... Our definition would not be credible if it did not include every commonly accepted form of the term 'disability'. But the definition—and, consequently, the law—would not be credible if it embraced people who were not fairly or generally recognised as disabled." (*Hansard*, H.C., Standing Committee E, col. 73).

One important consequence of the adoption of this "commonsense" approach is that the definition does not include certain categories of people who might well be considered "disabled" in a broader sense of the word. In particular, the definition does not extend to people who are mistakenly believed to be disabled (for example, a person with a slight speech impediment who is mistakenly assumed to be mentally handicapped), or who may become disabled in the future (for example, a person who has a latent condition or is pre-symptomatic). The Government was however persuaded during the Act's passage through Parliament to extend the definition to cover those who have in the past had a disability, but who are no longer disabled: see the note to s.2.

The definition in this section has been described as a framework definition, with the detailed interpretation left to the schedules. Schedule 1 in particular contains extensive powers for the Government to make regulations: "... to clarify and confirm the definition in the future, rather than leaving wide areas of vague legislation to be interpreted by courts differently at different times." (Minister for Social Security and Disabled People, *Hansard*, H.C., Standing Committee E, col. 73). The Minister emphasised that it was "most important ... to have adequate powers to ensure that the detail can be re-examined in the light of experience and changes in medical knowledge. A once-and-for-all definition would be inadequate. Parliament needs to have the regulatory powers to enable it to be specific and to keep up to date with future medical developments." (*ibid.* col. 74).

In addition, s.3 gives the Secretary of State wide powers to issue guidance in relation to the definition, which must be taken into account by courts and tribunals where relevant.

The definition of "disability" may be broken down into the following six elements:

Physical or mental impairment. These key concepts are not defined by the Act, although Sched. 1, para. 1(1) provides that "mental impairment" includes an impairment resulting from or consisting of a mental illness only if the illness is a "clinically well-recognised illness". The Secretary of State is empowered to issue regulations providing for conditions of a prescribed description to be treated as or as not amounting to impairments, as the case may be (Sched. 1, para. 1(2)).

Attempts to include in the definition an express reference to sensory impairments were resisted, on the grounds that its inclusion would not add to the legal or medical meaning: "sensory disorders are always either physical or mental, and the word sensory, therefore, does not represent a genuinely separate category ... The terms physical and mental are intended to be seen in their widest sense and should comprehensively cover all forms of impairment." (Minister for Social Security and Disabled People, *Hansard*, H.C., Standing Committee E, col. 71). In an attempt to put the matter beyond doubt, the Minister added: "... the Government have drafted the Bill so that it will cover sensory impairments. Anyone reading the record of our proceedings will be left in no doubt whatever that that was the intention of the Committee and the Government" (*ibid.* col. 72).

The requirement that mental illness be 'clinically well-recognised' in order to fall within the definition is further evidence of the medical model underlying the definition, and is designed to avoid "the possibility of claims based on obscure conditions unrecognised by reputable clinicians, which courts and tribunals would find extremely difficult to assess" (*ibid.* col. 104). The Minister indicated that a mental illness would be regarded as 'clinically well-recognised' if there is "a reasonably substantial body of practitioners who accept that a condition exists" (*ibid.* col. 100), and suggested that such illnesses "would include ... schizophrenia, manic depression, and severe and extended depressive psychoses." (*ibid.* col. 104). However, the Minister added: "We are clear ... that it is no function of the [Act] to cover moods or mild eccentricities and to say that they constitute a disability." (*ibid.* col. 104). The Minister also indicated that the Government intends to use its power to issue regulations in order to exclude certain psychopathic or anti-social disorders and addictions from the coverage of the Act (*ibid.* col. 105). Examples of the sorts of conditions which it intends to exclude are kleptomania, pyromania, paedophilia and personality disorders including psychopathic disorders (*ibid.* col. 109).

Long-term and substantial adverse effect. The protection of the Act is restricted to people with impairments which have a "substantial and long-term adverse effect" on their ability to carry out normal day-to-day activities. The intention is to exclude those with minor or trivial conditions, or conditions which, although disabling, are only temporary (for example, short-term illness). The Government considered that "... the law would begin to seem ridiculous if we did not ensure that it related to people who have a long-term impairment.... We must have a sense of time and of the long-term nature of disability" (Minister for Social Security and Disabled People, *Hansard*, H.C., Standing Committee E, col. 77). Ministers were however careful to acknowledge that it is the effect of the impairment which is important, not the severity of the impairment itself: "The [Act] covers disabilities which have a substantial and long-term or recurring effect on the ability to carry out normal day-to-day activities. Such effects may well be, and frequently will be, caused by disabilities which are not severe. The focus is thus on the effects and not on the disability itself." (Minister of State, *Hansard*, H.L., Vol. 564, col. 1650).

Schedule 1, para. 2(1) provides that the effect of an impairment will be deemed to be a long-term effect, if (a) it has lasted at least 12 months, (b) it is likely to last for at least 12 months, or (c) it is likely to last for the rest of the life of the person affected (the latter designed to cover a person suffering from a terminal illness who is unlikely to live for 12 months, who might otherwise fall outwith the Act's protection). A person suffering from a condition which is intermittent or sporadic (for example, conditions such as epilepsy or multiple sclerosis) may be covered by Sched. 1, para. 2(2), which provides that an impairment which stops having a substantial adverse effect on a person's ability to carry out normal day-to-day activities will be treated as continuing to have that effect, however long the intervening period of good health, where the disabling effects of the impairment are likely to recur. Again, there are regulation-making powers which enable the Government to prescribe circumstances in which the likelihood of an effect recurring is to be disregarded (para. 2(3)), or the effects are to be treated as being, or as not being, long-term effects (para. 2(4)). The Government has indicated that it intends to use these powers to exclude conditions "in which the effects may recur and be substantial for a brief time, but for the overwhelming majority of someone's life they would be non-existent or virtually so.... Severe hay fever is one example." (Minister for Social Security and Disabled People, *Hansard*, H.C., Standing Committee E, col. 113).

'Substantial' is not defined by the Act. Schedule 1, para. 3 does however provide that severe disfigurement will be treated as having a substantial adverse effect on a person's ability to carry out normal day-to-day activities, although once again regulations may provide for circumstances in which a severe disfigurement is not to be treated as having that effect. The Government has indicated that it intends to use this power to exclude those with deliberately acquired disfigurements, such as tattoos or body piercing (*ibid.* col. 111).

Normal day-to-day activities. The definition of disability revolves around the ability of a person to carry out normal day-to-day activities, yet it is a truism that what is normal for one person may not be normal for another. This phrase is intended to refer to the activities of an ordinary, average person rather than those of a person with specialised skills or abilities, for example, a mountaineer or a concert-pianist; "... we say 'normal day-to-day activities' to avoid people thinking that it covers ability to participate in some specialised sport or activity that most of us would not be capable of anyway and would not regard as part of normal day-to-day life." (Minister for Social Security and Disabled People, *Hansard*, H.C., Standing Committee E, col. 120.) Schedule 1, para. 4, lists the categories of activity which are to be treated as normal day-to-day activities for the purposes of the definition, namely, mobility; manual dexterity; physical co-ordination; continence; ability to lift, carry or otherwise move everyday objects; speech, hearing or eyesight; memory or ability to concentrate, learn or understand; or the perception of the risk of physical danger. The list is intended to be exhaustive (Minister of State, *Hansard*, H.L., Vol. 564, col. 1671), although it may be added to by regulations. Regulations may also provide for circumstances in which an impairment will be deemed to affect a person's ability to carry out normal day-to-day activities, and vice versa.

Effect of medical or other treatment. Specific provision is made in Sched. 1, para. 6, for cases where measures are being taken to treat or correct an impairment, for example, through medical treatment or the use of a prosthesis or other aid. An obvious example would be a potentially disabling condition such as epilepsy or diabetes which is controlled by medication. In such cases the impairment will be deemed to have a substantial adverse effect on a person's ability to carry out normal day-to-day activities, if it would be likely to have such an effect were it not for the medical treatment or corrective measures. In other words, the effect of the impairment must be considered without taking account of any medical treatment or other intervention which is being used to treat or correct it. This does not however extend to those with impaired sight where the impairment is correctable by spectacles or contact lenses or by some other prescribed method, whether or not those aids are in fact used. This exception reflects the fact that the correction of impaired sight by spectacles and contact lenses is usually so effective that "people who wear spectacles or contact lenses would not generally think of themselves as disabled." (Minister for Social Security and Disabled People, *Hansard*, H.C., Standing Committee E, col. 122). The Secretary of State may issue regulations making a similar exception in relation to other impairments:

"For example, at the moment, people wearing hearing aids will be covered by the definition because hearing aids usually provide only a partial correction of a disability. Those people are still usually, and should be, seen as disabled. But if at some future date, as a result of improved technology, hearing aids became as completely effective as spectacles or contact lenses are today, it might be appropriate to exclude people in that situation from the general definition of disability." (*ibid.* col. 122).

The Minister did however add: "There is no group that I intend to exclude in the immediately foreseeable future." (*ibid.* col. 122).

Persons deemed to be disabled. Schedule 1, para. 7 provides for a range of circumstances in which persons may be deemed to be disabled. In particular, para. 7(1) provides that a person who was registered as disabled under the Disabled Persons (Employment) Act 1944 on January 12, 1995, and who is still registered as disabled on the date when para. 7 comes into force, will be deemed to be a disabled person for an initial period of three years from that date; a certificate of registration issued under s.6 of the 1944 Act will be conclusive evidence of the matters certified therein (para. 7(3)), and a document purporting to be a certificate of registration will be deemed to be genuine and to have been validly issued unless proved to the contrary (para. 7(4)). In addition, there is a general power whereby prescribed descriptions of person may be deemed by regulation to be disabled for the purposes of the Act (para. 7(5)). In both cases, circumstances may be prescribed in which a person who has been deemed to be disabled under these provisions should no longer be deemed to be disabled (para. 7(6)).

Progressive conditions. One of the most controversial aspects of the definition of disability concerns its application to progressive conditions such as cancer, Parkinson's disease and multiple sclerosis. The problem here is that a considerable period of time may elapse between the diagnosis of a person as suffering from a progressive condition, and the point in time when that condition can be said to have a substantial adverse effect on that person's ability to carry out normal day-to-day activities—indeed, the condition may never reach that stage—yet the person may well face discrimination as a result of the medical prognosis long before that stage. It may also be very difficult in practice to define the point in time at which someone with a progressive condition becomes 'disabled' within the s.1 definition. The solution adopted is that where a person has a progressive condition which has resulted in an impairment which has *some* effect, but not necessarily a substantial effect, on his ability to carry out normal day-to-day activities, that person will be deemed to fall within the definition of a disabled person if the likely prognosis is that the condition will result in his having an impairment which has a substantial adverse effect on his ability to carry out normal day-to-day activities. Schedule 1, para. 8(1), gives cancer, multiple sclerosis, muscular dystrophy and infection by the human immunodeficiency virus (HIV) as examples of progressive conditions, and para. 8(2) empowers the Secretary of State to make regulations deeming other conditions to be or not to be progressive. The inclusion of HIV as an example of a progressive condition was a result of concerted pressure during the passage of the Bill.

Crucially, the protection for those suffering from progressive conditions only arises from the point in time when a condition becomes symptomatic, in the sense that it begins to have an effect on a person's ability to carry out normal day-to-day activities. The protection does not apply while a potentially disabling condition, although diagnosed, remains latent. It could be argued that if it is right that a person should be protected from discrimination once he or she begins to show symptoms of a potentially disabling condition, there is an equally strong case for protecting a person from discrimination before he or she begins to show any such symptoms. As matters stand, however, the Act permits discrimination against a person who has been diagnosed as suffering from or at risk of a progressive condition, as long as that person remains pre-symptomatic. This places a person at risk of a potentially disabling condition at a significant disadvantage compared with someone who has already developed such a condition, and could be said to provide a positive incentive to discriminate before such a person manifests any symptoms of the condition. This issue is likely to become increasingly significant as more sophisticated and reliable diagnostic techniques become available, and in particular with the development of tests for a genetic predisposition to conditions such as Huntingdon's chorea, Alzheimer's disease and certain forms of cancer. According to the Minister,

"... except in a few well-publicised cases, genetic tests are not as yet a useful indicator of future actual disability. Their inclusion would open up the [Act] to large numbers of people who are clearly not, and may never become, disabled ... we cannot wander into a situation whereby, for some reason or another, potentially the entire population could claim protection under the [Act]." (*Hansard*, H.C., Vol. 257, col. 887).

On the other hand, as Baroness Jay observed in the House of Lords:

"The paradox which is possible in the present situation is that where genetic counselling, genetic testing and identifying genetic markers is potentially one of the most exciting and liberating developments in medical science at the end of the 20th century, if it becomes the case that people feel that identifying those markers in their own personal situation will lead to discrimination, they will be less likely to take advantage of those extraordinary scientific advances which may help their own condition and in which medical science may be able to help future generations of children" (*Hansard*, H.L., Vol. 564, col. 1713).

Past disabilities

2.—(1) The provisions of this Part and Parts II and III apply in relation to a person who has had a disability as they apply in relation to a person who has that disability.

(2) Those provisions are subject to the modifications made by Schedule 2.

(3) Any regulations or order made under this Act may include provision with respect to persons who have had a disability.

(4) In any proceedings under Part II or Part III of this Act, the question whether a person had a disability at a particular time ("the relevant time") shall be determined, for the purposes of this section, as if the provisions of, or made under, this Act in force when the act complained of was done had been in force at the relevant time.

(5) The relevant time may be a time before the passing of this Act.

GENERAL NOTE

This section was added to the Bill in the House of Lords following sustained Opposition pressure. It extends the s.1 definition, for the purposes of Pts. I, II and III of the Act, to cover those who have had a disability but who are no longer disabled. Initially, the Government took the view that the protection of the Act should only apply to those who are "commonly accepted as being disabled", and should not therefore extend to those who have been disabled in the past. However, the Government was persuaded that the exclusion of those who have had a disability from the Act's coverage might allow discrimination against, for example, those with a history of mental illness who have made a full recovery, but who continue to suffer discrimination on account of their previous illness. As the Minister stated in introducing the amendment:

"It has become increasingly clear that people who have had a disability, although they may be no longer disabled as such, share with people who are currently disabled a need for protection against discrimination in relation to their disability .... It is clearly a very important part of the whole process of recovery that someone who has been disabled is able not only to participate fully in employment and social activities but to feel confident in doing so .... In addition, we have been persuaded that it is not always possible to tell when a person has fully recovered from a disability and when the condition is no longer likely to recur. The inclusion of people in the [Act] who have had a disability removes the need for individuals, businesses, courts and tribunals to have to deal with this grey area." (*Hansard*, H.L., Vol. 564, col. 1655).

Subs. (2)

Note that in order to fall within the extended definition, the past disability must have had a long-term effect, in the sense that it must have lasted for at least 12 months: see Sched. 2, para. 5.

Subs. (4)

This makes clear that if a person alleges discrimination in respect of a past disability, the question of whether that person had a disability will be decided by reference to the definition of disability in force at the time of the alleged act of discrimination: "This makes clear that the Bill will cover people who have recovered before the Bill has passed and it will also ensure consistency of treatment between people who are currently disabled and those who have recovered from the same treatment." (Minister of State, *Hansard*, H.L., Vol. 564, col. 1656).

Guidance

3.—(1) The Secretary of State may issue guidance about the matters to be taken into account in determining—

(a) whether an impairment has a substantial adverse effect on a person's ability to carry out normal day-to-day activities; or

(b) whether such an impairment has a long-term effect.

(2) The guidance may, among other things, give examples of—

(a) effects which it would be reasonable, in relation to particular activities, to regard for purposes of this Act as substantial adverse effects;

(b) effects which it would not be reasonable, in relation to particular activities, to regard for such purposes as substantial adverse effects;

(c) substantial adverse effects which it would be reasonable to regard, for such purposes, as long-term;

(d) substantial adverse effects which it would not be reasonable to regard, for such purposes, as long-term.

(3) A tribunal or court determining, for any purpose of this Act, whether an impairment has a substantial and long-term adverse effect on a person's ability to carry out normal day-to-day activities, shall take into account any guidance which appears to it to be relevant.

(4) In preparing a draft of any guidance, the Secretary of State shall consult such persons as he considers appropriate.

(5) Where the Secretary of State proposes to issue any guidance, he shall publish a draft of it, consider any representations that are made to him about the draft and, if he thinks it appropriate, modify his proposals in the light of any of those representations.

(6) If the Secretary of State decides to proceed with any proposed guidance, he shall lay a draft of it before each House of Parliament.

(7) If, within the 40-day period, either House resolves not to approve the draft, the Secretary of State shall take no further steps in relation to the proposed guidance.

(8) If no such resolution is made within the 40-day period, the Secretary of State shall issue the guidance in the form of his draft.

(9) The guidance shall come into force on such date as the Secretary of State may appoint by order.

(10) Subsection (7) does not prevent a new draft of the proposed guidance from being laid before Parliament.

(11) The Secretary of State may—

(a) from time to time revise the whole or part of any guidance and re-issue it;

(b) by order revoke any guidance.

(12) In this section—

"40-day period", in relation to the draft of any proposed guidance, means—

(a) if the draft is laid before one House on a day later than the day on which it is laid before the other House, the period of 40 days beginning with the later of the two days, and

(b) in any other case, the period of 40 days beginning with the day on which the draft is laid before each House,

no account being taken of any period during which Parliament is dissolved or prorogued or during which both Houses are adjourned for more than 4 days; and

"guidance" means guidance issued by the Secretary of State under this section and includes guidance which has been revised and re-issued.

GENERAL NOTE

This section gives the Secretary of State wide powers to issue guidance in relation to the definition of disability. Any such guidance must be taken into account by a court or tribunal where it appears to it to be relevant (subs. (3)). Subsections (4) to (12) lay down the detailed procedures for the issue, revision and revocation of guidance under this section, which is subject to the negative resolution procedure.

PART II

EMPLOYMENT

Discrimination by employers

Discrimination against applicants and employees

4.—(1) It is unlawful for an employer to discriminate against a disabled person—
  (a) in the arrangements which he makes for the purpose of determining to whom he should offer employment;
  (b) in the terms on which he offers that person employment; or
  (c) by refusing to offer, or deliberately not offering, him employment.

(2) It is unlawful for an employer to discriminate against a disabled person whom he employs—
  (a) in the terms of employment which he affords him;
  (b) in the opportunities which he affords him for promotion, a transfer, training or receiving any other benefit;
  (c) by refusing to afford him, or deliberately not affording him, any such opportunity; or
  (d) by dismissing him, or subjecting him to any other detriment.

(3) Subsection (2) does not apply to benefits of any description if the employer is concerned with the provision (whether or not for payment) of benefits of that description to the public, or to a section of the public which includes the employee in question, unless—
  (a) that provision differs in a material respect from the provision of the benefits by the employer to his employees; or
  (b) the provision of the benefits to the employee in question is regulated by his contract of employment; or
  (c) the benefits relate to training.

(4) In this Part "benefits" includes facilities and services.

(5) In the case of act which constitutes discrimination by virtue of section 55, this section also applies to discrimination against a person who is not disabled.

(6) This section applies only in relation to employment at an establishment in Great Britain.

GENERAL NOTE

This section makes it unlawful for an employer to discriminate against a disabled person (including a person who has had a disability: see s.2) in relation to employment. It is intended to be comprehensive in its coverage. It prohibits discrimination in all aspects of employment, including recruitment, terms of employment, promotion, training and dismissal, and is "intended to cover ... the use of standards, criteria, administrative methods, work practices or procedures that adversely affect a disabled person." (Parliamentary Under-Secretary of State, *Hansard*, H.C., Standing Committee E, col. 142). The wording closely follows that of the legislation outlawing discrimination in the employment field on grounds of sex and race (see the Sex Discrimination Act 1975 (c. 74), s.6, and the Race Relations Act 1976 (c. 65), s.4), and decisions on the interpretation of those provisions are likely to be in point here also.

The right not to be discriminated against covers employees and applicants for employment, including contract workers (see the note to s.12), apprentices, and self-employed people who contract personally to do any work (s.68(1)), but the protection only applies in relation to employment at an establishment in Great Britain (see below). There are specific exclusions in s.64 covering the armed forces, prison officers, firefighters and certain other occupations, and police officers also fall outside the scope of the Act's provisions, but the most significant limitation on the scope of the protection is undoubtedly the exclusion of employers with fewer than 20 employees (see the note to s.7). Curiously, while the Act covers partnerships in their capacity as employers, it does not prohibit discrimination for reasons relating to disability against partners or prospective partners themselves. This contrasts with the sex and race discrimination legislation, which expressly prohibits discrimination against partners or prospective partners, albeit only for firms consisting of six or more partners in the case of discrimination on racial ·

grounds (S.D.A., s.11; R.R.A., s.10). The Minister's explanation for the difference of approach in this context is not wholly convincing: "Since partners put their own resources into a firm, it is not clear how the question of the cost of adjustment should be dealt with, and in particular to what extent it would be reasonable for the disabled person to seek a contribution from the other partner or partners to meet the cost of the necessary adjustments." (*Hansard*, H.L., Vol. 564, col. 1782).

Employment at an establishment in Great Britain. This is to be construed in accordance with s.68(2) to (5).

Arrangements. According to the Minister, "The broad term 'arrangements' has deliberately been used [in s.4(1)(a) and s.6(1)] to cover anything done by or for an employer as part of his recruitment process or in making available opportunities in employment. It would not only include work practices and procedures, so far as such practices or procedures have any bearing on determining who is offered employment or to whom such opportunities are made available; it would go wider than that." (*Hansard*, H.C., Standing Committee E, col. 142).

There are specific provisions in s.11 relating to discriminatory job advertisements. If an advertisement indicates, or might reasonably be taken to indicate, that the employer might discriminate against a disabled applicant, then that advertisement will give rise to a presumption of discrimination. For such a presumption to arise, the disabled person must have applied for and been refused the employment in question, and must have presented a complaint to a tribunal under s.8 of the Act. Where these conditions are satisfied, the tribunal will presume that the employer's reason for not offering the employment to the complainant was related to his disability, unless the employer is able to prove to the contrary. See the note to s.11.

The Act contains no measures expressly dealing with medical examinations, despite evidence that pre-employment health screening is one of the most common ways in which disabled job applicants are discriminated against, by being screened out at an early stage in the selection process. At the Committee stage in the House of Commons, the Opposition tabled an amendment which would have made it unlawful for an employer, in advance of making an offer of employment, to require candidates to undergo a medical examination or to ask questions about the nature or severity of an applicant's disability, except in order to ascertain the applicant's ability to perform job related functions, or to conduct equal opportunities monitoring. The amendment was however rejected by the Government: "In general, employers should be free to use whatever recruitment procedures best meet their needs and to conduct medical examinations of employees where that seems appropriate." (Parliamentary Under-Secretary of State, *Hansard*, H.C., Standing Committee E, col. 151). In the Minister's view, forbidding medical examinations in all but the circumstances contemplated by the proposed amendment could have worked to the detriment of disabled applicants and employees: "For example, a prospective employer would not be able to ask questions about whether an applicant needed special arrangements to attend an interview, or about his ability to use ancillary facilities such as car parks and rest rooms. Perhaps more seriously, in some industries, an employer could not operate compulsory medical examinations for employees doing work involving a health risk." (*ibid.* col. 152). The Minister expressed sympathy "with the intention of avoiding the institution of a spurious system of medical examination intentionally designed to discriminate", but considered that the Act "deals with that possibility in other ways." (*ibid.* col. 160). Even in the absence of any specific restriction on pre-employment medical screening, an employer who insists on a medical check for a disabled applicant but not for other, non-disabled applicants might still be held to have discriminated unlawfully against the disabled applicant, as such a requirement would almost certainly be held to constitute less favourable treatment of that person for a reason relating to his or her disability; however, such treatment would only constitute unlawful discrimination if the employer could not show that his insistence on the medical check was justified, within the meaning of s.5(3): see the note to s.5 below.

Meaning of "discrimination"

5.—(1) For the purposes of this Part, an employer discriminates against a disabled person if—

(a) for a reason which relates to the disabled person's disability, he treats him less favourably than he treats or would treat others to whom that reason does not or would not apply; and

(b) he cannot show that the treatment in question is justified.

(2) For the purposes of this Part, an employer also discriminates against a disabled person if—

(a) he fails to comply with a section 6 duty imposed on him in relation to the disabled person; and

(b) he cannot show that his failure to comply with that duty is justified.

(3) Subject to subsection (5), for the purposes of subsection (1) treatment is justified if, but only if, the reason for it is both material to the circumstances of the particular case and substantial.

(4) For the purposes of subsection (2), failure to comply with a section 6 duty is justified if, but only if, the reason for the failure is both material to the circumstances of the particular case and substantial.

(5) If, in a case falling within subsection (1), the employer is under a section 6 duty in relation to the disabled person but fails without justification to comply with that duty, his treatment of that person cannot be justified under subsection (3) unless it would have been justified even if he had complied with the section 6 duty.

(6) Regulations may make provision, for purposes of this section, as to circumstances in which—

(a) treatment is to be taken to be justified;

(b) failure to comply with a section 6 duty is to be taken to be justified;

(c) treatment is to be taken not to be justified;

(d) failure to comply with a section 6 duty is to be taken not to be justified.

(7) Regulations under subsection (6) may, in particular—

(a) make provision by reference to the cost of affording any benefit; and

(b) in relation to benefits under occupational pension schemes, make provision with a view to enabling uniform rates of contributions to be maintained.

GENERAL NOTE

The definition of discrimination contained in this section differs in several important respects from that contained in the sex and race discrimination legislation. It retains the familiar concept of direct discrimination which is used in the Sex Discrimination Act 1975 and the Race Relations Act 1976, by providing that an employer discriminates against a disabled person if, for a reason which relates to that person's disability, he treats him less favourably than he treats or would treat others to whom that reason does not apply. However, in sharp contrast with direct discrimination on the grounds of sex or race, under these provisions less favourable treatment of a disabled person may be justified in certain circumstances. This difference reflects the fact that while a person's sex or race will rarely have a bearing on their ability to do a job, a person's disability may well have. Less favourable treatment of a disabled person is justified if the reason for it "is both material to the circumstances of the particular case and substantial" (subs. (3)).

The second major difference is that unlike the S.D.A. and the R.R.A., this definition does not expressly prohibit indirect discrimination (*i.e.* the application of a requirement or condition which has a disproportionate impact on a particular group or class). It does however provide, in subs. (2), that an employer discriminates against a disabled person if he fails to comply with the duty imposed on him under s.6 to make reasonable adjustments in relation to the disabled person (again, subject to a defence if the employer can show that the failure to comply with that duty is justified), and the Government has claimed that this provides effective protection against indirect discrimination:

"The right has been formulated to leave few, if any, of the ways in which disability can indirectly disadvantage a person outside the scope of the right. The intention is that any situation where an employer imposes a condition or requirement which might exclude a disabled person will be covered by the basic right and the duty on employers to make a reasonable adjustment." (White Paper, *Ending discrimination against disabled people*, Cm. 2729, 1995, para. 3.8).

Subs. (1)

Others to whom that reason does not or would not apply. The appropriate comparison for these purposes is with the treatment of a person to whom the reason for the less favourable treatment does not (or would not) apply, and not with the treatment of a person who does not have the disability in question. To use the example of an employee with arthritis who is refused employment because he or she cannot type, the appropriate comparison is with the treatment of a person to whom that reason does not apply (*i.e.* a person who is able to type), and not with a person who is unable to type because he or she has never learned to do so:

"... if the employer is rejecting people who cannot type, he will be treating more favourably those who can. The person with arthritis who did not get the job can show that he or she was treated less favourably than the person with typing abilities who did. The employer may well be able to justify that treatment—for example, if a disabled person was not adequately able to do the job, even taking account of any reasonable adjustment. But at least the disabled person would have to be given the consideration due under the [Act]." (Minister of State, *Hansard*, H.L. Vol. 566, col. 120).

If the comparison were with a person who is not disabled, the employer might have been able to argue that he was not treating the disabled applicant less favourably than a person without that disability, because he was treating all those who cannot type in the same way; the result would have been that the disabled applicant would have had no ground for complaint, even though the employment was refused for a reason which related to that person's disability.

Subss. (3) and (4)
Material to the circumstances of the particular case and substantial. Less favourable treatment of a disabled person is justified if the reason for it is both material to the circumstances of the particular case and substantial. This phrase was substituted for the original, more detailed version of the justification defence at a late stage in the Parliamentary proceedings. The earlier version focused on the employer's reasonable opinion as to the suitability of the disabled person for the employment in question, and was heavily criticised for its subjective approach (a similar approach is however retained for the purposes of Pt. III: see the note to s.20). Although not open to criticism on that particular ground, the present version offers precious little guidance as to the scope of the defence, although matters may become clearer if and when regulations are made under subs. (6) providing for circumstances in which an employer's actions are to be deemed to be, or not to be, justified. To be "material", a reason has to be related to the individual circumstances of the case in question, rather than, for example, being based on ill-informed assumptions about the effects of disability; and in the context of the duty to make adjustments, the Government has indicated that "substantial" is intended to exclude minor or trivial matters: see the note to s.6(1).

Subs. (5)
Where an employer has discriminated against a disabled person by treating that person less favourably for a reason relating to his or her disability, and has also failed without justification to comply with his duty under s.6 to make reasonable adjustments in relation to that person, the employer's treatment of that person cannot be justified under subs. (3), unless it would have been justified even if he had complied with his duty to make reasonable adjustments.

Subs. (7)
The power to make regulations under subs. (6) deeming less favourable treatment, or a failure to comply with a s.6 duty, to be justified in certain circumstances, includes the power to stipulate that discrimination may be justified by reference to the cost of affording a benefit, and, in relation to benefits under occupational pension schemes, to make provision enabling uniform rates of contributions to be maintained. These provisions form part of a series of measures in the Act designed to address the specific issue of discrimination in relation to occupational pension benefits (see the notes to s.6(11) and s.17). They reflect the Government's view that employers should in appropriate circumstances be allowed to justify less favourable treatment of disabled people on account of the increased risks and extra costs of providing such benefits:
"Where a disabled applicant [to an occupational pension scheme] has a pre-existing medical condition which is likely to increase the risk of ill-health retirement or death in service it is important that employers should be able to take just as much account of that as they would if the person were not disabled." (Minister of State, *Hansard*, H.L., Vol. 566, col. 995).
However, since it would clearly run counter to the whole philosophy of the legislation if the less favourable treatment of a disabled person could be justified on the basis of assumptions about that person's health and life expectancy which were ill-founded, the Government has been at pains to stress that any such assumptions must be based on sound evidence if they are to play a part in the calculation of risk in relation to disabled people:
"... employers will want to ensure that their decisions are based on sound evidence; for example, actuarial or medical evidence. Many disabled people have disabilities which do not affect their life expectancy or likelihood of ill-health retirement and these [provisions] will make sure they can no longer be unfairly denied access to an employer's pension scheme." (Minister of State, *ibid.* col. 995).
During the Bill's passage through the House of Lords, the Minister, rejecting an opposition amendment which sought to disapply the power to deem less favourable treatment in relation to

occupational pension schemes to be justified, suggested that there might be two types of case in which occupational benefits for a disabled person might justifiably be less than those for a non-disabled person:

"The first is that pensions are almost always linked to pay. If there is a justifiable difference in pay received by the two workers—perhaps, for example, because the disability means that the disabled person has to work fewer hours—it must be right that the pension can also reflect that difference ... The second reason is that the disability might create actuarial risks which the employer or the pension fund should not have to take. For example, depending on the circumstances, we believe that an employer who takes on an employee who is terminally ill can be justified in refusing such a person cover under any scheme he operates for death-in-service benefits. The removal of any justification in the case of these benefits and payments would place quite unwarranted burdens on employers." (Minister of State, *Hansard*, H.L., Vol. 566, cols. 169 and 170).

The Government intends to consult on the use of the regulation-making powers, and in particular on what kind of additional cost might justify less favourable treatment of a disabled person; in moving the amendments at Third Reading in the House of Lords, the Minister declared his wish to "put on the record the fact that we have absolutely no intention legislating for what might be trivial costs." (*ibid*. col. 1000).

Duty of employer to make adjustments

6.—(1) Where—
  (a) any arrangements made by or on behalf of an employer, or
  (b) any physical feature of premises occupied by the employer,
place the disabled person concerned at a substantial disadvantage in comparison with persons who are not disabled, it is the duty of the employer to take such steps as it is reasonable, in all the circumstances of the case, for him to have to take in order to prevent the arrangements or feature having that effect.

(2) Subsection (1)(a) applies only in relation to—
  (a) arrangements for determining to whom employment should be offered;
  (b) any term, condition or arrangements on which employment, promotion, a transfer, training or any other benefit is offered or afforded.

(3) The following are examples of steps which an employer may have to take in relation to a disabled person in order to comply with subsection (1)—
  (a) making adjustments to premises;
  (b) allocating some of the disabled person's duties to another person;
  (c) transferring him to fill an existing vacancy;
  (d) altering his working hours;
  (e) assigning him to a different place of work;
  (f) allowing him to be absent during working hours for rehabilitation, assessment or treatment;
  (g) giving him, or arranging for him to be given, training;
  (h) acquiring or modifying equipment;
  (i) modifying instructions or reference manuals;
  (j) modifying procedures for testing or assessment;
  (k) providing a reader or interpreter;
  (l) providing supervision.

(4) In determining whether it is reasonable for an employer to have to take a particular step in order to comply with subsection (1) regard shall be had, in particular, to—
  (a) the extent to which taking the step would prevent the effect in question;
  (b) the extent to which it is practicable for the employer to take the step;
  (c) the financial and other costs which would be incurred by the employer in taking the step and the extent to which taking it would disrupt any of his activities;
  (d) the extent of the employer's financial and other resources;

(e) the availability to the employer of financial or other assistance with respect to taking the step.

This subsection is subject to any provision of regulations made under subsection (8).

(5) In this section, "the disabled person concerned" means—

(a) in the case of arrangements for determining to whom employment should be offered, any disabled person who is, or has notified the employer that he may be, an applicant for that employment;

(b) in any other case, a disabled person who is—

(i) an applicant for the employment concerned; or

(ii) an employee of the employer concerned.

(6) Nothing in this section imposes any duty on an employer in relation to a disabled person if the employer does not know, and could not reasonably be expected to know—

(a) in the case of an applicant or potential applicant, that the disabled person concerned is, or may be, an applicant for the employment; or

(b) in any case, that that person has a disability and is likely to be affected in the way mentioned in subsection (1).

(7) Subject to the provisions of this section, nothing in this Part is to be taken to require an employer to treat a disabled person more favourably than he treats or would treat others.

(8) Regulations may make provision, for the purposes of subsection (1)—

(a) as to circumstances in which arrangements are, or a physical feature is, to be taken to have the effect mentioned in that subsection;

(b) as to circumstances in which arrangements are not, or a physical feature is not, to be taken to have that effect;

(c) as to circumstances in which it is reasonable for an employer to have to take steps of a prescribed description;

(d) as to steps which it is always reasonable for an employer to have to take;

(e) as to circumstances in which it is not reasonable for an employer to have to take steps of a prescribed description;

(f) as to steps which it is never reasonable for an employer to have to take;

(g) as to things which are to be treated as physical features;

(h) as to things which are not to be treated as such features.

(9) Regulations made under subsection (8)(c), (d), (e) or (f) may, in particular, make provision by reference to the cost of taking the steps concerned.

(10) Regulations may make provision adding to the duty imposed on employers by this section, including provision of a kind which may be made under subsection (8).

(11) This section does not apply in relation to any benefit under an occupational pension scheme or any other benefit payable in money or money's worth under a scheme or arrangement for the benefit of employees in respect of—

(a) termination of service;

(b) retirement, old age or death;

(c) accident, injury, sickness or invalidity; or

(d) any other prescribed matter.

(12) This section imposes duties only for the purpose of determining whether an employer has discriminated against a disabled person; and accordingly a breach of any such duty is not actionable as such.

GENERAL NOTE

This section contains the all-important provisions which set out the duty of an employer to make reasonable adjustments to his or her employment arrangements and premises in order to help a disabled person overcome the practical effects of a disability. The duty exists where any arrangements made by or on behalf of the employer, or any physical feature of premises occupied by the employer, place a disabled person at a "substantial disadvantage" in comparison with people who are not disabled. The duty does not however arise in the abstract: employers are not required to adapt their working arrangements or their premises "in anticipation of possibly having a disabled applicant or employee at some point in the future." (White Paper, *Ending discrimination against disabled people,* Cm. 2729, 1995, para. 3.7). Rather, the duty only arises in respect of a disabled person who is an employee of the employer concerned, or who has applied (or notified the employer that he may apply) for the employment in question (subs. (5)). In the case of applicants (including potential applicants) for employment, the employer is not under a duty to make adjustments if he does not know, and could not reasonably be expected to know, that the disabled person concerned is or may be an applicant for the employment (subs. (6)(b)). In general, a disabled person is protected from unlawful discrimination whether or not the employer knows of that person's disability (see the note to s.5); however, the duty to make adjustments does not arise unless the employer knows, or could reasonably be expected to know, that the person has a disability which is likely to place him or her at a substantial disadvantage in comparison with persons who are not disabled (subs. (6)(a)).

The duty of adjustment, as expressed in subs. (1), requires the employer to take any steps which it is reasonable for him or her to have to take in order to overcome any substantial disadvantage to a disabled applicant or employee caused by the employer's employment arrangements or premises. This may involve the employer in taking one step, or perhaps a combination of steps, in order to comply with this duty. Subsection (3) gives a number of examples of steps, one or more of which might be appropriate in particular circumstances, while subs. (4) lists a number of factors encompassing issues of practicability, cost and effectiveness which must be considered in determining whether it is reasonable for an employer to have to take a particular step or combination of steps. They are:

(a) *the extent to which taking the step would prevent the effect in question.* It might not be reasonable to require an employer to take a step which involves little benefit to the disabled employee.

(b) *the extent to which it is practicable for the employer to take the step.* During the Bill's passage through Parliament, the Minister of State commented: "it might not be reasonable for an employer needing an employee urgently to have to wait for an adjustment to be made to allow a disabled person to be employed. That is more likely to be the case with smaller employers but could apply to larger ones." (*Hansard,* H.C., Vol. 566, col. 185).

(c) *the financial and other costs which would be incurred by the employer in taking the step and the extent to which taking it would disrupt any of his activities.* Many adjustments will involve little or no cost to the employer (see below). "[I]t would not normally be reasonable for an employer to spend fewer resources on retaining a disabled person than on recruiting a replacement." (*ibid.* col. 185).

(d) *the extent of the employer's financial and other resources.* "Although the size of a business is not necessarily an indication of the resources available, it is more reasonable for an employer with considerable resources to make an adjustment with a significant cost than for an employer with few resources." (*ibid.* col. 185).

(e) *the availability to the employer of financial or other assistance with respect to taking the step.* "A step is not unreasonable if the availability of help from an outside organisation or from the disabled person would compensate for the factors that would have made it unreasonable. For example, it might be unreasonable on grounds of costs for a particular employer to provide a laptop computer with a Braille keyboard. However, if a suitable one could be loaned or borrowed when needed, for example under the Access to Work scheme, or if the individual has a suitable one he could provide, then the employer could not successfully claim that provision of the laptop was unreasonable because of the cost." (*ibid.* col. 185).

Subsection (8) contains a number of powers to make regulations relating to the duty of reasonable adjustment. Regulations may provide, for example, for circumstances in which arrangements or physical features must be deemed to place, or not to place, a disabled person at a substantial disadvantage, and may prescribe steps which are or are not reasonable for an employer to have to take in specific circumstances, and steps which it is always or never reasonable for an employer to have to take. There is a specific provision in subs. (9) which allows the issue of reasonableness to be determined by reference to the cost of taking the steps concerned. The Government indicated during the passage of the Bill that it has no immediate intention of using this power to put a financial ceiling on the concept of reasonable adjustment in employment cases, preferring to leave the issue of the extent of reasonable cost to the judgment of industrial tribunals on general principles (including those set out in subs. (4)), in conjunction with the guidance in the forthcoming Code of Practice:

"We believe that the concept of 'reasonable' will ensure that employers are not faced with an undue cost burden in making adjustments, but wish nonetheless to have regulation-making powers available in case that should prove not to be the case ... The Government have made clear from the outset that, while there is no upper financial limit to the duty on the employer to make a reasonable adjustment, should the need arise, Ministers would be prepared to consider setting a financial cap." (Minister of State, *Hansard*, H.L., Vol. 564, cols. 1761, 1768). A financial limit is however planned for the provisions relating to goods, facilities and services in Pt. III (see the note to s.21).

It seems that the Government took the decision not to impose a financial ceiling on adjustments in employment cases in the light of evidence that in most cases adjustments will have a nil or minimal cost. The Compliance Cost Assessment for the Act assumes an average cost of £200 per disabled employee for the 10 per cent of cases where a disabled employee is likely to require an adjustment. In those relatively few cases where the cost of an adjustment would be much higher, the question of whether an employer should be required to make that adjustment will be decided in accordance with the general test of reasonableness, taking into account the extent of the employer's resources, the availability of outside financial assistance, etc. The experience of the United States under the Americans with Disabilities Act 1990 suggests that in most cases the necessary adaptations can be made at modest cost. The Minister reported during the debates on the Bill that in 43 per cent of cases under the A.D.A., reasonable accommodation by the employer cost nothing, merely involving the moving of furniture or the introduction of different working hours. A survey by the Job Accommodation Network in 1987 revealed that the average cost of adjustments made by employers in the United States amounted to only $200, while 68 per cent of adjustments cost less than $500; in only 5 per cent of cases did the cost exceed $5,000 (*Evaluation Survey*, President's Commission on Employment of People with Disabilities, Washington, D.C., 1987).

A failure on the part of an employer to comply with the duty to make reasonable adjustments in relation to a disabled person will itself be an act of unlawful discrimination under s.4, unless the employer can show that his failure to comply with that duty is justified, in the sense that the reason for the failure is both material to the circumstances of the particular case and substantial (see the note to s.5). Where an employer has discriminated against a disabled person by treating that person less favourably for a reason relating to his or her disability, and has also failed without justification to comply with his duty to make reasonable adjustments in relation to that person, the employer's treatment of that person cannot be justified under s.5(3), unless it would have been justified even if he had complied with his duty to make reasonable adjustments under this section: see s.5(5).

It is now widely accepted that disability is a social construct, in that disabled people are handicapped not so much by their impairments as by the organisation and structure of the society in which they live and work. This was acknowledged in the report of the Committee on Restrictions against Disabled People (CORAD, 1982), which stated:
"There is no direct relationship between the degree of disability and the degree of handicap; adverse social and environmental factors can place the mildly disabled at a severe disadvantage and an enabling environment can reduce any disadvantage experienced by a severely disabled individual ... the frustrating experience of almost all disabled people is that not only are they often restricted by their own physical limitations, but they have imposed on them additional restrictions by the structure of the society in which they live." (paras. 2.2 and 2.3).
The duty to make reasonable adjustments in this section is a recognition of the fact that, while "the majority of disabled people who want to work need no, or only very modest help ... some disabled people need practical help to enable them to get a job." (White Paper, *Ending discrimination against disabled people*, Cm. 2729, 1995, para. 3.5).

Subs. (1)
Arrangements made by or on behalf of an employer. The term "arrangements", as defined in subs. (2), applies only in relation to arrangements for determining who should be offered employment, and to any term, condition or arrangements on which employment, promotion, transfer, training or any other benefit is offered or afforded. According to the Minister; "The broad term 'arrangements' has deliberately been used [in s.4(1)(a) and subs. (1)] to cover anything done by or for an employer as part of his recruitment process or in making available opportunities in employment. It would not only include work practices and procedures, so far as such practices or procedures have any bearing on determining who is offered employment or to whom such opportunities are made available; it would go wider than that." (*Hansard*, H.C., Standing Committee E, col. 142). Examples of arrangements which might place a disabled person at a disadvantage include: working times which are inconvenient because of the needs of carers or the difficulty of negotiating rush-hour crowds; instructions which are difficult to understand for a person with a learning disability; or, where the employer has car parking facilities, not allocating a parking space to a disabled employee who finds it very difficult to use public trans-

port. There is a power in subs. (8) to make regulations as to the circumstances in which arrangements are or are not to be taken to place a disabled person at a substantial disadvantage.

Premises occupied by the employer. The duty of employers to make reasonable adjustments to premises where some physical feature of those premises causes substantial disadvantage to a disabled person applies only in relation to premises which are occupied by the employer:

"employers are not under a duty to make reasonable adjustments in respect of, for example, features of the disabled person's private house. It would also not apply to some other employer's premises in the case, say, of a travelling salesman or to the disabled person's home in the case of a homeworker." (Minister of State, *Hansard,* H.L., Vol. 566, col. 184).

Examples of physical features of premises which might place a disabled person at a disadvantage include: doors that are too narrow for someone using a wheelchair; taps that someone with arthritis cannot turn; or lighting too dim for someone with restricted vision.

The duty of an employer to make reasonable adjustments to premises may present problems where the employer occupies premises under a lease, the terms of which prevent or restrict the occupier from making alterations to the premises. In those circumstances, the terms of the lease are overridden by s.16 of the Act, which entitles the occupier to alter the premises, with the written consent of the landlord, in order to comply with a duty to make adjustments under this section. See the note to s.16.

Part M of the Building Regulations 1988 (revised in 1991) contains mandatory requirements for new non-domestic buildings (including substantial extensions) relating to the provision of access and facilities for disabled people. In the Bill as originally published, the duty to make adjustments did not apply to a physical feature of a building or extension erected in compliance with any requirement of the Building Regulations relating to disabled people. That exemption was subsequently dropped from the Bill at Report stage in the House of Commons (*Hansard*, H.C., Vol. 257, col. 891), but the Government is considering making regulations under subs. (8)(e) to similar effect. The effect would be that where a building or extension was constructed in accordance with Building Regulations relating to disabled people, the duty to make adjustments would not apply to any aspect of a feature specifically covered by those regulations (*e.g.* the width of a door), as long as that feature continued to meet the requirements which were in force when the building or extension was constructed (an important *caveat* in view of the fact that Pt. M contains no mechanism for continuing control over buildings). The exemption would not apply to other aspects of physical features which were not covered by Building Regulations. The Government is contemplating the introduction of a similar exemption for buildings or extensions constructed in accordance with a requirement of the British Standard on "Access for the disabled to buildings" (BS5810).

Substantial disadvantage. The duty to make adjustments only arises where the employer's arrangements or premises place a disabled person at a "substantial disadvantage" in comparison with people who are not disabled. In Committee, the Minister indicated that the use of the term "substantial" is intended to exclude minor and trivial disadvantage:

"To a lawyer, the word 'substantial' literally means of substance. It does not necessarily mean the large, grand, highly significant object that a layman might imagine. ... The word 'substantial' is included to remove the possibility of the most minor things being brought into play." (Parliamentary Under-Secretary of State, *Hansard*, H.C., Standing Committee E, col. 196).

Subs. (3)

Other examples of steps which it might be reasonable for an employer to take are: providing signers, hearing aid-compatible telephones or minicom facilities, or allocating a dedicated parking space.

Subs. (11)

This subsection disapplies the duty of reasonable adjustment in relation to benefits under occupational pension schemes and certain other similar benefits, and should be read together with the provisions in s.5(7) which allow less favourable treatment of disabled employees in certain circumstances: see the note to s.5 above. The case for excluding the duty was explained in the following terms:

"Where a disabled person has been lawfully refused access to part of an occupational pension scheme—for example, based on a reasonable belief that his health condition presents an unreasonable risk—the employer will not have to consider ways in which his overall remuneration package can be brought up to the level enjoyed by other employees; for example, by increasing his salary." (Minister of State, *Hansard*, H.L., Vol. 566, col. 1001).

So, for example, if regulations were to be made under s.5(7)(b) enabling employers to maintain uniform rates of contribution in relation to occupational pension schemes, so that a disabled person could be required to pay the same rate of contributions as other employees although not eligible for some of the benefits of the scheme, an employer would not be required to make a reasonable adjustment to overcome the disadvantage to the disabled employee.

Exemption for small businesses

7.—(1) Nothing in this Part applies in relation to an employer who has fewer than 20 employees.

(2) The Secretary of State may by order amend subsection (1) by substituting a different number (not greater than 20) for the number for the time being specified there.

(3) In this section—

"anniversary" means the anniversary of the coming into force of this section; and

"review" means a review of the effect of this section.

(4) Before making any order under subsection (2), the Secretary of State shall conduct a review.

(5) Unless he has already begun or completed a review under subsection (4), the Secretary of State shall begin to conduct a review immediately after the fourth anniversary.

(6) Any review shall be completed within nine months.

(7) In conducting any review, the Secretary of State shall consult—

(a) such organisations representing the interests of employers as he considers appropriate; and

(b) such organisations representing the interests of disabled persons in employment or seeking employment as he considers appropriate.

(8) If, on completing a review, the Secretary of State decides to make an order under subsection (2), he shall make such an order to come into force not later than one year after the commencement of the review.

(9) If, on completing a review, the Secretary of State decides not to make such an order, he shall not later than one year after the commencement of the review lay before Parliament a report—

(a) summarising the results of the review; and

(b) giving the reasons for his decision.

(10) Any report made by the Secretary of State under subsection (9) shall include a summary of the views expressed to him in his consultations.

GENERAL NOTE

The exemption of small businesses (*i.e.* employers with fewer than 20 employees) from the employment provisions of the Act is one of its most controversial measures. The effect of the exemption is to exclude 96 per cent of employers from the duty not to discriminate against disabled persons, and while Government statistics indicate that 83 per cent of employees will be covered by the Act (Parliamentary Under-Secretary of State, *Hansard*, H.C., Standing Committee E, col. 248), if one includes self-employed workers (who come within the scope of the protection where they contract personally to do any work: s.68(1)), the coverage falls to 65 per cent (Prescott-Clarke, *Employment and Handicap*, 1990, SCPR, London). There is a similar exemption in the Disabled Persons (Employment) Act 1944 (c. 10), in that the provisions in s.9 of that Act requiring employers to employ a 3 per cent quota of registered disabled employees only apply to those employing 20 or more employees (s.9 and the associated provisions are prospectively repealed by s.62(7), from a date to be announced). The Government has indicated that 20 was chosen as the appropriate figure for the cut-off because that is the figure which applies under the 1944 Act (Parliamentary Under-Secretary of State, *Hansard*, H.C., Standing Committee E, col. 246). In the context of the 1944 Act, an exemption for small employers was perhaps inevitable, because statistically it is difficult to apply a 3 per cent quota to small firms (in a firm of 17 employees or less, 3 per cent rounded to the nearest whole number is zero). Such technical considerations do not apply where legislation is based on a principle of non-discrimination rather than on the enforcement of a quota. The main reason for the exemption of small employers from the new provisions is a desire on the part of the Government to reduce the administrative and cost burdens on small employers.

The Government has not sought to justify the small business exemption on the grounds of compliance cost alone. It would have been difficult to do so, given the evidence that in most cases, the necessary adjustments will have a nil or minimal cost (see the note to s.6). The Government's own Compliance Cost Assessment for the Act assumes an average cost of £200 per disabled employee for the 10 per cent of cases where a disabled employee is likely to require an adjustment. In some cases the cost of an adjustment may of course be much higher, but it can be argued that the interests of small businesses are adequately protected, without the need for a blanket exemption, by the fact that employers are only required to make *reasonable* adjustments, taking into account the extent of the employer's resources, the availability of outside financial assistance, etc. The Government also has the power to place a financial limit on adjustments, but significantly it decided not to impose any such cap in employment cases (unlike in cases involving the supply of goods and services) because it was not persuaded that a financial limit was necessary in view of the likely cost burden on employers.

During the passage of the Bill through Parliament, the Government placed greater emphasis on the administrative burden of complying with the legislation:

"the Government have no desire that small businesses should discriminate against disabled people or any other group of people ... but we want it recognised that small firms are subject to many constraints, not least that they cannot be expected to have the personnel resources—the range of abilities, knowledge, competence and time—to allow them to concern themselves with the minutiae of legislation. That is why ... we maintain the view that businesses with fewer than 20 employees should be exempted from the legislation." (Parliamentary Under-Secretary of State, *Hansard*, H.C., Standing Committee E, col. 248).

This argument was anticipated in the White Paper, *Ending discrimination against disabled people*, which stated that the proposed exemption for small employers "... reflects the Government's recognition that it may be more difficult and burdensome for smaller firms without specialist personnel to get to grips with the new right and obtain the advice they need in particular cases." (Cm. 2729, 1995, para. 3.10). There is however, no exemption from the complex provisions of Pt. III of the Act for small suppliers of goods and services (*e.g.* the proverbial corner shop), even though an argument based on administrative burdens would seem to apply with equal if not greater force in that context. Neither is there any exemption for small employers from the sex and race discrimination legislation, or from the health and safety legislation. The Minister's claim that the comparison with the S.D.A. and the R.R.A. is misleading because "they are much more simple, straightforward pieces of legislation, and are much easier for a small business man to grasp than the implications of [this Act]" (*Hansard*, H.C., Vol. 257, col. 730) may well ring hollow with employers who have had to grapple with, for example, equal value claims under the Equal Pay Act 1970 (c. 41).

The Secretary of State has the power to change the threshold of 20 employees, but only to a lower number (subs. (2)), and he must conduct a review of the effect of the exemption before making any changes (subs. (4)). The exemption must in any event be reviewed after the employment provisions of the Act have been in force for four years (subs. (5)), unless it has been reviewed earlier, and the results of the review must be reported to Parliament a year after that (subs. (9)). Given that the Government's explanation for the exemption relies in part at least on the difficulty for small employers in getting to grips with the new provisions, it may not be unduly optimistic to expect that the current threshold of 20 will be reduced as the Act's provisions become more familiar: "It is unrealistic to expect [the small-scale employer] to know what might or might not be reasonable, to take advice or follow case law as it develops, *especially in the early years of an Act's implementation*." (Parliamentary Under-Secretary of State, *Hansard*, H.C., Vol. 257, col. 728, emphasis added).

Subs. (1)
An employer who has fewer than 20 employees. In calculating the number of employees, any apprentices and self-employed workers who contract personally to do any work must be included (s.68(1)). The threshold applies to the number of employees which the employer has. Unlike the small employer threshold which applies in some other areas of employment law (*e.g.* under ss.146(4B) and s.56A of the Employment Protection (Consolidation) Act 1978 (c. 44)), employees who are employed by associated employers are not to be included in the calculation. The Minister confirmed during debates on the Bill that, for these purposes, "Each individual company within a group is a separate employer." (Minister of State, *Hansard*, H.L., Vol. 564, col. 1917).

Although not expressly spelt out in the Act, it seems that the relevant date for determining whether or not the exemption applies is the date on which the discriminatory act complained of took place (Parliamentary Under-Secretary of State, *Hansard*, H.C., Standing Committee E, col. 227). A small firm which expands above the threshold will therefore have to fulfil the obligations imposed by the Act (including the duty to make reasonable adjustments) from that point in time onwards, unless and until the number of employees falls below the threshold once again. Difficult problems are likely to arise in the case of firms with fluctuating workforces where the number of employees oscillates above and below the threshold, or where a seasonal influx of casual workers takes a small firm over the threshold for a limited period. If the exemption ceases to apply, the protection against disability discrimination applies to all employees, not just to those who are newly employed: "Once the firm [has] expanded to 20 employees or more, it would have to fulfil the obligations that we propose. That would include reassessing a previous series of acts in the light of the new obligations and ceasing any form of discrimination." (Parliamentary Under-Secretary of State, *Hansard*, H.C., Standing Committee E, col. 249). However, that protection will be lost if the number falls below the threshold again, along with the entitlement to any adjustments made by the employer, unless the employee had a contractual entitlement to the adjustment. It is unclear whether, in a case where an employer's workforce fluctuates above and below the threshold, a tribunal will be able to take that fact into account in determining whether it would be reasonable to require the employer to make an adjustment.

Enforcement etc.

Enforcement, remedies and procedure

8.—(1) A complaint by any person that another person—
(a) has discriminated against him in a way which is unlawful under this Part, or
(b) is, by virtue of section 57 or 58, to be treated as having discriminated against him in such a way,
may be presented to an industrial tribunal.

(2) Where an industrial tribunal finds that a complaint presented to it under this section is well-founded, it shall take such of the following steps as it considers just and equitable— ,
(a) making a declaration as to the rights of the complainant and the respondent in relation to the matters to which the complaint relates;
(b) ordering the respondent to pay compensation to the complainant;
(c) recommending that the respondent take, within a specified period, action appearing to the tribunal to be reasonable, in all the circumstances of the case, for the purpose of obviating or reducing the adverse effect on the complainant of any matter to which the complaint relates.

(3) Where a tribunal orders compensation under subsection (2)(b), the amount of the compensation shall be calculated by applying the principles applicable to the calculation of damages in claims in tort or (in Scotland) in reparation for breach of statutory duty.

(4) For the avoidance of doubt it is hereby declared that compensation in respect of discrimination in a way which is unlawful under this Part may include compensation for injury to feelings whether or not it includes compensation under any other head.

(5) If the respondent to a complaint fails, without reasonable justification, to comply with a recommendation made by an industrial tribunal under subsection (2)(c) the tribunal may, if it thinks it just and equitable to do so—
(a) increase the amount of compensation required to be paid to the complainant in respect of the complaint, where an order was made under subsection (2)(b); or
(b) make an order under subsection (2)(b).

(6) Regulations may make provision—
(a) for enabling a tribunal, where an amount of compensation falls to be awarded under subsection (2)(b), to include in the award interest on that amount; and
(b) specifying, for cases where a tribunal decides that an award is to include an amount in respect of interest, the manner in which and the periods and rate by reference to which the interest is to be determined.

(7) Regulations may modify the operation of any order made under paragraph 6A of Schedule 9 to the Employment Protection (Consolidation) Act 1978 (power to make provision as to interest on sums payable in pursuance of

industrial tribunal decisions) to the extent that it relates to an award of compensation under subsection (2)(b).

(8) Part I of Schedule 3 makes further provision about the enforcement of this Part and about procedure.

GENERAL NOTE

As with complaints of discrimination on grounds of sex and race, complaints of unlawful disability discrimination under Pt. II must be made to an industrial tribunal. The detailed procedures, and the remedies available, are similar to those which apply in complaints under the Sex Discrimination Act 1975 and the Race Relations Act 1976. There are however some important differences; in particular, the Act makes no provision for the enforcement of the employment provisions, or for the assistance of individual complainants, by a body equivalent to the Equal Opportunities Commission or the Commission for Racial Equality. The National Disability Council established under Pt. VI is only empowered to advise the Government on general issues relating to discrimination against disabled people. It has no power to investigate complaints of discrimination, to provide assistance to individuals in enforcing their rights before the courts and tribunals, or to take strategic enforcement action of its own accord (see the note to s.50). Predictably, this has been a major source of criticism of the Act's provisions. There is however provision, as in claims of sex and race discrimination, for the Secretary of State to issue a questionnaire which a potential complainant may serve on the employer to help him or her decide whether to make a complaint, and if so, to formulate and present the case in the most effective manner: see the note to s.56. The employer's replies to these questions will be admissible in evidence in any subsequent tribunal proceedings, and a tribunal may draw adverse inferences from a failure to reply, or a reply which is evasive or equivocal. Special provision is also made for the application of reporting restrictions where evidence of a personal nature is likely to be heard by the tribunal hearing the complaint: see the notes to ss.62 and 63. There is an appeal to the Employment Appeal Tribunal on a point of law from the decision of an industrial tribunal under this Act: Sched. 6, para. 2, amending the E.P.(C.)A. 1978, s.136(1).

Subs. (1)
Presented to an industrial tribunal. Complaints under Pt. II must be presented to an industrial tribunal before the end of the period of three months beginning when the act complained of was done (Sched. 3, para. 3(1)), although the tribunal may consider a complaint which is out of time "if, in all the circumstances of the case, it considers that it is just and equitable to do so" (*ibid.* para. 3(2)). This discretionary power of the tribunal to extend the time-limit is more flexible than the escape clause normally used in employment protection legislation (*e.g.* in complaints of unfair dismissal under the E.P.(C.)A. 1978, s.67), which focuses on whether it was "reasonably practicable" for the complaint to be brought in time. Where the act of discrimination is attributable to a contract term, the discriminatory act will be treated as extending throughout the duration of the contract; an act "extending over a period" (see below) will be treated as done at the end of that period; and a deliberate omission will be treated as done when the person decided upon it (Sched. 3, para. 3(3)). A person will be taken to have decided upon an omission when he or she does an act inconsistent with doing the omitted act, or, if no such inconsistent act has been done, at the expiry of the period within which he or she might reasonably have been expected to do the omitted act, if it was to be done (*ibid.* para. 3(4)).

These provisions mirror those in the S.D.A., s.76, and the R.R.A., s.68, and decisions on the interpretation of those provisions are likely to be in point here also. In cases under the S.D.A. and R.R.A., the following points, *inter alia,* have emerged:
  (i)   the question of whether it is just and equitable to extend the three-month time limit has been held to be a question of fact for the tribunal (*Foster v. South Glamorgan Health Authority* [1988] I.R.L.R. 277), and the decision of the tribunal on this point is likely to be difficult to challenge on appeal (*Hutchinson v. Westward Television* [1977] I.R.L.R. 69).
  (ii) the discovery of facts indicating possible discrimination after the expiry of the three-month time-limit may be a good reason to allow an application out of time: see for example, *Clarke v. Hampshire Electro-Plating Co.* [1991] I.R.L.R. 490; *Berry v. Ravensbourne National Health Service Trust* [1993] I.C.R. 871.
  (iii) in cases involving dismissal, the time-limit runs from the date on which the complainant actually finds himself or herself out of a job, and not (as in unfair dismissal complaints) from the effective date of termination: see *Lupetti v. Wrens Old House* [1984] I.C.R. 348, a case under the R.R.A., which was applied in the context of the S.D.A. in *Gloucester Working Men's Club & Institute v. James* [1986] I.C.R. 603; see also *Adekeye v. Post Office* [1993] I.R.L.R. 324, where the time limit was held to run from the rejection of an internal appeal, rather than from the date of the dismissal.

(iv) the rule concerning acts "extending over a period" has been held to apply only to a *continuing* act of discrimination, and not to a situation where a *single* act or event of discrimination has continuing *consequences*. So, for example, in *Amies v. Inner London Education Authority* [1977] I.C.R. 308, a case under the S.D.A., s.76(6)(b), the E.A.T. rejected the complainant's argument that the employer's failure to appoint her to a particular post was a continuing act of discrimination; in contrast, in *Calder v. James Findlay Corporation (Note)* [1989] I.R.L.R. 55, the employer's refusal to allow the complainant access to a mortgage subsidy scheme was held by the E.A.T. to be a continuing discrimination against her, so that she was entitled to bring her complaint more than three months after the refusal. These cases were approved by the House of Lords in *Barclays Bank v. Kapur* [1991] I.R.L.R. 136, a case under the R.R.A., s. 68(7)(c), in which the employer's refusal to recognise the complainant's previous service for pensions purposes was held to be a continuing act of discrimination. That decision was followed in *Littlewoods Organisation v. Traynor* [1993] I.R.L.R. 154, where the employer's failure to take promised remedial action in relation to a complaint of discrimination was held to constitute a continuing act of discrimination, but was distinguished in *Sougrin v. Haringey Health Authority* [1991] I.R.L.R. 447, affirmed [1992] I.R.L.R. 416 where the employer's decision on grading was held to be a single event, not a continuing act of discrimination. See also *Owusu v. London Fire & Civil Defence Authority* [1995] I.R.L.R. 574.

(v) in *Swithland Motors v. Clarke* [1994] I.C.R. 231, a case under the S.D.A., s.76(6)(c), involving an alleged deliberate omission to offer employment, the E.A.T. held that "decided" means "decided at a time and in circumstances when [the person] was in a position to implement that decision."

Subss. (2)–(5)

The remedies available for an act of unlawful discrimination are similar to those which apply under S.D.A., s.65, and R.R.A., s.56: the tribunal may make a declaration as to the rights of the parties, order the respondent to pay the complainant compensation, and/or recommend that the respondent take, within a specified period, action which appears to the tribunal to be reasonable, in all the circumstances, for the purpose of obviating or reducing the adverse effect of the unlawful conduct on the complainant.

Compensation. There is no upper limit on the compensation which may be awarded in a complaint under this section, in line with the equivalent provisions under the S.D.A. and the R.R.A., where the upper limits were removed by the Sex Discrimination and Equal Pay (Remedies) Regulations 1993 (S.I. 1993 No. 2798), and the Race Relations (Remedies) Act 1994 (c. 10), respectively. As in cases under the S.D.A. and R.R.A., compensation is to be assessed by applying the principles applicable to the calculation of damages in tort or, in Scotland, reparation for breach of statutory duty (subs. (3)), and may include compensation for injury to feelings (subs. (4)). Amounts awarded for injury to feelings in cases under the S.D.A. and R.R.A. have traditionally tended to be low, although in *Noone v. North West Thames Regional Health Authority* [1988] I.R.L.R. 195, the Court of Appeal awarded £3,000 under that head in a case of unlawful race discrimination where it considered that the injury to feelings was severe. More recently, in *Sharifi v. Strathclyde Regional Council* [1992] I.R.L.R. 259, the E.A.T. indicated that £500 was "at or near the minimum" for an award of damages for injury to feelings in race discrimination cases, and in *Ministry of Defence v. Sullivan* [1994] I.C.R. 193, the E.A.T. said that there would be an award for injury to feelings in most sex discrimination cases, and approved an award of £750. For detailed guidance from the Court of Appeal on the assessment of compensation in cases under the R.R.A., see *Alexander v. Home Office* [1988] I.R.L.R. 190; I.C.R. 685.

In some earlier Court of Appeal decisions in cases under the S.D.A. and the R.R.A., it was assumed that exemplary damages could be awarded in sex and race discrimination cases (see for example, *Alexander v. Home Office* (above), and *Bradford City Metropolitan Council v. Arora* [1989] I.C.R. 719). However, in *Deane v. Ealing London Borough Council* [1993] I.R.L.R. 209, the E.A.T. held that a tribunal has no power to make an award of exemplary damages under the R.R.A., following the decision of the Court of Appeal in *Gibbons v. South Western Water Services* [1993] 1 All E.R. 609 that exemplary damages may only be awarded for torts recognised as existing before the decision of the House of Lords in *Rookes v. Barnard* [1964] A.C. 1129. For a similar ruling with respect to exemplary damages under the S.D.A., see *Ministry of Defence v. Meredith* [1995] I.R.L.R. 539. It follows that exemplary damages may not be awarded under this section. The E.A.T. in *Deane* upheld an award of aggravated damages under the R.R.A., and in *Meredith* the E.A.T. confirmed that aggravated damages may also be awarded under the S.D.A.

Action appearing to the tribunal to be reasonable. The tribunal is also empowered to recommend that the respondent takes certain specified remedial action. This discretion is not unfettered, as the recommendation must be for the purpose of remedying the matter to which the complaint relates. In *Noone v. North West Thames Regional Health Authority (No 2)* [1988] I.R.L.R. 550, the Court of Appeal held, under the similar provisions of the R.R.A., that a tribunal had no power to recommend that an applicant who had not been promoted because of unlawful discrimination should be appointed to the next available vacancy, or be given preferential treatment in the selection procedure; indeed, any such response on the part of the employer might constitute an act of unlawful positive discrimination (see for example, *British Gas v. Sharma* [1991] I.R.L.R. 101). Curiously, whereas under the S.D.A. and R.R.A. the tribunal may recommend that the respondent take "action appearing to the tribunal to be *practicable*", this section refers to "action appearing to the tribunal to be *reasonable*"; unfortunately it is not clear whether the difference in wording is intended to be of any significance. If the respondent fails without reasonable justification to comply with a recommendation, the tribunal may increase the amount of compensation already awarded, or may make such an award, if it thinks it is just and equitable to do so (subs. (5)).

Subs. (8)
  Schedule 3, para. 1 makes provision for conciliation through ACAS, as with complaints under the S.D.A. and the R.R.A.; para. 2 provides that the remedies available for an infringement of Pt. II are (with the exception of judicial review) exclusively those provided by this section; para. 3 makes provision for time-limits (see the note to subs. (1)); and para. 4 concerns certification by Ministers: see the note to s.59.

Validity of certain agreements

  9.—(1) Any term in a contract of employment or other agreement is void so far as it purports to—
  (a) require a person to do anything which would contravene any provision of, or made under, this Part;
  (b) exclude or limit the operation of any provision of this Part; or
  (c) prevent any person from presenting a complaint to an industrial tribunal under this Part.
  (2) Paragraphs (b) and (c) of subsection (1) do not apply to an agreement not to institute proceedings under section 8(1), or to an agreement not to continue such proceedings, if—
  (a) a conciliation officer has acted under paragraph 1 of Schedule 3 in relation to the matter; or
  (b) the conditions set out in subsection (3) are satisfied.
  (3) The conditions are that—
  (a) the complainant must have received independent legal advice from a qualified lawyer as to the terms and effect of the proposed agreement (and in particular its effect on his ability to pursue his complaint before an industrial tribunal);
  (b) when the adviser gave the advice there must have been in force a policy of insurance covering the risk of a claim by the complainant in respect of loss arising in consequence of the advice; and
  (c) the agreement must be in writing, relate to the particular complaint, identify the adviser and state that the conditions are satisfied.
  (4) In this section—
  "independent", in relation to legal advice to the complainant, means that it is given by a lawyer who is not acting for the other party or for a person who is connected with that other party; and
  "qualified lawyer" means—
        (a) as respects proceedings in England and Wales, a barrister (whether in practice as such or employed to give legal advice) or a solicitor of the Supreme Court who holds a practising certificate; and
        (b) as respects proceedings in Scotland, an advocate (whether in practice as such or employed to give legal advice) or a solicitor who holds a practising certificate.
  (5) For the purposes of subsection (4), any two persons are to be treated as connected if—

(a) one is a company of which the other (directly or indirectly) has control, or

(b) both are companies of which a third person (directly or indirectly) has control.

GENERAL NOTE
This section places restrictions on contracting out of the Act's provisions. It renders void any term in a contract of employment or other agreement if it, (a) requires a person to contravene this Part of the Act; (b) attempts to exclude or limit the operation of this Part of the Act; or (c) attempts to prevent a person from presenting a complaint to an industrial tribunal under this Part of the Act. Exception is however made in the case of an agreement not to institute or continue proceedings, where that agreement has been reached with the assistance of an ACAS conciliation officer, or where the parties have made a valid compromise contract.

The requirements for a valid compromise contract are set out in subs. (3); they mirror the corresponding provisions introduced into the S.D.A. and the R.R.A. by the Trade Union Reform and Employment Rights Act 1993 (c. 19), s.39 and Sched. 6. The principal requirements are that the complainant must have received independent legal advice from a qualified lawyer as to the terms and effect of the proposed agreement, and its effect on his ability to pursue his complaint before a tribunal; the adviser must be covered by appropriate insurance at the time when the advice is given; and the agreement must be in writing, relate to the particular complaint, identify the adviser and state that these conditions are satisfied.

Charities and support for particular groups of persons

10.—(1) Nothing in this Part—

(a) affects any charitable instrument which provides for conferring benefits on one or more categories of person determined by reference to any physical or mental capacity; or

(b) makes unlawful any act done by a charity or recognised body in pursuance of any of its charitable purposes, so far as those purposes are connected with persons so determined.

(2) Nothing in this Part prevents—

(a) a person who provides supported employment from treating members of a particular group of disabled persons more favourably than other persons in providing such employment; or

(b) the Secretary of State from agreeing to arrangements for the provision of supported employment which will, or may, have that effect.

(3) In this section—

"charitable instrument" means an enactment or other instrument (whenever taking effect) so far as it relates to charitable purposes;

"charity" has the same meaning as in the Charities Act 1993;

"recognised body" means a body which is a recognised body for the purposes of Part I of the Law Reform (Miscellaneous Provisions) (Scotland) Act 1990; and

"supported employment" means facilities provided, or in respect of which payments are made, under section 15 of the Disabled Persons (Employment) Act 1944.

(4) In the application of this section to England and Wales, "charitable purposes" means purposes which are exclusively charitable according to the law of England and Wales.

(5) In the application of this section to Scotland, "charitable purposes" shall be construed in the same way as if it were contained in the Income Tax Acts.

GENERAL NOTE
This section contains specific exemptions from Pt. II for charities and for the providers of supported employment. Subsection (1) is designed to enable charities which confer benefits on particular categories of disabled people in pursuance of their charitable purposes, to continue to do so without fear of infringing the provisions of Pt. II. It means, for example, that an organisation like the Royal National Institute for the Deaf will continue to be able to employ people with hearing impairments in preference to people with other kinds of disability "because of their

experience or the techniques they have learned in coping with their specific impairment. They may also wish to encourage the employment of people with such disabilities by setting a personal example of doing so themselves." (Minister of State, *Hansard*, H.L., Vol. 564, col. 1932).

Subsection (2) provides an exemption for the providers of supported employment who treat members of a particular group of disabled persons more favourably that other persons in providing such employment. The supported employment programme was set up under the Disabled Persons (Employment) Act 1944, s.15 to provide employment opportunities for severely disabled people who would otherwise be unlikely to obtain employment because of the nature or severity of their disability. The provisions in the 1944 Act on supported employment are to continue, notwithstanding the repeal of much of that Act: see the note to s.61.

Charity. The exemption is not restricted to registered charities.

Advertisements suggesting that employers will discriminate against disabled persons

11.—(1) This section applies where—

(a) a disabled person has applied for employment with an employer;
(b) the employer has refused to offer, or has deliberately not offered, him the employment;
(c) the disabled person has presented a complaint under section 8 against the employer;
(d) the employer has advertised the employment (whether before or after the disabled person applied for it); and
(e) the advertisement indicated, or might reasonably be understood to have indicated, that any application for the advertised employment would, or might, be determined to any extent by reference to—
    (i) the successful applicant not having any disability or any category of disability which includes the disabled person's disability; or
    (ii) the employer's reluctance to take any action of a kind mentioned in section 6.

(2) The tribunal hearing the complaint shall assume, unless the contrary is shown, that the employer's reason for refusing to offer, or deliberately not offering, the employment to the complainant was related to the complainant's disability.

(3) In this section "advertisement" includes every form of advertisement or notice, whether to the public or not.

GENERAL NOTE

This section tackles the difficult issue of discriminatory job advertisements. It provides that where a job advertisement suggests (or might reasonably be taken to suggest) that the employer might discriminate against disabled applicants, then in any complaint by a disabled person under s.8 of the Act, the tribunal must assume, unless the contrary is shown, that the employer's reason for not offering the employment to the complainant was related to his or her disability. This assumption applies where the job advertisement indicated (or might be understood to have indicated) that the outcome of any application for the job would, or might be determined to any extent, by reference to the successful applicant not having any disability, or the kind of disability which the complainant has, or to the employer's reluctance to make a reasonable adjustment. The complainant must have sought and been refused the employment to which the advertisement relates, but it does not matter whether the employment was advertised before or after the complainant applied for it. It can be seen that the only significance of a discriminatory job advertisement under this section is that it gives rise to an assumption of discrimination in a complaint under s.8. As such a complaint may not be brought against an employer with fewer than 20 employees, it follows that there is nothing in this section which prevents a small employer from placing an advertisement which clearly demonstrates an intention to discriminate against disabled applicants.

The approach to discriminatory advertisements in this section differs significantly from that taken in the sex and race discrimination legislation, under which it is unlawful to publish or cause to be published an advertisement which indicates or might reasonably be understood as indicating an intention to commit an unlawful act of discrimination (S.D.A., s.38; R.R.A., s.29). Enforcement under those Acts is placed in the hands of the Equal Opportunities Commission and the Commission for Racial Equality, which may seek a declaration or, if the defendant appears likely to commit further unlawful acts, an injunction, or alternatively may serve a non-discrimination notice on the defendant. One obvious explanation for the difference in approach lies in the lack of a suitable body to bring enforcement proceedings in this context, the role of the National Disability Council being confined to the giving of advice to Ministers: see the note to s.50.

The approach of this section more closely resembles that of the Trade Union and Labour Relations (Consolidation) Act 1992 (c. 52), s.137, to job advertisements which discriminate on grounds of union membership. There are however some important differences: first, a job advertisement is only caught by the T.U.L.R.A. provisions where it indicates (or might reasonably be understood as indicating) that a particular job "is open only to a person who is, or is not, a union member"; in contrast, the provisions in this section apply where the advertisement indicates (or might reasonably be understood as indicating) that an application "would or might be determined to any extent by reference to" the applicant not having a disability, etc. Secondly, under the T.U.L.R.A. provisions, a person who does not satisfy the condition regarding union membership and who applies unsuccessfully for the job is conclusively presumed to have been refused it unlawfully, regardless of any other reason there may have been for the employer's decision not to appoint that person, whereas under this section the employer has the opportunity of rebutting the presumption by showing that the reason the employment was not offered to the complainant was not related to his or her disability. Furthermore, even if the employer fails to rebut the presumption, he may be able to show that the refusal of employment is justified within the meaning of s.5.

A major source of controversy in this area is the mentioning of health requirements in job advertisements. The Government's view is that a blanket ban on mentioning health requirements in job advertisements would be inappropriate, because there might be legitimate reasons why an employer would wish to mention such requirements in an advertisement, for example, where they are relevant to the job (Minister of State, *Hansard*, H.L., Vol. 566, col. 176). "What is important is to cover the problem of employers trying to dissuade disabled people from applying for jobs that they might be able to do ..." (Minister of State, *Hansard*, H.L., Vol. 564, col. 1935). However, the Minister also emphasised that, while employers should be able to advise potential applicants of the genuine physical and mental requirements of a specific job, "employers will be well advised to consider the duty of reasonable adjustment in identifying health requirements which might be overcome by such an adjustment." (Minister of State, *Hansard*, H.L., Vol. 566, col. 176).

Subs. (3)
Advertisement. The same definition is also applied for the purposes of T.U.L.R.A., s.137: see T.U.L.R.A., s.143(1). The definition is a broad one, encompassing every form of advertisement or notice, whether public or not. It is certainly wide enough to cover notices on company notice-boards and in internal newsletters, as well as advertisements in the press.

Discrimination by other persons

Discrimination against contract workers

12.—(1) It is unlawful for a principal, in relation to contract work, to discriminate against a disabled person—

(a) in the terms on which he allows him to do that work;
(b) by not allowing him to do it or continue to do it;
(c) in the way he affords him access to any benefits or by refusing or deliberately omitting to afford him access to them; or
(d) by subjecting him to any other detriment.

(2) Subsection (1) does not apply to benefits of any description if the principal is concerned with the provision (whether or not for payment) of benefits of that description to the public, or to a section of the public which includes the contract worker in question, unless that provision differs in a material respect from the provision of the benefits by the principal to contract workers.

(3) The provisions of this Part (other than subsections (1) to (3) of section 4) apply to any principal, in relation to contract work, as if he were, or would be, the employer of the contract worker and as if any contract worker supplied to do work for him were an employee of his.

(4) In the case of an act which constitutes discrimination by virtue of section 55, this section also applies to discrimination against a person who is not disabled.

(5) This section applies only in relation to contract work done at an establishment in Great Britain (the provisions of section 68 about the meaning of "employment at an establishment in Great Britain" applying for the purposes of this subsection with the appropriate modifications).

(6) In this section—

"principal" means a person ("A") who makes work available for doing by individuals who are employed by another person who supplies them under a contract made with A;

"contract work" means work so made available; and

"contract worker" means any individual who is supplied to the principal under such a contract.

GENERAL NOTE

In common with the sex and race discrimination legislation, this section extends the prohibition on discrimination against disabled persons to the hirer of contract labour, by placing hirers under a duty of non-discrimination similar to the duty imposed on employers by s.4 of the Act. The provisions apply where workers ("contract workers") are supplied under contract by their employer to a third party hirer (the "principal") who makes "contract work" available for them. Subsection (1) provides that it is unlawful for a principal, in relation to contract work, to discriminate against a disabled person (a) in the terms on which he allows that person to do contract work, (b) by not allowing that person to do or to continue to do contract work, (c) in the way in which that person is given access to any benefits, or by refusing or deliberately omitting to give him access to those benefits (unless benefits of that description are also provided by the principal to the public at large within subs. (2)) or (d) by subjecting that person to any other detriment. In all other respects, the provisions of Pt. II (for example, in relation to the definition of discrimination, the duty to make reasonable adjustments and the defence of justification) apply to the hirer of a contract worker as if that person were the employer of that worker (subs. (3)). However, the duty of a principal to make reasonable adjustments for a contract worker is bound to reflect the fact that the relationship between principal and contract worker is not the same as the relationship between employer and employee: "Clearly what would be reasonable in the case of the hirer would depend on the hirer's circumstances and this would necessarily take account of the often much more limited relationship between the hirer and worker. For example, there might be very few types of adjustment a principal could reasonably be required to make for people hired for only a couple of weeks or for people whom the employer needed at very short notice." (Minister of State, *Hansard*, H.L., Vol. 566, col. 222).

There is of course a potential overlap where the duty to make reasonable adjustments is imposed on both the principal and the employment business which is the contract worker's employer. It seems that the principal's duty of reasonable adjustment "would include the hirer co-operating as far as was reasonable with adjustments made by the employment business" (*ibid.* col. 222), and the Government has indicated that it intends to make regulations to provide in detail for the allocation of the duty to make reasonable adjustments between the two organisations. Although not expressly stated in the Act, it would appear that the small business exemption applies to a hirer of contract labour under this section as it applies to an employer, by virtue of subs. (3); "The provisions of this Part ... apply to any Principal ... as if he were, or would be, the employer of the contract worker...". This gives rise to a confusing variety of permutations: circumstances may arise where the contract worker's employer is exempt from the Act's provisions because he has fewer than 20 employees, but the hirer is not, and vice versa; alternatively both parties, or neither party, may be exempt, depending on the numbers employed or hired (as the case may be) by each of them at the relevant time. To make matters worse, the position as regards exemption may change from day to day, as the numbers employed or hired by the parties changes. It is to be hoped that the regulations will clarify exactly where the duty to make reasonable adjustments lies in such cases.

For the equivalent provisions in relation to sex and race discrimination, see the S.D.A., s.9, and the R.R.A., s.7.

Who supplies them under a contract. Under the equivalent provisions in the S.D.A., s.9, the E.A.T. has held that there must be an undertaking by the supplier to supply the workers in question to the principal: *Rice v. Fon-a-Car* [1980] I.C.R. 133.

Discrimination by trade organisations

13.—(1) It is unlawful for a trade organisation to discriminate against a disabled person—
   (a) in the terms on which it is prepared to admit him to membership of the organisation; or
   (b) by refusing to accept, or deliberately not accepting, his application for membership.

(2) It is unlawful for a trade organisation, in the case of a disabled person who is a member of the organisation, to discriminate against him—
   (a) in the way it affords him access to any benefits or by refusing or deliberately omitting to afford him access to them;
   (b) by depriving him of membership, or varying the terms on which he is a member; or
   (c) by subjecting him to any other detriment.

(3) In the case of an act which constitutes discrimination by virtue of section 55, this section also applies to discrimination against a person who is not disabled.

(4) In this section "trade organisation" means an organisation of workers, an organisation of employers or any other organisation whose members carry on a particular profession or trade for the purposes of which the organisation exists.

GENERAL NOTE

Trade organisations are covered by s.4 of the Act in their relationship with their employees or prospective employees; in line with the legislation which prohibits discrimination on grounds of sex and race, this section prohibits discrimination by trade organisations against disabled members or prospective members. As defined in subs. (4), "trade organisation" means an organisation of workers (such as a trade union), an organisation of employers (such as an employers' association), or any other organisation whose members carry on a particular profession or trade for the purposes of which the organisation exists (for example, a professional association such as the Institute of Personnel and Development). It is unlawful for any such organisation to discriminate against a disabled person in relation to the terms on which it is prepared to admit that person into membership, or by refusing to accept or deliberately not accepting that person's application for membership (subs. (1)). It is also unlawful for a trade organisation to discriminate against a disabled member in relation to that person's access to any benefits, or by depriving that person of membership or varying the terms of his membership, or by subjecting that person to any other detriment (subs. (2)). "Discrimination" in relation to trade organisations is defined in s.14 in the same terms as discrimination in relation to employers under s.5, and s.15 places trade organisations under a duty to make reasonable adjustments similar to that which applies to employers under s.6. As with the provisions relating to employers, less favourable treatment of a disabled person by a trade organisation may be justified in certain circumstances: "For example, in the case of a trade union delegation to inaccessible premises not controlled by the union it might be necessary to leave out a wheelchair user" (Minister of State, *Hansard*, H.L., Vol. 566, col. 225). The duty to make reasonable adjustments might, for example, require a trade union "to ensure that, where it is reasonable, visually impaired members could get union literature in braille and members with hearing impairments could have signers at meetings" (*ibid.* col. 225).

For the equivalent provisions in relation to sex and race discrimination, see the S.D.A., s.12, and the R.R.A., s.11.

Trade; business. As defined in s.68(1), "profession" includes any vocation or occupation, and "trade" includes any business.

Meaning of "discrimination" in relation to trade organisations

14.—(1) For the purposes of this Part, a trade organisation discriminates against a disabled person if—
   (a) for a reason which relates to the disabled person's disability, it treats him less favourably than it treats or would treat others to whom that reason does not or would not apply; and

(b) it cannot show that the treatment in question is justified.

(2) For the purposes of this Part, a trade organisation also discriminates against a disabled person if—

(a) it fails to comply with a section 15 duty imposed on it in relation to the disabled person; and

(b) it cannot show that its failure to comply with that duty is justified.

(3) Subject to subsection (5), for the purposes of subsection (1) treatment is justified if, but only if, the reason for it is both material to the circumstances of the particular case and substantial.

(4) For the purposes of subsection (2), failure to comply with a section 15 duty is justified if, but only if, the reason for the failure is both material to the circumstances of the particular case and substantial.

(5) If, in a case falling within subsection (1), the trade organisation is under a section 15 duty in relation to the disabled person concerned but fails without justification to comply with that duty, its treatment of that person cannot be justified under subsection (3) unless the treatment would have been justified even if the organisation had complied with the section 15 duty.

(6) Regulations may make provision, for purposes of this section, as to circumstances in which—

(a) treatment is to be taken to be justified;

(b) failure to comply with a section 15 duty is to be taken to be justified;

(c) treatment is to be taken not to be justified;

(d) failure to comply with a section 15 duty is to be taken not to be justified.

GENERAL NOTE

The definition of discrimination in relation to trade organisations in this section is substantially the same as that which applies to employers under s.5: see the note to that section. As to discrimination by trade organisations generally, see the note to s.13.

Appeal against refusal of exemption certificate

15.—(1) Where—

(a) any arrangements made by or on behalf of a trade organisation, or

(b) any physical feature of premises occupied by the organisation,

place the disabled person concerned at a substantial disadvantage in comparison with persons who are not disabled, it is the duty of the organisation to take such steps as it is reasonable, in all the circumstances of the case, for it to have to take in order to prevent the arrangements or feature having that effect.

(2) Subsection (1)(a) applies only in relation to—

(a) arrangements for determining who should become or remain a member of the organisation;

(b) any term, condition or arrangements on which membership or any benefit is offered or afforded.

(3) In determining whether it is reasonable for a trade organisation to have to take a particular step in order to comply with subsection (1), regard shall be had, in particular, to—

(a) the extent to which taking the step would prevent the effect in question;

(b) the extent to which it is practicable for the organisation to take the step;

(c) the financial and other costs which would be incurred by the organisation in taking the step and the extent to which taking it would disrupt any of its activities;

(d) the extent of the organisation's financial and other resources;

(e) the availability to the organisation of financial or other assistance with respect to taking the step.

This subsection is subject to any provision of regulations made under subsection (7).

(4) In this section "the disabled person concerned" means—

(a) in the case of arrangements for determining to whom membership should be offered, any disabled person who is, or has notified the organisation that he may be, an applicant for membership;

(b) in any other case, a disabled person who is—

(i) an applicant for membership; or

(ii) a member of the organisation.

(5) Nothing in this section imposes any duty on an organisation in relation to a disabled person if the organisation does not know, and could not reasonably be expected to know that the disabled person concerned—

(a) is, or may be, an applicant for membership; or

(b) has a disability and is likely to be affected in the way mentioned in subsection (1).

(6) Subject to the provisions of this section, nothing in this Part is to be taken to require a trade organisation to treat a disabled person more favourably than it treats or would treat others.

(7) Regulations may make provision for the purposes of subsection (1) as to any of the matters mentioned in paragraphs (a) to (h) of section 6(8) (the references in those paragraphs to an employer being read for these purposes as references to a trade organisation).

(8) Subsection (9) of section 6 applies in relation to such regulations as it applies in relation to regulations made under section 6(8).

(9) Regulations may make provision adding to the duty imposed on trade organisations by this section, including provision of a kind which may be made under subsection (7).

(10) This section imposes duties only for the purpose of determining whether a trade organisation has discriminated against a disabled person; and accordingly a breach of any such duty is not actionable as such.

GENERAL NOTE

This section places trade organisations under a duty to make reasonable adjustments to their arrangements and premises to prevent disabled people from being placed at a substantial disadvantage in comparison with people who are not disabled. The duty of trade organisations to make adjustments under this section is substantially the same as the duty placed on employers under s.6: see the note to that section. Unlike s.6, however, this section does not contain a list of examples of steps which a trade organisation may have to take in relation to a disabled person in order to comply with the duty to make adjustments. As to discrimination by trade organisations generally, see the note to s.13.

Premises occupied under leases

Alterations to premises occupied under leases

16.—(1) This section applies where—

(a) an employer or trade organisation ("the occupier") occupies premises under a lease;

(b) but for this section, the occupier would not be entitled to make a particular alteration to the premises; and

(c) the alteration is one which the occupier proposes to make in order to comply with a section 6 duty or section 15 duty.

(2) Except to the extent to which it expressly so provides, the lease shall have effect by virtue of this subsection as if it provided—

(a) for the occupier to be entitled to make the alteration with the written consent of the lessor;

(b) for the occupier to have to make a written application to the lessor for consent if he wishes to make the alteration;

(c) if such an application is made, for the lessor not to withhold his consent unreasonably; and

(d) for the lessor to be entitled to make his consent subject to reasonable conditions.

(3) In this section—

"lease" includes a tenancy, sub-lease or sub-tenancy and an agreement for a lease, tenancy, sub-lease or sub-tenancy; and

"sub-lease" and "sub-tenancy" have such meaning as may be prescribed.

(4) If the terms and conditions of a lease—

(a) impose conditions which are to apply if the occupier alters the premises, or

(b) entitle the lessor to impose conditions when consenting to the occupier's altering the premises,

the occupier is to be treated for the purposes of subsection (1) as not being entitled to make the alteration.

(5) Part I of Schedule 4 supplements the provisions of this section.

GENERAL NOTE

The duty of an employer or trade organisation to make reasonable adjustments for the benefit of disabled people under ss.6 and 15 of the Act may necessitate the alteration of premises, but this could present problems for employers and organisations who occupy premises under a lease, where the terms of the lease prevent or restrict them from making alterations to those premises. This section, which was added to the Bill at Third Reading in the House of Lords, overrides the terms of the lease in such circumstances by entitling the occupier, with the written consent of the landlord, to alter the premises to comply with a s.6 or s.15 duty. The occupier must apply in writing to the landlord seeking his consent for the alterations, and the landlord must not withhold that consent unreasonably, although the consent may be made subject to reasonable conditions (subs. (2)). An occupier of premises who fails to apply to the landlord for consent to make the alterations will not be able to claim that he was prevented by the terms of the lease from making a reasonable adjustment to the premises (Sched. 4, para. 1). In a complaint under s.8, the complainant or the occupier may ask the tribunal to join the landlord as a party to the proceedings, and if the tribunal finds that the landlord has unreasonably refused consent to the alterations, or has imposed unreasonable conditions, it may do one or more of the following: make a declaration; make an order authorising the occupier to make the alterations specified in the order (subject to any specified conditions); or order the landlord to pay compensation to the complainant. Any such order may be instead of or in addition to an order made against the occupier under s.8(2), although if the tribunal orders the landlord to pay compensation, it cannot order the occupier to do so (Sched. 4, para. 2).

According to the Government: "This approach [will] ensure that the lease will not operate to frustrate the duty of adjustment. It also has the advantage of protecting the landlord where he has a legitimate objection to allowing an alteration to premises." (Minister of State, *Hansard*, H.L., Vol. 566, col. 1016).

The Secretary of State may make regulations specifying circumstances in which it would or would not be reasonable for a landlord to withhold his consent to adjustments, and whether a condition imposed by the landlord is to be taken to be reasonable or unreasonable (Sched. 4, para. 3). "Obviously, if the building was listed and there were concerns about making alterations, it would be perfectly reasonable to refuse consent on those grounds." (Minister of State, *ibid.* col. 1018). Regulations may also make provision for cases where premises are occupied under a sub-lease or sub-tenancy (*ibid.* para. 4).

Occupational pension schemes and insurance services

Occupational pension schemes

17.—(1) Every occupational pension scheme shall be taken to include a provision ("a non-discrimination rule")—

(a) relating to the terms on which—

(i) persons become members of the scheme; and

(ii) members of the scheme are treated; and

(b) requiring the trustees or managers of the scheme to refrain from any act or omission which, if done in relation to a person by an employer, would amount to unlawful discrimination against that person for the purposes of this Part.

(2) The other provisions of the scheme are to have effect subject to the non-discrimination rule.

(3) Without prejudice to section 67, regulations under this Part may—

(a) with respect to trustees or managers of occupational pension schemes make different provision from that made with respect to employers; or

(b) make provision modifying the application to such trustees or managers of any regulations made under this Part, or of any provisions of this Part so far as they apply to employers.

(4) In determining, for the purposes of this section, whether an act or omission would amount to unlawful discrimination if done by an employer, any provision made under subsection (3) shall be applied as if it applied in relation to the notional employer.

GENERAL NOTE

Entitlement to occupational pension benefits under the contract of employment is covered by s.4(2) of the Act, which prohibits discrimination by an employer against a disabled person in the terms of employment and in the opportunities for receiving any other benefit (subject to certain modifications in ss.5(7) and 6(11) which take account of the particular problems raised by occupational pension benefits in this context: see the notes to ss.5 and 6). This section extends those principles to the trustees and managers of occupational pension schemes, by implying into every such scheme a "non-discrimination rule". The effect of this rule is that any discrimination by the trustees or managers of an occupational pension scheme in relation to the terms on which people become members of the scheme, or the way in which members of the scheme are treated, will be treated as a breach of the rules of the scheme (subs. (1)). For these purposes, an act or omission by the trustees or managers will be contrary to the rules of the scheme if it would amount to unlawful discrimination under this Part of the Act if done by an employer, although regulations made under subs. (3) may make provision for trustees and managers which is different from that made for employers. Unlike the provisions prohibiting unlawful discrimination by employers, a complaint of unlawful discrimination against the trustees or managers of an occupational pension scheme does not lie to an industrial tribunal. Rather, a disabled person who is affected by an infringement of the non-discrimination rule "will be able to seek redress through the dispute resolution mechanisms which already exist for pensions (sic) schemes." (Minister of State, *Hansard*, H.L., Vol. 566, col. 994).

Occupational pension scheme. This has the same meaning as in the Pension Schemes Act 1993 (c. 48).

Insurance services

18.—(1) This section applies where a provider of insurance services ("the insurer") enters into arrangements with an employer under which the employer's employees, or a class of his employees—

(a) receive insurance services provided by the insurer; or

(b) are given an opportunity to receive such services.

(2) The insurer is to be taken, for the purposes of this Part, to discriminate unlawfully against a disabled person who is a relevant employee if he acts in relation to that employee in a way which would be unlawful discrimination for the purposes of Part III if—

(a) he were providing the service in question to members of the public; and

(b) the employee was provided with, or was trying to secure the provision of, that service as a member of the public.

(3) In this section—

"insurance services" means services of a prescribed description for the provision of benefits in respect of—

(a) termination of service;

(b) retirement, old age or death;

(c) accident, injury, sickness or invalidity; or

(d) any other prescribed matter; and

"relevant employee" means—

(a) in the case of an arrangement which applies to employees of the employer in question, an employee of his;

(b) in the case of an arrangement which applies to a class of employees of the employer, an employee who is in that class.

(4) For the purposes of the definition of "relevant employee" in subsection (3), "employee", in relation to an employer, includes a person who has applied for, or is contemplating applying for, employment by that employer or (as the case may be) employment by him in the class in question.

GENERAL NOTE

This section provides for the situation where an employer enters into arrangements with an insurance company for insurance services (for example, private health insurance) to be received by the employer's employees. It provides that the insurer will be taken to have discriminated unlawfully against a disabled employee if it treats that person in a way which would be unlawful discrimination under Pt. III if it were providing the service in question to the employee as a member of the public: "That means that refusal to insure a disabled employee, or levying a higher premium, will be unlawful unless it is justified; for example, where there are reasonable grounds for supposing that the disabled person represents a higher risk than normal." (Minister of State, *Hansard*, H.L., Vol. 566, col. 995). "Insurance services", as defined in subs. (3), include the provision of benefits in respect of termination of service, retirement, old age, death, accident, injury, sickness, invalidity or any other matter that may be prescribed by regulations. A complaint of an infringement of this section lies to an industrial tribunal under s.8.

PART III

DISCRIMINATION IN OTHER AREAS

Goods, facilities and services

Discrimination in relation to goods, facilities and services

19.—(1) It is unlawful for a provider of services to discriminate against a disabled person—

(a) in refusing to provide, or deliberately not providing, to the disabled person any service which he provides, or is prepared to provide, to members of the public;

(b) in failing to comply with any duty imposed on him by section 21 in circumstances in which the effect of that failure is to make it impossible or unreasonably difficult for the disabled person to make use of any such service;

(c) in the standard of service which he provides to the disabled person or the manner in which he provides it to him; or

(d) in the terms on which he provides a service to the disabled person.

(2) For the purposes of this section and sections 20 and 21—

(a) the provision of services includes the provision of any goods or facilities;

(b) a person is "a provider of services" if he is concerned with the provision, in the United Kingdom, of services to the public or to a section of the public; and

(c) it is irrelevant whether a service is provided on payment or without payment.

(3) The following are examples of services to which this section and sections 20 and 21 apply—

(a) access to and use of any place which members of the public are permitted to enter;

(b) access to and use of means of communication;
(c) access to and use of information services;
(d) accommodation in a hotel, boarding house or other similar establishment;
(e) facilities by way of banking or insurance or for grants, loans, credit or finance;
(f) facilities for entertainment, recreation or refreshment;
(g) facilities provided by employment agencies or under section 2 of the Employment and Training Act 1973;
(h) the services of any profession or trade, or any local or other public authority.

(4) In the case of an act which constitutes discrimination by virtue of section 55, this section also applies to discrimination against a person who is not disabled.

(5) Except in such circumstances as may be prescribed, this section and sections 20 and 21 do not apply to—
(a) education which is funded, or secured, by a relevant body or provided at—
    (i) an establishment which is funded by such a body or by a Minister of the Crown; or
    (ii) any other establishment which is a school as defined in section 14(5) of the Further and Higher Education Act 1992 or section 135 (1) of the Education (Scotland) Act 1980;
(b) any service so far as it consists of the use of any means of transport; or
(c) such other services as may be prescribed.

(6) In subsection (5) "relevant body" means—
(a) a local education authority in England and Wales;
(b) an education authority in Scotland;
(c) the Funding Agency for Schools;
(d) the Schools Funding Council for Wales;
(e) the Further Education Funding Council for England;
(f) the Further Education Funding Council for Wales;
(g) the Higher Education Funding Council for England;
(h) the Scottish Higher Education Funding Council;
(i) the Higher Education Funding Council for Wales;
(j) the Teacher Training Agency;
(k) a voluntary organisation; or
(l) a body of a prescribed kind.

GENERAL NOTE
This section introduces a right of access for disabled people, by making it unlawful for a service provider to discriminate against a disabled person in the provision of goods, facilities or services. The right is "a universal, all-embracing right of non-discrimination against disabled people ... applicable to all providers of goods, facilities and services to the general public, with the specific exclusions of transport and education" (Minister for Social Security and Disabled People, *Hansard*, H.C., Standing Committee E, col. 290). The new right of access "will not only prohibit discriminatory behaviour but also require positive action which is reasonable and readily achievable to overcome the physical and communication barriers that impede disabled people's access" (White Paper, *Ending discrimination against disabled people*, Cm. 2729, 1995, para. 4.4).

The new right imposes four main duties on service providers. First, it makes it unlawful for a service provider to discriminate against a disabled person by refusing to provide goods, facilities or services which he provides to other members of the public, or by providing them on different terms or to a different standard. So, for example, it might be unlawful for a supermarket owner to refuse to serve someone whose disability means that they shop slowly, or for a restaurant owner to insist that a person with a facial disfigurement sits out of sight of other customers, or for a travel agent to ask a disabled person for a bigger deposit when they are booking a holiday (*A Brief Guide to the Disability Discrimination Act*, DL40, p.6). Secondly, it places a duty on a service provider to take reasonable steps to change any practice, policy or procedure which makes it impossible or unreasonably difficult for disabled people to make use of a service which he provides to other members of the public. Thirdly, it places a duty on a service provider to take reasonable steps to remove or alter any physical barrier which makes it impossible or unreasonably difficult for disabled people to make use of such a service, or to provide some alternative means of making the service accessible to a disabled person. Fourthly, it places a duty on a service provider to take reasonable steps to provide auxiliary aids or services (*e.g.* information on tape or in braille) which would make it easier for disabled people to use their services.

Subsection (1) makes it unlawful for a service provider to discriminate against a disabled person by failing to comply with any of the above duties. The duty to make reasonable adjustments to practices, policies and procedures, to remove to physical barriers and to provide auxiliary aids, is contained in s.21 (see the notes to that section). A similar duty is placed on employers under Pt. II, although in that context the duty arises where a disabled person is put at a "substantial disadvantage" by the employer's arrangements or premises. Surprisingly, the Act does not contain any express prohibition on discriminatory advertisements for goods, facilities and services to mirror the provisions in s.11 outlawing discriminatory job advertisements. This contrasts with the corresponding provisions in the sex and race discrimination legislation, which apply both to advertisements for employment and for goods and services. The Government were not persuaded that there was a problem which needed to be addressed in this area, and suggested that any discriminatory advertisement for goods and services would be covered by the s.21 duty to make adjustments:

"[Section 21] puts a duty on service providers to change any policy, practice or procedure which makes it impossible or unreasonably difficult for a disabled person to make use of their services. Given the need to adjust such policies, it seems most unlikely that a trader, determined to evade this requirement, would advertise his or her failure to comply with the law." (Minister of State, *Hansard*, H.L., Vol. 565, col. 676).

Discrimination is defined for the purposes of this section in s.20. As with the provisions relating to employment, the definition is in two parts: a service provider discriminates against a disabled person (a) if he treats that person less favourably, for a reason which relates to his or her disability or (b) if he fails to comply with a duty to make reasonable adjustments. In both cases, the discriminatory conduct may be justified, but the justification defence which applies here differs significantly from that which applies in the case of employment, and it has been argued that the grounds upon which discriminatory conduct may be justified (danger to health and safety, lack of informed consent, preserving the service for other members of the public, etc.) are so wide and subjective as to render the right not to be discriminated against almost worthless.

That *caveat* aside, these provisions are very broad in their scope. They apply to the provision of any service (including the provision of goods and facilities) by a person concerned with the provision in the U.K. of such services to the public or a section of the public, whether or not for payment (subs. (2)). The breadth of coverage is illustrated by the list of examples in subs. (3) which, with the exception of heads (b) and (c), corresponds to the lists contained in the equivalent provisions in the Sex Discrimination Act 1975 and the Race Relations Act 1976; heads (b) and (c) were added to reflect the importance of communication and information services to disabled people, although the list is not exhaustive (Minister for Social Security and Disabled People, *Hansard*, H.C., Standing Committee E, col. 291). Unlike the sex and race discrimination legislation, there are specific exclusions in subs. (5) for educational establishments and transport vehicles, despite vigorous Opposition attempts to include those areas in this Part of the Act. The Government were however persuaded to make some important concessions in those areas: see Pts. IV and V.

At the time of writing, the implementation date for the duties contained in this Part of the Act had yet to be announced. The Government has however made it clear that the duties are to be phased in over a number of years, with the right not to be refused service coming into force first, towards the end of 1996, and the duties relating to auxiliary aids and the removal of physical barriers being brought into force over a longer period of up to ten years, to allow service providers enough time to prepare for and make the necessary changes (Minister of State, *Hansard*, H.L., Vol. 564, cols. 803, 1696).

Subs. (1)
Provider of services. This is defined in subs. (2)(b) as a person concerned with the provision, in the U.K., of "services to the public or to a section of the public". For the interpretation of this phrase in the context of discrimination in the provision of goods, facilities and services on grounds of race, see *Charter v. Race Relations Board* [1973] A.C. 868 (a case under the R.R.A. 1968, s.2, the forerunner of the provisions now contained in the R.R.A., s.20), where it was held that the provisions did not apply to situations of a purely private character; see also *Dockers' Labour Club and Institute v. Race Relations Board* [1976] A.C. 285. It follows that this section does not apply to the provision of services to their members by trade unions and other similar

organisations; separate provision for discrimination by trade organisations is made in s.13: see the note to that section.

The provision of services includes the provision of any goods or facilities (subs. (2)(a)). Manufacturers and designers who supply their services directly to the public will be covered by this section as service providers, but the Government has made clear that the Act is not intended to cover the design and manufacture of products: "It is one thing to give an individual a legal right of access to goods and services as the [Act] does; but it is quite another to give him a right to products of a certain type or design." (Minister of State, *Hansard*, H.L., Vol. 566, col. 241; and see *ibid*. Vol. 564, col. 1768). "This is the case even where the product could be regarded as "information"; for example, newspapers, books and television programmes. There will therefore be no requirement for those items to be made available in an accessible format." (*ibid*. Vol. 566, col. 251). Nor does the Act require manufacturers to provide information on products (operating instructions, etc.) in accessible formats (*ibid*.).

Although not specifically mentioned in subs. (3), "services" is intended to include legal services provided to members of the public by courts, tribunals, solicitors, the Legal Aid Board and other agencies of the criminal justice system (Minister of State, *Hansard*, H.L., Vol. 566, col. 260). Service as a juror is not covered by Pt. III, since that cannot be construed as a service being provided to members of the public (*ibid*. col. 261); the position of witnesses is however less clear: "The fact that witnesses are classed as users of the court services (*i.e.* for the purposes of the National Survey of Court Users) does not mean that they are receiving a service within the meaning of the [Act]." (*ibid*. col. 262). The Government has also confirmed that "services" includes all medical and health care services (Minister of State, *Hansard*, H.L., Vol. 564, col. 1952).

Refusing to provide, or deliberately not providing. For the interpretation of the phrase "refusing or deliberately omitting to provide" as it appears in the equivalent provisions outlawing discrimination in the provision of goods, facilities and services in the S.D.A., s.29, see *Gill v. El Vino Co.* [1983] Q.B. 425.

Meaning of "discrimination"

20.—(1) For the purposes of section 19, a provider of services discriminates against a disabled person if—

(a) for a reason which relates to the disabled person's disability, he treats him less favourably than he treats or would treat others to whom that reason does not or would not apply; and

(b) he cannot show that the treatment in question is justified.

(2) For the purposes of section 19, a provider of services also discriminates against a disabled person if—

(a) he fails to comply with a section 21 duty imposed on him in relation to the disabled person; and

(b) he cannot show that his failure to comply with that duty is justified.

(3) For the purposes of this section, treatment is justified only if—

(a) in the opinion of the provider of services, one or more of the conditions mentioned in subsection (4) are satisfied; and

(b) it is reasonable, in all the circumstances of the case, for him to hold that opinion.

(4) The conditions are that—

(a) in any case, the treatment is necessary in order not to endanger the health or safety of any person (which may include that of the disabled person);

(b) in any case, the disabled person is incapable of entering into an enforceable agreement, or of giving an informed consent, and for that reason the treatment is reasonable in that case;

(c) in a case falling within section 19(1)(a), the treatment is necessary because the provider of services would otherwise be unable to provide the service to members of the public;

(d) in a case falling within section 19(1)(c) or (d), the treatment is necessary in order for the provider of services to be able to provide the service to the disabled person or to other members of the public;

(e) in a case falling within section 19(1)(d), the difference in the terms on which the service is provided to the disabled person and those on which it is provided to other members of the public reflects the greater cost to the provider of services in providing the service to the disabled person.

(5) Any increase in the cost of providing a service to a disabled person which results from compliance by a provider of services with a section 21 duty shall be disregarded for the purposes of subsection (4)(e).

(6) Regulations may make provision, for purposes of this section, as to circumstances in which—

(a) it is reasonable for a provider of services to hold the opinion mentioned in subsection (3)(a);

(b) it is not reasonable for a provider of services to hold that opinion.

(7) Regulations may make provision for subsection (4)(b) not to apply in prescribed circumstances where—

(a) a person is acting for a disabled person under a power of attorney;

(b) functions conferred by or under Part VII of the Mental Health Act 1983 are exercisable in relation to a disabled person's property or affairs; or

(c) powers are exercisable in Scotland in relation to a disabled person's property or affairs in consequence of the appointment of a curator bonis, tutor or judicial factor.

(8) Regulations may make provision, for purposes of this section, as to circumstances (other than those mentioned in subsection (4)) in which treatment is to be taken to be justified.

(9) In subsections (3), (4) and (8) "treatment" includes failure to comply with a section 21 duty.

GENERAL NOTE

The definition of discrimination which is used for the purposes of the right of access to goods, facilities and services is similar to that which applies in employment cases under Pt. II (see the note to s.5). It adopts the same two-fold approach, by providing that a service provider discriminates against a disabled person if (a) he treats that person less favourably than he treats or would treat others, for a reason which relates to that person's disability or (b) he fails to comply with a duty imposed on him under s.21 to make reasonable adjustments in relation to the provision of services to disabled persons. As in the employment provisions, the Act departs from the approach which is normally taken in anti-discrimination legislation by allowing a service provider to argue that the less favourable treatment, or the failure to make adjustments, is justified. However, while the justification defence in employment cases takes an objective approach, focusing on whether the reason for the employer's conduct "is both material to the circumstances of the particular case and substantial" (see s.5(3)), in this context a more detailed and more subjective test of justification is used, which turns on the service provider's reasonable opinion as to whether certain conditions are satisfied (subs. (3)). A similar test was originally intended for the employment provisions, but in a late amendment to s.5 that test was substituted by the "material and substantial" test, after concern was expressed that the original version was too complex and allowed too much discretion to employers. The explanation for the difference in approach was explained in the following terms: "Service providers often have to take very quick and perhaps less informed decisions when serving someone. So an opinion-based approach remains appropriate." (Minister of State, *Hansard*, H.L., Vol. 566, col. 119).

By subs. (3), discriminatory treatment of a disabled person may be justified if, in the reasonable opinion of the service provider, one or more of the following conditions set out in subs. (4) are satisfied:

(a) the treatment is necessary in order not to endanger health and safety. It is not unlawful for a service provider to refuse to provide a service, or to do so on different terms, if the health and safety of the disabled person or of other people would be put in danger: "An example of this could be if a swimming instructor, taking an adult beginners class, has to focus most of his attention on a disabled person and cannot cover the programme for each class. Other members of the class might be put at risk." (Minister of State, *Hansard*, H.L., Vol. 566, col. 1025).

(b) the treatment is reasonable because the disabled person is incapable of entering into an enforceable agreement or of giving an informed consent. Concern has been expressed by organisations such as MIND and Mencap that the subjective nature of this test might enable it to be used as a general justification for refusing to serve people with mental impairments, reinforcing the widespread misunderstanding which exists in society about the ability of mentally ill people and people with learning difficulties to manage their own affairs. The Government has indicated that this justification is intended to be narrow in its scope, and is not intended to be used as a loophole to allow people to refuse to serve disabled persons:

"It will not be reasonable for service providers to cite this justification when the purchase of a product or service would not normally be the subject of a written agreement. For example, it cannot be used in relation to buying groceries in a supermarket. The subsection will apply only to major purchases—a motor car perhaps—or credit agreements, and it is meant to apply only in a few cases." (Minister for Social Security and Disabled People, *Hansard*, H.C., Standing Committee E, col. 350; see also *Hansard*, H.C., Vol. 257, col. 893).

Regulations may be made under subs. (4) disapplying this justification for discrimination where someone is acting on behalf of a disabled person under a power of attorney, or where a person's property or affairs are under the management of the Court of Protection under Pt. VII of the Mental Health Act 1983 (c. 20).

(c) it is necessary to refuse to serve a disabled person because otherwise the service provider would be unable to provide that service to other customers. This defence has been described as "the strictest test of all. It applies only in circumstances in which, if a service provider were to serve a particular disabled person, he would not be able to continue to provide his service at all. That is our intention. . . . the use of the word necessary would be a tough test, with a meaning akin to essential. That is intended to be its legal meaning." (Minister for Social Security and Disabled People, *Hansard*, H.C., Standing Committee E, col. 354). The defence would not apply where providing the service to a disabled person would merely delay or disrupt the provision of the service to other customers (*ibid.* col. 355).

(d) it is necessary to provide the service to a disabled person on different terms or to a different standard in order to be able to provide that service to that person or to other customers.

(e) where a service is provided to a disabled person on different terms, the difference in those terms reflects the greater cost to the service provider in providing that service to a disabled person. On the face of it, this seems to give a service provider the right to surcharge disabled customers for providing, for example, information in an accessible format, or otherwise making their services more accessible. However, subs. (5) makes it clear that any increase in the cost of providing a service to a disabled person which results from compliance with a duty under s.21 to make that service more accessible may not be passed on to the disabled customer under this head. The Government has confirmed that subs. (4)(e) is not intended to "give businesses the opportunity to load opportunity costs on to a disabled person or allow service providers to charge more to a disabled person where they have to make their services more accessible to suit his or her disability . . . It is certainly not our intention that, for example, a large organisation which had to produce information in an alternative format for some of its disabled customers should be able to charge them more for it." (Minister of State, *Hansard*, H.L., Vol. 564, col. 2009). The defence is therefore much narrower in scope than it might initially seem to be, covering those who provide specialised goods or services for disabled people:

"I have in mind a shoemaker who is asked by a disabled person to make a shoe to an unusual pattern or using an unusual fabric. The task might take the shoemaker longer than usual and require a special order for equipment and materials. That would amount to a different, more specialised service than he would usually provide, and it is reasonable that he should be able to charge more." (Minister for Social Security and Disabled People, *Hansard*, H.C., Standing Committee E, col. 357).

Regulations may specify circumstances in which it is or is not reasonable for a service provider to believe that one or more of these conditions are satisfied (subs. (6)), and may also provide for other circumstances in which discriminatory treatment by service providers will be deemed to be justified (subs. (8)). The Government has indicated that it intends to make regulations permitting insurance companies to charge higher premiums to disabled customers "to the extent that the extra charge is based on actuarial data or other good reasons." (White Paper, *Ending discrimination against disabled people*, Cm. 2729, 1995, para. 4.4), while at the same time declaring its intention of eliminating unfair discrimination in insurance:

"we have been convinced that disabled people, when they seek insurance cover, sometimes face unfair discrimination, whether in the form of a loaded premium or a refusal to provide cover at all. We want to ensure that the treatment of disabled customers is based on a reasonable assessment of risk rather than on any prejudicial assumptions of the insurer." (Minister of State, *Hansard*, H.L., Vol. 564, col. 2013).

In common with employment provisions in Pt. II, the definition of discrimination in this section does not expressly prohibit indirect discrimination (*i.e.* the application of a requirement or condition which has a disproportionate impact on a particular group or class). As in that context, however, the Government's view is that the duty to make reasonable adjustments will protect disabled people against indirect discrimination in the provision of goods, facilities and services: "Indirect discrimination typically occurs where a practice or condition of access has a disproportionately adverse effect, often unintended, on a particular section of society. Because disabled people constitute a very diverse group, a general prohibition of indirect discrimination against them could have unforeseen consequences which were unfairly burdensome for businesses. Nonetheless, the Government accepts that there may be particular practices, indirectly denying disabled people access to goods and services, which should be prevented. Banning animals, for example, has a disproportionate effect on those blind people who rely on guide dogs. The Government will therefore require practical modifications to such practices [*i.e.* under s.21] so that disabled people are not unjustifiably denied access." (White Paper, *Ending discrimination against disabled people*, Cm. 2729, 1995, para. 4.5).

Subs. (1)
Others to whom that reason does not or would not apply. See the note to s.5(1).

Duty of providers of services to make adjustments

21.—(1) Where a provider of services has a practice, policy or procedure which makes it impossible or unreasonably difficult for disabled persons to make use of a service which he provides, or is prepared to provide, to other members of the public, it is his duty to take such steps as it is reasonable, in all the circumstances of the case, for him to have to take in order to change that practice, policy or procedure so that it no longer has that effect.

(2) Where a physical feature (for example, one arising from the design or construction of a building or the approach or access to premises) makes it impossible or unreasonably difficult for disabled persons to make use of such a sentence, it is the duty of the provider of that service to take such steps as it is reasonable, in all the circumstances of the case, for him to have to take in order to—

(a) remove the feature;

(b) alter it so that it no longer has that effect;

(c) provide a reasonable means of avoiding the feature; or

(d) provide a reasonable alternative method of making the service in question available to disabled persons.

(3) Regulations may prescribe—

(a) matters which are to be taken into account in determining whether any provision of a kind mentioned in subsection (2)(c) or (d) is reasonable; and

(b) categories of providers of services to whom subsection (2) does not apply.

(4) Where an auxiliary aid or service (for example, the provision of information on audio tape or of a sign language interpreter) would—

(a) enable disabled persons to make use of a service which a provider of services provides, or is prepared to provide, to members of the public, or

(b) facilitate the use by disabled persons of such a service,

it is the duty of the provider of that service to take such steps as it is reasonable, in all the circumstances of the case, for him to have to take in order to provide that auxiliary aid or service.

(5) Regulations may make provision, for the purposes of this section—

(a) as to circumstances in which it is reasonable for a provider of services to have to take steps of a prescribed description;

(b) as to circumstances in which it is not reasonable for a provider of services to have to take steps of a prescribed description;

(c) as to what is to be included within the meaning of "practice, policy or procedure";

(d) as to what is not to be included within the meaning of that expression;

(e) as to things which are to be treated as physical features;

(f) as to things which are not to be treated as such features;

(g) as to things which are to be treated as auxiliary aids or services;

(h) as to things which are not to be treated as auxiliary aids or services.

(6) Nothing in this section requires a provider of services to take any steps which would fundamentally alter the nature of the service in question or the nature of his trade, profession or business.

(7) Nothing in this section requires a provider of services to take any steps which would cause him to incur expenditure exceeding the prescribed maximum.

(8) Regulations under subsection (7) may provide for the prescribed maximum to be calculated by reference to—

(a) aggregate amounts of expenditure incurred in relation to different cases;

(b) prescribed periods;

(c) services of a prescribed description;

(d) premises of a prescribed description; or

(e) such other criteria as may be prescribed.

(9) Regulations may provide, for the purposes of subsection (7), for expenditure incurred by one provider of services to be treated as incurred by another.

(10) This section imposes duties only for the purpose of determining whether a provider of services has discriminated against a disabled person; and accordingly a breach of any such duty is not actionable as such.

GENERAL NOTE

This section places a duty on service providers to make reasonable adjustments to overcome any barriers that make it impossible or unreasonably difficult for disabled people to gain access to goods, facilities and services. A similar duty is placed on employers under Pt. II of the Act, although in that context the duty arises where a disabled person is put at a "substantial disadvantage" by the employer's arrangements or premises: see the note to s.6.

The duty to make adjustments is in three parts. First, subs. (1) provides that a service provider has a duty to take reasonable steps to change any practice, policy or procedure which makes it impossible or unreasonably difficult for disabled people to make use of a service which he provides to other members of the public, so that it no longer has that effect. For example, it would be unlawful for a restaurant which does not allow animals to refuse admission to a disabled person with a guide dog. The Government has insisted that service providers "will not be able to get away with treating disabled people without the same dignity and respect as any other customer. If, for example, a cafe proprietor does have to change a 'no dogs' rule it will not be good enough for him to suggest that he is happy to see the animal tied up outside with a bowl of water!" (Minister of State, *Hansard*, H.L., Vol. 566, col. 266). Regulations made under subs. (5) may define what is or is not to count as a "practice, policy or procedure" for these purposes.

Secondly, subs. (2) provides that a service provider has a duty to take reasonable steps to remove or alter any physical feature (for example, a physical barrier) which makes it impossible or unreasonably difficult for disabled people to make use of a service which he provides to other members of the public, or to provide a reasonable method of avoiding the feature or of making the service available to disabled people in some other way. For example, a supplier of goods might be required to widen entrance doors, remove steps or install a lift to make its premises accessible to people in wheelchairs; alternatively, it might be reasonable to provide an illustrated catalogue and order form, or to arrange for items to be brought down to the disabled person. The Government has conceded that this may result in a wheelchair user having less choice than other customers, and therefore receiving a lower standard of service: "The requirement ... is to provide access to a service as close as it is reasonably possible to get to the standard normally offered." (Minister of State, *Hansard*, H.L., Vol. 566, col. 267). Provided the Act's requirements are satisfied, it is for service providers themselves to decide how best their services can be made accessible to disabled people. The Government rejected an Opposition amendment which sought to provide that the use of an alternative means of providing a service should be allowed only as a last resort when physical alterations were unreasonably difficult:

"the legislation has been deliberately drafted in a way that ensures that sensible, low-cost accessibility solutions are encouraged wherever possible, so long as they are reasonable. The amendment could impose much unnecessary cost on businesses in situations where to contemplate expensive building work which might be considered reasonable in its own right would be to fly in the face of common sense if, as a prior option, a work-around solution could not be considered as well." (Minister of State, *Hansard*, H.L., Vol. 564, col. 2022).

The Minister did however concede that in some situations (*e.g.* restaurants, theatres and art galleries) physical alterations to premises would be the only reasonable solution "because physical access to premises is a fundamental attribute of the service... It would clearly not be reasonable for the proprietor of a cafe to suggest that a take-away meal was a suitable alternative to making an adjustment to the layout or construction of his premises which would allow disabled people to enter." (*ibid*). The Minister also confirmed that the means of entrance must also be reasonable in such cases: "It would not be reasonable ... to expect a wheelchair user to have to negotiate the rubbish bins and general detritus of a back alley to be let into a restaurant via the kitchens..." (*ibid*. col. 2023).

Any physical alterations remain subject to the control of the planning and highway authorities, by virtue of the provisions in s.59 which provide that obligations under the Act are subordinate to other enactments. Concern has been expressed over the possible impact which the duty to make physical alterations might have on historic buildings, and the need to balance the reasonable expectations of disabled people as regards access with the desire to preserve the fabric of such buildings. In the White Paper, *Ending discrimination against disabled people* (Cm. 2729, 1995, at para. 4.10), the Government indicated that it was considering an exemption from the new right for listed buildings where the alterations would damage the essential character for which the building is protected. The Government has since concluded that any such exemption is unnecessary, since s.59 will prevent a service provider having to act without listed building consent in order to comply with the Act: "So if, for example, listed building consent to replace a medieval archway with a pair of sliding doors was refused, the service provider who then declined to install the new doorway could not be held to have discriminated against a disabled person for whom the building remained consequently inaccessible." (Minister of State, *Hansard*, H.L., Vol. 564, col. 2023). Physical adjustments for which listed building consent would be granted would however have to be considered.

The duty of a service provider to make reasonable adjustments to physical features may present problems where the premises are occupied under a lease, the terms of which prevent or restrict the occupier from making alterations to the premises. In those circumstances, the terms of the lease are overridden by s.27 of the Act, which entitles the occupier to alter the premises, with the written consent of the landlord, in order to comply with a duty to make adjustments under this section. See the note to s.27.

Part M of the Building Regulations 1988 (revised in 1991) contains mandatory requirements for new non-domestic buildings and substantial extensions concerning the provision of access and facilities for disabled people. In the Bill as originally published, there was a specific exemption from the duty to make physical adjustments for buildings and extensions erected in compliance with any requirement of the Building Regulations relating to disabled people:

"The Government takes the view that service providers should be able to rely on Part M of the building regulations as representing a bona fide national standard of accessibility for disabled people... It is only natural justice that a service provider who sets up in a new building which complies with building regulations should be entitled to believe that his premises have been certified as accessible." (Minister of State, *Hansard*, H.L., Vol. 564, col. 2026).

That exemption was dropped from the Bill at Committee stage in the House of Lords: "We now recognise that the subsection as drafted is something of a blunt instrument and that the problem needs to be tackled in a rather more sophisticated way." (Minister of State, *Hansard*, H.L., Vol. 564, col. 2026). The Government has indicated that it intends to make regulations under subs. (5) addressing the issue. For the Government's proposals in relation to the Building Regulations and the duty to make adjustments under Pt. II of the Act, see the note to s.6.

Thirdly, subs. (4) provides that a service provider has a duty to take reasonable steps to provide auxiliary aids or services which would enable disabled people to make use of their services, or make it easier for them to do so. For example, a service provider might be expected to provide information on tape or in braille for visually impaired customers, an induction loop for people with hearing aids, or a handrail for those who have difficulty walking up stairs.

"The extent to which a provider must provide auxiliary aids depends on the goods, facilities and services available. For example, a catalogue company that offers a telephone ordering service could reasonably be expected to provide a minicom service for deaf people, but a local butcher's shop that does not offer anyone a telephone ordering service could not reasonably be expected to provide minicom." (Minister for Social Security and Disabled People, *Hansard*, H.C., Standing Committee E, col. 292).

Regulations made under subs. (5) may provide that certain things are or are not to be treated as "auxiliary aids or services" for these purposes.

It is unlawful for a service provider to discriminate against a disabled person by failing to comply with any of these duties where the effect of that failure is to make it "impossible or unreasonably difficult" for the disabled person to make use of the service in question (s.19(1)(b)), unless the service provider can show that his failure to comply with the duty is justified within the meaning of s.20 (see the note to that section). The Government has denied that this test of discrimination is insufficiently tough on service providers:

"[I]n this context, the term 'service' includes the concept of service as far as possible to the same standard as that received by other people. There is no question of service providers being able to get away with providing access to a lower standard than normal *unless there are inescapable reasons*." (Minister of State, *Hansard*, H.L., Vol. 566, col. 266, emphasis added).

However, this assurance sits uneasily with the views of the Minister, quoted above, on the desirability of encouraging low-cost accessibility solutions, which suggests that the choice of access solution may be driven primarily by considerations of cost rather than standard of service. Ultimately, the extent of the duty on service providers will turn upon how the phrase "impossible or unreasonably difficult" is interpreted by the courts, and on whether, in each individual case, the court considers that the service provider has taken "such steps as it is reasonable, in all the circumstances of the case, for him to have to take" to enable a disabled person to make use of the service in question.

There are two further limitations on the scope of the duty to make adjustments imposed by this section. First, subs. (6) provides that a service provider is not required to take any steps which would fundamentally alter the nature of the service in question or the nature of his trade, business or profession. For example, the owner of a night club would not be expected to raise lighting levels for visually-impaired people; and a trainer of champion athletes would still be entitled to exclude the majority of the population from his classes (White Paper, *Ending discrimination against disabled people*, Cm. 2729, 1995, para. 4.4). Secondly, subs. (7) provides that a service provider is not required to take any steps which would cause him to incur expenditure over a prescribed maximum amount. At the time of writing, the Government had yet to announce what the limit on the expenditure on adjustments would be. Subsection (8) allows the maximum to be calculated according to aggregate amounts of expenditure on adjustments, the period over which the expenditure is made, the type of service and premises, and other as yet unspecified criteria, while subs. (9) allows expenditure incurred by one service provider to be treated as incurred by another. Regulations may also be made under subss. (3) and (5), fleshing out the details of the duty to make adjustments. In particular, subs. (3)(b) allows certain prescribed categories of service provider to be exempted from the duty to remove physical barriers.

Premises

Discrimination in relation to premises

22.—(1) It is unlawful for a person with power to dispose of any premises to discriminate against a disabled person—

(a) in the terms on which he offers to dispose of those premises to the disabled person;

(b) by refusing to dispose of those premises to the disabled person; or

(c) in his treatment of the disabled person in relation to any list of persons in need of premises of that description.

(2) Subsection (1) does not apply to a person who owns an estate or interest in the premises and wholly occupies them unless, for the purpose of disposing of the premises, he—

(a) uses the services of an estate agent, or

(b) publishes an advertisement or causes an advertisement to be published.

(3) It is unlawful for a person managing any premises to discriminate against a disabled person occupying those premises—

(a) in the way he permits the disabled person to make use of any benefits or facilities;

(b) by refusing or deliberately omitting to permit the disabled person to make use of any benefits or facilities; or

(c) by evicting the disabled person, or subjecting him to any other detriment.

(4) It is unlawful for any person whose licence or consent is required for the disposal of any premises comprised in, or (in Scotland) the subject of, a tenancy to discriminate against a disabled person by withholding his licence or consent for the disposal of the premises to the disabled person.

(5) Subsection (4) applies to tenancies created before as well as after the passing of this Act.

(6) In this section—

"advertisement" includes every form of advertisement or notice, whether to the public or not;

"dispose", in relation to premises, includes granting a right to occupy the premises, and, in relation to premises comprised in, or (in Scotland) the subject of, a tenancy, includes—

(a) assigning the tenancy, and

(b) sub-letting or parting with possession of the premises or any part of the premises;

and "disposal" shall be construed accordingly;

"estate agent" means a person who, by way of profession or trade, provides services for the purpose of finding premises for persons seeking to acquire them or assisting in the disposal of premises; and

"tenancy" means a tenancy created—

(a) by a lease or sub-lease,

(b) by an agreement for a lease or sub-lease,

(c) by a tenancy agreement, or

(d) in pursuance of any enactment.

(7) In the case of an act which constitutes discrimination by virtue of section 55, this section also applies to discrimination against a person who is not disabled.

(8) This section applies only in relation to premises in the United Kingdom.

GENERAL NOTE

This section makes it unlawful for a person with the power to dispose of premises to discriminate against a disabled person in the sale, letting and management of those premises, for example, by refusing to sell or rent property to a disabled person, by offering the property on worse terms than would be offered to anyone else, or by preventing a disabled tenant from using any benefits or facilities. It mirrors the corresponding provisions in the Sex Discrimination Act 1975, s.30, and the Race Relations Act 1976, s.21, and, in common with those provisions, is subject to an exemption in the case of small dwellings (see s.23). Discrimination is defined for these purposes in broadly similar terms to those which apply in the case of goods, facilities and services (see s.24), but with the important difference that, in this context, there is no duty on a person selling, renting or managing property to make adjustments to the property to make it accessible to a disabled person.

Exemption for small dwellings

23.—(1) Where the conditions mentioned in subsection (2) are satisfied, subsection (1), (3) or (as the case may be) (4) of section 22 does not apply.

(2) The conditions are that—

(a) the relevant occupier resides, and intends to continue to reside, on the premises;

(b) the relevant occupier shares accommodation on the premises with persons who reside on the premises and are not members of his household;

(c) the shared accommodation is not storage accommodation or a means of access; and

(d) the premises are small premises.

(3) For the purposes of this section, premises are "small premises" if they fall within subsection (4) or (5).

(4) Premises fall within this subsection if—

(a) only the relevant occupier and members of his household reside in the accommodation occupied by him;

(b) the premises comprise, in addition to the accommodation occupied by the relevant occupier, residential accommodation for at least one other household;

(c) the residential accommodation for each other household is let, or available for letting, on a separate tenancy or similar agreement; and

(d) there are not normally more than two such other households.

(5) Premises fall within this subsection if there is not normally residential accommodation on the premises for more than six persons in addition to the relevant occupier and any members of his household.

(6) For the purposes of this section "the relevant occupier" means—

(a) in a case falling within section 22(1), the person with power to dispose of the premises, or a near relative of his;

(b) in a case falling within section 22(4), the person whose licence or consent is required for the disposal of the premises, or a near relative of his.

(7) For the purposes of this section—

"near relative" means a person's spouse, partner, parent, child, grandparent, grandchild, or brother or sister (whether of full or half blood or by affinity); and

"partner" means the other member of a couple consisting of a man and a woman who are not married to each other but are living together as husband and wife.

GENERAL NOTE

This section contains an exemption for small dwellings similar to that found in the Sex Discrimination Act 1975, s.32, and the Race Relations Act 1976, s.22.

Meaning of "discrimination"

24.—(1) For the purposes of section 22, a person ("A") discriminates against a disabled person if—

(a) for a reason which relates to the disabled person's disability, he treats him less favourably than he treats or would treat others to whom that reason does not or would not apply; and

(b) he cannot show that the treatment in question is justified.

(2) For the purposes of this section, treatment is justified only if—

(a) in A's opinion, one or more of the conditions mentioned in subsection (3) are satisfied; and

(b) it is reasonable, in all the circumstances of the case, for him to hold that opinion.

(3) The conditions are that—

(a) in any case, the treatment is necessary in order not to endanger the health or safety of any person (which may include that of the disabled person);

(b) in any case, the disabled person is incapable of entering into an enforceable agreement, or of giving an informed consent, and for that reason the treatment is reasonable in that case;

(c) in a case falling within section 22(3)(a), the treatment is necessary in order for the disabled person or the occupiers of other premises forming part of the building to make use of the benefit or facility;

(d) in a case falling within section 22(3)(b), the treatment is necessary in order for the occupiers of other premises forming part of the building to make use of the benefit or facility.

(4) Regulations may make provision, for purposes of this section, as to circumstances in which—

(a) it is reasonable for a person to hold the opinion mentioned in subsection 2(a);

(b) it is not reasonable for a person to hold that opinion.

(5) Regulations may make provision, for purposes of this section, as to circumstances (other than those mentioned in subsection (3)) in which treatment is to be taken to be justified.

GENERAL NOTE

Discrimination is defined for the purposes of s.22 in broadly similar terms to those which apply in the case of access to goods, facilities and services (see s.20), save that in this context there is no duty to make reasonable adjustments to the property. Less favourable treatment of a disabled person may be justified if the person renting or selling property believes that one or more of the conditions in subs. (3) is satisfied, and it is reasonable for him to hold that opinion. So, for example, by virtue of subs. (3)(a), it may be justifiable for a landlord to refuse to let a flat to a disabled person if that person is unable to negotiate the stairs in safety or use the fire escape in an emergency.

Enforcement, etc.

Enforcement, remedies and procedure

25.—(1) A claim by any person that another person—

(a) has discriminated against him in a way which is unlawful under this Part; or

(b) is by virtue of section 57 or 58 to be treated as having discriminated against him in such a way,

may be made the subject of civil proceedings in the same way as any other claim in tort or (in Scotland) in reparation for breach of statutory duty.

(2) For the avoidance of doubt it is hereby declared that damages in respect of discrimination in a way which is unlawful under this Part may include compensation for injury to feelings whether or not they include compensation under any other head.

(3) Proceedings in England and Wales shall be brought only in a county court.

(4) Proceedings in Scotland shall be brought only in a sheriff court.

(5) The remedies available in such proceedings are those which are available in the High Court or (as the case may be) the Court of Session.

(6) Part II of Schedule 3 makes further provision about the enforcement of this Part and about procedure.

GENERAL NOTE

Claims of unlawful discrimination under this Part of the Act must be brought in a county court (or, in Scotland, a sheriff court), and the remedies available are those available in the High Court (or, in Scotland, the Court of Session). The court may award damages, which may include compensation for injury to feelings (subs. (2)). There is no limit on the amount of damages which may be awarded for financial loss under this section. There is however a power in Sched. 3, para. 7 to set an upper limit on the damages available for injury to feelings. This contrasts with the employment provisions in Pt. II, and with the position under the Sex Discrimination Act 1975 and the Race Relations Act 1976, where there is no upper limit on the damages which may be awarded for injury to feelings, or indeed for any other head of recoverable loss. The Government has indicated that it intends to set the limit "close to or at the level which applies at any time to claims which fall to be considered by the small claims court" (Minister of State, *Hansard*, H.L., Vol. 565, col. 735). The upper limit for the small claims procedure is currently set at £3,000:

"We want to ensure that as many cases as possible can be resolved without recourse to the court system. However, where that becomes inevitable, we want the system for redress to be as informal and easy to use as possible. . . . we wish to set the limit on the amount payable for injured feelings so as to help ensure that the vast majority of cases can be dealt with under the small claims procedure, with its advantages of cheap and informal resolution." (Minister of State, *Hansard*, H.L., Vol. 566, col. 1065).

At the present time, legal aid is not available for claims under £1,000. The National Disability Council established under Pt. VI of the Act has no power to investigate complaints of discrimination in the provision of goods, facilities and services, or to assist individuals in enforcing their rights before the courts (see the note to s.50). However, provision is made in s.28 for the establishment by the Government of an advisory service "to provide free advice to help disabled people and businesses to resolve individual disputes arising from the right of access ... without recourse to legal action." (White Paper, *Ending discrimination against disabled people*, Cm. 2729, 1995, para. 4.8).

As to compensation for injury to feelings and the award of exemplary damages in sex and race discrimination cases, see the note to s.8.

Subs. (6)

Schedule 3, para. 5 provides that the remedies available for an infringement of Pt. III are (with the exception of judicial review) exclusively those provided by this section; para. 6 makes provision for time limits (see below); para. 7 allows an upper limit to be placed on damages for injury to feelings (see the General Note to this section); and para. 8 concerns certification by Ministers (see the note to s.59).

Period within which proceedings must be brought. Proceedings in respect of a claim under Pt. III must be instituted before the end of the period of six months beginning when the act complained of was done (Sched. 3, para. 6(1)), although that period may be extended for a further two months where an adviser appointed by the Secretary of State under s.28 is approached before the end of the initial six-month period in relation to actual or prospective proceedings under this section (*ibid*. para. 6(2)). A court may consider a claim which is out of time "if, in all the circumstances of the case, it considers that it is just and equitable to do so" (*ibid*. para. 6(3)). Where a discriminatory act is attributable to a contract term, that act will be treated as extending throughout the duration of the contract; an act extending over a period will be treated as done at the end of that period; and a deliberate omission will be treated as done when the person decided upon it (Sched. 3, para. 6(4)). A person will be taken to have decided upon an omission when he or she does an act inconsistent with doing the omitted act, or, if no such inconsistent act has been done, at the expiry of the period within which he or she might reasonably have been expected to do the omitted act, if it was to be done (*ibid*. para. 6(5)).

For the likely interpretation of these provisions, see the note to s.8(1), which examines the approach taken to the parallel provisions in the S.D.A., s.76, and the R.R.A., s.68.

Validity and revision of certain agreements

26.—(1) Any term in a contract for the provision of goods, facilities or services or in any other agreement is void so far as it purports to—

(a) require a person to do anything which would contravene any provision of, or made under, this Part,

(b) exclude or limit the operation of any provision of this Part, or

(c) prevent any person from making a claim under this Part.

(2) Paragraphs (b) and (c) of subsection (1) do not apply to an agreement settling a claim to which section 25 applies.

(3) On the application of any person interested in an agreement to which subsection (1) applies, a county court or a sheriff court may make such order as it thinks just for modifying the agreement to take account of the effect of subsection (1).

(4) No such order shall be made unless all persons affected have been—

(a) given notice of the application; and

(b) afforded an opportunity to make representations to the court.

(5) Subsection (4) applies subject to any rules of court providing for that notice to be dispensed with.

(6) An order under subsection (3) may include provision as respects any period before the making of the order.

GENERAL NOTE

This section provides that any term in a contract for the provision of goods, facilities or services or in any other agreement is void if it: (a) requires a person to contravene this Part of the

Act; (b) attempts to exclude or limit the operation of this Part of the Act; or (c) attempts to prevent a person from making a claim under this Part of the Act (subs. (1)). As usual, an exception is made in the case of an agreement to settle a claim under s.25 (subs. (2)). The court may modify a contract to take account of the effect of subs. (1), on the application of any interested person, having first notified all those affected of the application and given them an opportunity to make representations (subss. (3) to (6)). For the equivalent provisions as they apply to claims of sex and race discrimination, see the S.D.A. 1975, s.77 and the R.R.A. 1976, s.72 respectively.

Alterations to premises occupied under leases

27.—(1) This section applies where—
- (a) a provider of services ("the occupier") occupies premises under a lease;
- (b) but for this section, he would not be entitled to make a particular alteration to the premises; and
- (c) the alteration is one which the occupier proposes to make in order to comply with a section 21 duty.

(2) Except to the extent to which it expressly so provides, the lease shall have effect by virtue of this subsection as if it provided—
- (a) for the occupier to be entitled to make the alteration with the written consent of the lessor;
- (b) for the occupier to have to make a written application to the lessor for consent if he wishes to make the alteration;
- (c) if such an application is made, for the lessor not to withhold his consent unreasonably; and
- (d) for the lessor to be entitled to make his consent subject to reasonable conditions.

(3) In this section—
> "lease" includes a tenancy, sub-lease or sub-tenancy and an agreement for a lease, tenancy, sub-lease or sub-tenancy; and
> "sub-lease" and "sub-tenancy" have such meaning as may be prescribed.

(4) If the terms and conditions of a lease—
- (a) impose conditions which are to apply if the occupier alters the premises, or
- (b) entitle the lessor to impose conditions when consenting to the occupier's altering the premises,

the occupier is to be treated for the purposes of subsection (1) as not being entitled to make the alteration.

(5) Part II of Schedule 4 supplements the provisions of this section.

GENERAL NOTE

This section entitles a service provider who occupies leased premises to alter those premises in order to comply with a duty to make reasonable adjustments under s.21. It is in substantially the same terms as the provisions in s.16 of the Act which entitle an employer or a trade organisation to alter leased premises, and reference should therefore be made to the notes on that section. Note, however, that under this section, if an occupier has applied in writing to the lessor for consent to alter the premises, and that consent has been refused or has been given subject to conditions, the occupier (or a disabled person who has an interest in the proposed alteration to the premises being carried out) may refer the matter to the county court, and if the court decides that the lessor's refusal, or any condition imposed by him on his consent, was unreasonable, it may make a declaration or an order authorising the occupier to make the alteration specified in the order. Any such order may also require the occupier to comply with any conditions specified therein (Sched. 4, para. 6).

Advice and assistance

28.—(1) The Secretary of State may make arrangements for the provision of advice and assistance to persons with a view to promoting the settlement of disputes arising under this Part otherwise than by recourse to the courts.

(2) Any person appointed by the Secretary of State in connection with arrangements made under subsection (1) shall have such duties as the Secretary of State may direct.

(3) The Secretary of State may pay to any person so appointed such allowances and compensation for loss of earnings as he considers appropriate.

(4) The Secretary of State may make such payments, by way of grants, in respect of expenditure incurred, or to be incurred, by any person exercising functions in accordance with arrangements made by the Secretary of State under this section as he considers appropriate.

(5) The approval of the Treasury is required for any payment under subsection (3) or (4).

GENERAL NOTE

This section provides for the establishment of an advisory service to offer advice and assistance to individuals alleging discrimination by those providing goods and services, and to promote the settlement of disputes. In the context of sex and race discrimination, this function may be performed by the Equal Opportunities Commission and the Commission for Racial Equality, but the National Disability Council established under Pt. VI of the Act only has the power to advise the Government; it is not empowered to provide advice, information or guidance on an individual basis to disabled persons or service providers (see the note to s.50). This service is intended to fill that gap. Advice in relation to the employment of people with disabilities will continue to be provided by the Employment Service's Placing, Assessment and Counselling Teams (PACTs) and the Advisory, Conciliation and Arbitration Service (ACAS).

The detailed nature of the advisory service to be established under this section is to be the subject of consultation, but at the time of writing it appeared that the Government were contemplating a combined approach involving a telephone helpline to provide general information to disabled people and service providers, and a "second tier" advice and assistance service which would complement the work of the existing advice agencies such as the Citizens Advice Bureaux and DIAL (the Disability Information and Advice Line Service), and would help the existing disability advisers in their work:

"In other words, what is required is a secondary tier of advice to give help and assistance to those who have the day-to-day contact with disabled people: in essence, a team of full-time disability advisers who, whether situated centrally or regionally, will together form a pool of expertise which can be utilised to stop disputes escalating to the point where court action is necessary." (Minister of State, *Hansard*, H.L., Vol. 566, col. 1029).

Under this scheme, the existing advice agencies would continue to be the primary source of advice and assistance for disabled people and service providers. In more complicated cases, or where the parties cannot reach agreement, the guidance of the advisers could be sought, and in very difficult cases the case could be referred on to the advice service (*ibid.* col. 1030).

PART IV

EDUCATION

GENERAL NOTE

As originally published, the Bill did not apply to education. The right of access to goods, facilities and services in Pt. III of the Act contains an exemption in s.19(5) for education framed in very broad terms, and the Government successfully resisted Opposition attempts to include education within the range of facilities and services covered by the right of access in Pt. III. This resistance was not unexpected, given that the education of children with special educational needs and of students with learning difficulties and disabilities was tackled comparatively recently in the Education Act 1993, the Further and Higher Education Act 1992 and the Code of Practice on the Identification and Assessment of Special Educational Needs. The Government's strategy in this area, as explained in the White Paper, *Ending discrimination against disabled people*, Cm. 2729, 1995, has been to consolidate the approach of the 1992 and 1993 Acts, which attempt to strike a balance between choice, needs and resources, rather than to give disabled pupils and students a right of access to an educational institution of their choice:

"It is an inescapable fact that, to make the best and the most efficient provision for the individual needs of pupils and students with a wide spectrum of special educational needs, a degree of planning and concentration of resources is essential. The Education Acts strike a balance between the important rights of parents and students to choice about their education and the need to have planning and concentration of resources. That is the way in which finite resources are used to best effect. The inclusion of education in the Bill could lead to those resources being spread too thinly." (Minister for Social Security and Disabled People, *Hansard*, H.C., Standing Committee E, col. 328).

The Government was however persuaded to make some modest amendments to the Education Acts, mainly in connection with the provision of information by governing bodies and local education authorities as to arrangements and facilities for disabled pupils and students, while leaving intact the structure of the existing legislation.

One of the principal areas of controversy in this area has been whether disabled pupils should have a right to receive an integrated education in a mainstream (*i.e.* a non-special) school. Section 160 of the Education Act 1993 imposes a qualified duty to educate a child with special educational needs in an ordinary school rather than a special school, building on the integration duty previously contained in the Education Act 1981, but this duty only arises if the conditions set out in s.160(2) of the 1993 Act are satisfied. The conditions are that an integrated education must be compatible with (i) the child receiving the special educational provision which his learning difficulty calls for, (ii) the provision of efficient education for the children with whom he will be educated, and (iii) the efficient use of resources. This third condition in particular has been widely used by local education authorities as a justification for denying disabled pupils access to mainstream education, and its use has been described by the Independent Panel for Special Educational Advice as "Overused, subjective, secretive and practically unchallengeable." (*Half Measures: RADAR's Response to the Consultation Document on Government Measures to Tackle Discrimination Against Disabled People*, 1994, para. 2.21).

The duty to integrate a child with special educational needs into a mainstream school is also subject to the wishes of the child's parents. Section 160(1) of the 1993 Act provides that, subject to the conditions referred to above, a child with special educational needs must be educated in an ordinary school "unless that is incompatible with the wishes of the parent", which in effect gives a parent a veto on a child's integration into mainstream education. However, the 1993 Act does not give parents any right to choose an integrated education for their child, nor does it place any legal obligation on schools or local education authorities to take positive action to widen access for children with special educational needs. Local education authorities are merely required to "keep under review" their arrangements for special educational provision (Education Act 1993, s.159), and grant-maintained schools and local education authorities have a duty to collect information on the provision of education for children with special educational needs (*ibid.* s.21).

The 1993 Act therefore falls a long way short of giving disabled children a right of access to mainstream schools. There has been little significant change in the rate of integration of children with special educational needs into mainstream education since the duty to integrate was first introduced in 1981, and there is evidence of considerable variation across the country in the proportion of children with special educational needs who are educated in ordinary schools. Research conducted for the Centre for Studies on Integration in Education indicates that children with special educational needs are six times less likely to receive an integrated education in the London Borough of Lambeth than if they live in Barnsley or Cornwall (*ibid.* para. 2.18). A survey conducted by Coopers and Lybrand in 1993 for the Spastics Society and the National Union of Teachers to assess the extent of disabled access in schools in England and Wales found that 16 per cent of primary schools and seven per cent of secondary schools were completely inaccessible to disabled people, while 26 per cent and 10 per cent respectively reported being fully accessible; only 18 per cent of secondary schools were reported as being 75 per cent accessible, and 65 per cent of primary and 55 per cent of secondary schools had no suitably adapted toilet facilities.

Education of disabled persons

29.—(1) In section 161(5) of the Education Act 1993 (information relating to pupils with special educational needs to be included in annual report), omit the words from "and in this subsection" to the end.

(2) After section 161(5) of that Act insert—

"(6) The annual report for each county, voluntary or grant-maintained school shall include a report containing information as to—

(a) the arrangements for the admission of disabled pupils;

(b) the steps taken to prevent disabled pupils from being treated less favourably than other pupils; and

(c) the facilities provided to assist access to the school by disabled pupils.

(7) In this section—

"annual report" means the report prepared under the articles of government for the school in accordance with section 30 of the Education (No. 2) Act 1986 or, as the case may be, paragraph 8 of Schedule 6 to this Act; and

"disabled pupils" means pupils who are disabled persons for the purposes of the Disability Discrimination Act 1995."

(3) In section 1 of the Education Act 1994 (establishment of the Teacher Training Agency) add, at the end—

"(4) In exercising their functions, the Teacher Training Agency shall have regard to the requirements of persons who are disabled persons for the purposes of the Disability Discrimination Act 1995."

GENERAL NOTE

Section 161 of the 1993 Act places a number of duties on governing bodies in relation to pupils with special educational needs. In particular, governing bodies must "use their best endeavours" to ensure that the necessary special educational provision is made, and must ensure, so far as is reasonably practicable and subject to certain conditions, that a child with special educational needs takes part in the activities of the school together with children who do not have special educational needs. Section 161(5) provides that the annual report of the governing body must contain prescribed information about the implementation of the governing body's policy for pupils with special educational needs. Schools are required to formulate and publish information about their policy for children with special educational needs. This section adds to s.161, by providing that the annual report for each county, voluntary or grant-maintained (but not maintained special) school must in future also include information as to the arrangements for the admission of disabled pupils, the steps taken to prevent disabled pupils from being discriminated against, and the facilities provided to assist access to the school by disabled pupils (subs. (2)). As the Minister commented in introducing the new clauses in the House of Lords:

"Schools which are inaccessible to disabled pupils will have to admit it. The need to do so will be a spur for them to consider how they might become accessible cost effectively ... Schools should not merely pay lip service to the integration of disabled pupils; rather they should do everything they can to achieve genuine and full integration. I am convinced that this measure will encourage such integration, underpinned by the statutory duty to integrate pupils within mainstream schools as far as is possible." (Minister of State, *Hansard*, H.L., Vol. 564, col. 1994).

In addition, subs. (3) amends the Education Act 1994 to require the Teacher Training Agency to "have regard to the requirements of persons who are disabled persons" in exercising its functions. This falls a long way short of the equal right of access to courses of initial teacher training for suitably qualified disabled people, which was advocated by RADAR in its response to the Government's 1994 Consultation Document.

Further and higher education of disabled persons

30.—(1) The Further and Higher Education Act 1992 is amended as set out in subsections (2) to (6).

(2) In section 5 (administration of funds by further education funding councils), in subsection (6)(b), after "may" insert ", subject to subsection (7A) below,".

(3) After section 5(7) insert—

"(7A) Without prejudice to the power to impose conditions given by subsection (6)(b) above, the conditions subject to which a council gives financial support under this section to the governing body of an institution within the further education sector—

(a) shall require the governing body to publish disability statements at such intervals as may be prescribed; and

(b) may include conditions relating to the provision made, or to be made, by the institution with respect to disabled persons.

(7B) For the purposes of subsection (7A) above—

"disability statement" means a statement containing information of a prescribed description about the provision of facilities for education made by the institution in respect of disabled persons;

"disabled persons" means persons who are disabled persons for the purposes of the Disability Discrimination Act 1995; and

"prescribed" means prescribed by regulations."

(4) In section 8 (supplementary functions) add, at the end—

"(6) As soon as is reasonably practicable after the end of its financial year, each council shall make a written report to the Secretary of State on—

(a) the progress made during the year to which the report relates in the provision of further education for disabled students in their area; and

(b) their plans for the future provision of further education for disabled students in their area.

(7) In subsection (6) above—

"disabled students" means students who are disabled persons for the purposes of the Disability Discrimination Act 1995; and

"financial year" means the period of twelve months ending with 31st March 1997 and each successive period of twelve months."

(5) In section 62 (establishment of higher education funding councils), after subsection (7) insert—

"(7A) In exercising their functions, each council shall have regard to the requirements of disabled persons.

(7B) In subsection (7A) "disabled persons" means persons who are disabled persons for the purposes of the Disability Discrimination Act 1995."

(6) In section 65 (administration of funds by higher education funding councils), after subsection (4) insert—

"(4A) Without prejudice to the power to impose conditions given by subsection (3) above, the conditions subject to which a council makes grants, loans or other payments under this section to the governing body of a higher education institution shall require the governing body to publish disability statements at such intervals as may be specified.

(4B) For the purposes of subsection (4A) above—

"disability statement" means a statement containing information of a specified description about the provision of facilities for education and research made by the institution in respect of persons who are disabled persons for the purposes of the Disability Discrimination Act 1995; and

"specified" means specified in the conditions subject to which grants, loans or other payments are made by a council under this section."

(7) The Education Act 1944 is amended as set out in subsections (8) and (9).

(8) In section 41 (functions of local education authorities in respect of further education), after subsection (2) insert—

"(2A) It shall be the duty of every local education authority to publish disability statements at such intervals as may be prescribed.

(2B) For the purposes of subsection (2A) above—

"disability statement" means a statement containing information of a prescribed description about the provision of facilities for further education made by the local education authority in respect of persons who are disabled persons for the purposes of the Disability Discrimination Act 1995; and

"prescribed" means prescribed by regulations made by the Secretary of State."

(9) In section 41(7), (8) and (11), for "this section" substitute "subsections (1) and (6) above".

GENERAL NOTE

This section amends the Further and Higher Education Act 1992, which, *inter alia*, established the Further and Higher Education Funding Councils. Section 4(2) of the 1992 Act requires the Further Education Funding Councils for England and Wales to "have regard to the requirements of persons having learning difficulties", which includes a person who has a disability which prevents or hinders him from making use of education facilities (*ibid.* s.4(7)). Under s.5 of the 1992 Act, the Further Education Funding Councils may give financial support to the governing body of an institution "on such terms and conditions as the council think fit". Subsection (3) of this section places a duty on the funding councils to require institutions in the further education sector, as a condition of the provision of such financial support, to publish "disability statements" containing information about the provision of facilities for education for students with disabilities. Local education authorities are under a similar duty to publish disability statements in respect of facilities for further education provided by them: see subss. (7) to (9), amending the Education Act 1994, s.41. The funding councils may also make the grant of financial support subject to conditions relating to the provision made by the institution for disabled persons. The frequency and content of disability statements is to be prescribed by regulations, after consultation with the funding councils. The Government has indicated that: "Information is likely to include physical access, the provision of specialist equipment, facilities which may help students with particular disabilities, admission policies, counselling and welfare arrangements." (Minister of State, *Hansard*, H.L., Vol. 564, col. 1991). In addition, subs. (4) places a duty on the funding councils to produce an annual report to the Secretary of State on the progress made during the year in the provision of further education for students with disabilities, and their plans for future provision.

In respect of higher education, subs. (5) imposes a duty on the Higher Education Funding Councils "to have regard to the requirements of disabled persons" in exercising their functions, similar to the duty placed on the Further Education Funding Councils under s.4(2) of the 1992 Act; more significantly, as in the case of further education, subs. (6) places a duty on the Higher Education Funding Councils to make grants, loans or payments to higher education institutions conditional on the publication by the governing bodies of those institutions of disability statements containing information about the provision of facilities for education and research for students with disabilities. Unlike the provisions on further education, the frequency and content of disability statements are to be specified by the funding councils, rather than being prescribed by regulations. According to the Minister:

"The intention is that the statements would assist disabled students and funding councils generally in understanding the provision available for education and research in the particular institution. ... The statements would thus go wider than simply including information about physical facilities. It will be a matter for the funding councils, in consultation, to determine how to specify the information needed in the statements to achieve that in a viable and cost-effective way." (Minister of State, *Hansard*, H.L., Vol. 564, col. 1993).

During the debates in the House of Lords on the scope of the disability statements, concern was expressed that the new requirements might interfere with the academic autonomy of the universities over matters such as admissions arrangements, structure and content of the curriculum, and assessment procedures. In replying, the Minister emphasised that the purpose of the disability statements is to assist disabled students to understand what provision will be available for them, not to require a university to change its admissions arrangements, modify its course structures or alter its assessment procedures in order to meet the needs of disabled students:

"I am happy to state the Government's considered view that [the new measures] are not meant to do so and that they do not do so. Nor is it the Government's intention that the disability statements should be used to put pressure on the universities or the higher education funding councils to change policies on the curriculum or admissions. Such matters are quite properly academic matters which are the responsibility of the institutions to determine. Naturally, we hope that universities will be as receptive as they can to the needs of disabled students, and we believe that the need to set out information about their policies will help focus their attention on this issue. But it will remain for universities to determine their own policies." (Minister of State, *Hansard*, H.L., Vol. 566, col. 1036).

Further and higher education of disabled persons: Scotland

31.—(1) The Further and Higher Education (Scotland) Act 1992 is amended as follows.

(2) In section 37 (establishment of Scottish Higher Education Funding Council) after subsection (4) insert—

"(4A) In exercising their functions, the Council shall have regard to the requirements of disabled persons.

(4B) In subsection (4A) above, "disabled persons" means persons who are disabled persons for the purpose of the Disability Discrimination Act 1995."

(3) In section 40 (administration of funds by the Council), after subsection (4) insert—

"(5) Without prejudice to the power to impose conditions given by subsection (3) above, the conditions subject to which the Council make grants, loans or other payments under this section to the governing body of an institution within the higher education sector shall require the governing body to publish disability statements at such intervals as may be specified.

(6) For the purposes of subsection (5) above—

"disability statement" means a statement containing information of a specified description about the provision of facilities for education and research made by the institution in respect of persons who are disabled persons for the purpose of the Disability Discrimination Act 1995; and

"specified" means specified in the conditions subject to which grants, loans or other payments are made by the Council under this section."

PART V

PUBLIC TRANSPORT

GENERAL NOTE

Part V of the Act contains a wide-ranging set of enabling provisions which empower the Secretary of State for Transport to establish a timetable for achieving a fully accessible public transport system through the introduction of regulations setting minimum access standards for buses, trains, taxis and other public service vehicles. As originally drafted, the Bill made no provision for access to public transport, an omission which caused widespread dismay among campaigners for disabled people's rights, many of whom argued that the right of access to employment and to goods and services conferred by the Act would be undermined if steps were not also taken to ensure that disabled people had the opportunity to travel to where those jobs, goods or services were available. The force of this argument was acknowledged in the Consultation Document on *Measures to Tackle Discrimination Against Disabled People* (July 1994), which stated that: "A fully accessible transport system and pedestrian environment are key elements for enabling disabled people to become fully integrated into society."

The Government was eventually persuaded to use the opportunity presented by the Act to tackle the question of access to public transport, and the measures contained in Pt. V were introduced into the Bill in the House of Lords. The provisions empower the Secretary of State to set minimum access standards for accessible taxis, public service vehicles and rail vehicles, with a timetable for implementation. The Government's stated intention is that the access requirements will only apply to new vehicles, in view of the cost and technical difficulty of applying them retrospectively (Minister of State, *Hansard*, H.L., Vol. 565, col. 715). The new provisions do not extend to travel by air or sea, the Government's view being that the international dimension of air and sea travel would make domestic legislation in those cases of limited value (Mr William Hague, Minister for Social Security and Disabled People, *Hansard*, H.C., Vol. 257, col. 858).

Of the 6.5 million disabled people in the U.K., 4.5 million have a mobility disability, yet progress towards accessible public transport has been slow. The Disabled Persons Transport Advisory Committee (DPTAC), an advisory body set up under the Transport Act 1985 (c. 67) to advise the Secretary of State for Transport, estimated in 1989 that between 10 and 12 per cent of the population were unable to access the public transport system adequately (*Public Transport and the Missing Six Millions: What Can be Learned?* London, DPTAC, 1989). Trains are now being designed and built to provide improved access and facilities for disabled people, but the overall position is still poor. Accommodation for wheelchair users is often restricted to one designated space per train, which means that two wheelchair users cannot travel together, and it is still commonplace for wheelchair users to be relegated to the guard's van. Lack of accessible toilet facilities on trains is a further major problem for disabled travellers. Under the Railways Act 1993 (c. 43), the operators of passenger and station services are under a duty to "have regard" to the interests of disabled travellers as a condition of being granted a licence to operate, but that Act does not impose any requirement to take positive steps to improve access. Section 70 of the 1993 Act required the Regulator to prepare and publish a code of practice for protecting the interests of disabled users of railway passenger services or station services, and to encourage the adoption and implementation of the code, but as the code of practice has no legal force there is no obligation on passenger or station operators to comply with its recommendations. The ban on people in wheelchairs from using the London underground system (except for certain above-ground stations) was removed in 1993, but access is still extremely difficult. Significant progress has been made in improving access to taxis in several major cities. So for example, in London all new licensed taxis have had to be wheelchair-accessible since 1989, and all licensed taxis are required to be wheelchair-accessible by the year 2000; similar requirements apply in Liverpool, Manchester and Edinburgh, but elsewhere the picture is more patchy. Some local authorities have adopted a policy of insisting on accessible taxis before issuing or renewing licences, but there has been no overall co-ordination of policy. The survey conducted by the Office of Population Censuses and Surveys in 1986 revealed that 1.1 million people were unable to use buses because of their disabilities. Most buses and coaches are inaccessible to wheelchair-users, and to many people with mobility restrictions, because of the height of their steps. There has however been some experimentation with wheelchair-accessible low-floor buses on urban bus-routes in London, Liverpool and Tyneside, and the Government has confirmed its commitment to ensuring that, from a date to be fixed, all new buses will be of low-floor construction, as far as is technically feasible. Most new buses already incorporate the design features contained in the Bus Specifications drawn up by DPTAC (*Making Buses More Suitable for Elderly and Ambulant Disabled People*, London, DPTAC, 1988), but they represent only a small proportion of the total number of buses in service. Ease of access to the transport system is of course a benefit to all travellers, not just those with disabilities.

The technical and financial implications for public transport operators of a requirement of fully accessible transport systems are very considerable. It may be prohibitively expensive or simply technically impracticable to require adaptations to be made to existing vehicles, although worthwhile improvements can sometimes be made at relatively little cost (*e.g.* the provision of portable ramps at railway stations). It is usually easier and more cost-effective to provide disabled access in new vehicles or facilities, or as part of a major refurbishment, a point acknowledged in the White Paper, *Ending Discrimination against Disabled People*, at para. 5.3. The Government has therefore been at pains to stress that the new access standards will only apply to new vehicles, enabling transport operators to comply with the duty to provide full access as and when vehicles are replaced (Minister of State, *Hansard*, H.L., Vol. 566, col. 463). The new measures have also been drafted so as to provide maximum flexibility in tailoring the access requirements to different modes of transport. The regulation-making powers therefore allow for the imposition of different standards and access solutions, with different time scales, to reflect the particular circumstances of different geographical areas and locations, and the wide range of modes of transport. The exclusion of existing vehicles from the accessibility requirements, coupled with the broad powers to apply different standards and to grant exemptions, means that, for certain types of transport and in certain areas, full accessibility is unlikely to be achieved until well into the next century.

Taxis

Taxi accessibility regulations

32.—(1) The Secretary of State may make regulations ("taxi accessibility regulations") for the purpose of securing that it is possible—
  (a) for disabled persons—
            (i) to get into and out of taxis in safety;
            (ii) to be carried in taxis in safety and in reasonable comfort; and
  (b) for disabled persons in wheelchairs—
            (i) to be conveyed in safety into and out of taxis while remaining in their wheelchairs; and
            (ii) to be carried in taxis in safety and in reasonable comfort while remaining in their wheelchairs.
  (2) Taxi accessibility regulations may, in particular—
  (a) require any regulated taxi to conform with provisions of the regulations as to—
            (i) the size of any door opening which is for the use of passengers;
            (ii) the floor area of the passenger compartment;

         (iii) the amount of headroom in the passenger compartment;

         (iv) the fitting of restraining devices designed to ensure the stability of a wheelchair while the taxi is moving;

    (b) require the driver of any regulated taxi which is plying for hire, or which has been hired, to comply with provisions of the regulations as to the carrying of ramps or other devices designed to facilitate the loading and unloading of wheelchairs;

    (c) require the driver of any regulated taxi in which a disabled person who is in a wheelchair is being carried (while remaining in his wheelchair) to comply with provisions of the regulations as to the position in which the wheelchair is to be secured.

  (3) The driver of a regulated taxi which is plying for hire, or which has been hired, is guilty of an offence if—

    (a) he fails to comply with any requirement imposed on him by the regulations; or

    (b) the taxi fails to conform with any provision of the regulations with which it is required to conform.

  (4) A person who is guilty of such an offence is liable, on summary conviction, to a fine not exceeding level 3 on the standard scale.

  (5) In this section—

    "passenger compartment" has such meaning as may be prescribed;

    "regulated taxi" means any taxi to which the regulations are expressed to apply;

    "taxi" means a vehicle licensed under—

        (a) section 37 of the Town Police Clauses Act 1847, or

        (b) section 6 of the Metropolitan Public Carriage Act 1869,

    but does not include a taxi which is drawn by a horse or other animal.

DEFINITIONS

  "disabled person": s.1(2).
  "passenger compartment": subs. (5).
  "regulated taxi": s.68(1); subs. (5).
  "regulations": s.68(1).
  "standard scale": Criminal Justice Act 1982, s.37(2).
  "taxi": s.68(1); subs. (5).
  "taxi accessibility regulations": s.68(1); subs. (1).

GENERAL NOTE

  This is the first of eight sections in the Act concerning the accessibility of taxis. It empowers the Secretary of State for Transport to make regulations ("taxi accessibility regulations") laying down detailed specifications for taxis to ensure that they are fully accessible to all disabled persons, whether or not they are wheelchair users, and requiring taxi drivers to comply with any requirements as to the carrying and use of special equipment (*e.g.* ramps). The new requirements will generally apply only to licensed taxis (*i.e.* vehicles which are licensed as taxis under the Town Police Clauses Act 1847 (c. 89), s.37, or the Metropolitan Public Carriage Act 1869 (c. 115), s.6), not to private hire vehicles. However, in recognition of the growing trend whereby private hire companies are granted concessions to operate taxi services from certain locations (for example, as is the case at Gatwick Airport), the Secretary of State is empowered to extend the new requirements to hire car services provided under franchise agreements at ports, airports, railway stations and bus stations (s.33). The new requirements will not apply (in the first instance, at least) to existing taxis: "We have no intention of introducing the requirements over such a period as would undermine the viability of the taxi trade" (Minister of State, *Hansard*, H.L., Vol. 564, col. 2047). Section 34 makes the issue of new taxi licences (which require renewal on an annual basis) conditional on compliance with the taxi accessibility regulations, but allows a non-accessible vehicle which is already licensed as a taxi to be re-licensed, unless and until the Secretary of State decides to remove that concession. To ensure that the new requirements do not jeopardise the viability of the taxi trade in a particular area, s.35 gives the Secretary of State a broad power to make exemption regulations under which he may grant an order exempting a licensing authority from the new requirements where, because of the specific circumstances of an area, it would be inappropriate to impose the new requirements, and where to do so would result in an unacceptable reduction in the number of taxis in the area.

Requiring taxis to be accessible to passengers in wheelchairs would be of limited utility if taxi drivers were not required to carry those passengers. Section 36 therefore places the driver of a regulated taxi which has been hired by or for a disabled person in a wheelchair under a duty to carry the disabled passenger, to take steps to ensure his safety and comfort, and to assist him in getting himself and his luggage into or out of the taxi. A driver who fails to comply with these duties commits an offence, although it will not be unlawful to refuse to carry a disabled person if the circumstances are such that it would otherwise be lawful for the driver to refuse to carry that person. Drivers can seek exemption from these duties on medical grounds, or on the grounds that their physical condition makes it impossible or unreasonably difficult to comply with them. In addition, all drivers of licensed taxis (not just those who drive regulated taxis) are placed under a duty by s.37 to convey a disabled person accompanied by a guide dog or a hearing dog, without any additional charge, subject to a narrow exemption on medical grounds (*e.g.* where the driver has a medical condition such as asthma which is aggravated by dogs).

The purpose of the taxi accessibility regulations is to ensure that in due course all licensed taxis will be fully accessible to disabled persons, whether or not they are travelling in a wheelchair. Subsection (1) provides that accessibility for these purposes means ensuring that it is possible for disabled persons to get into and out of taxis in safety, and to be carried in taxis in safety and in reasonable comfort; for disabled persons in wheelchairs, these requirements must be satisfied while they remain in their wheelchairs. Significantly, the parallel provisions in s.40 concerning the accessibility of public service vehicles (for example, buses) provide that it must be possible for disabled persons to get on and off such vehicles in safety "and without unreasonable difficulty".

Subsection (2) provides that the regulations may contain detailed specifications covering, *inter alia*, the size of passenger door-openings, the floor area and amount of headroom in the passenger compartment, and the fitting of restraining devices to ensure that wheelchairs remain stable while the taxi is moving; the regulations may also require taxi drivers to comply with any requirements concerning the carrying of ramps or other equipment designed to facilitate the loading or unloading of wheelchairs, or the position in which wheelchairs must be secured. A taxi driver who fails to comply with any requirement imposed on him by the regulations, or whose taxi fails to conform with any provision of the regulations with which it is required to conform, is liable on summary conviction to a fine not exceeding level 3 on the standard scale (subss. (3) and (4)).

It seems likely that the requirement that all taxis become fully accessible will necessitate the development of a new generation of purpose-built taxi to meet the needs of the full range of people with disabilities. The currently-available designs of purpose-built taxi (the Metrocab and Fairway) can be adapted to provide access for most wheelchair users, but they are difficult for some non-wheelchair users to enter and exit, particularly those with arthritis. Ordinary saloon cars used as taxis are completely inaccessible to wheelchair users, although they can be modified (*e.g.* by fitting a swivelling passenger seat) to allow for easier access by ambulant disabled passengers. The new requirements will eventually bring to an end the use of saloon cars as licensed taxis, but the cost implications of requiring a change-over to purpose-built taxis are such that the Secretary of State is expected to allow existing non-accessible vehicles to be re-licensed for at least a 10-year period, to allow those vehicles to reach the end of their useful life (see the note to s.34). It remains to be seen whether, when that time finally comes, the cost of buying an accessible vehicle will cause owner-drivers of licensed taxis to move to the private hire sector. Ministers have indicated that the concession for existing non-accessible vehicles is unlikely to apply in areas such as London, Manchester, Liverpool and Edinburgh, where earlier target-dates for accessibility have already been set (Minister for Social Security and Disabled People, H.C., Standing Committee E, col. 447).

Taxi. With one exception (see the note to s.33), the taxi accessibility regulations apply only to vehicles licensed to ply for hire as hackney carriages under the Town Police Clauses Act 1847, s.37, or the Metropolitan Public Carriage Act 1869, s.6, not to minicabs or other private hire vehicles. The 1869 Act governs the licensing of hackney carriages in the Metropolitan Police District and the City of London, while the 1847 Act makes provision for the licensing of hackney carriages in those parts of England and Wales outside the area to which the 1869 Act applies. The 1869 Act, s.4, defines a "hackney carriage" as "any carriage for the conveyance of passengers which plies for hire" within the limits of that Act; and the London Hackney Carriage Act 1831 (c. 22), s.35, provides that a hackney carriage found standing in any street or place shall, unless actually hired, be deemed to be plying for hire. The 1847 Act, s.37, similarly defines a "hackney carriage" as a "wheeled carriage ... used in standing or plying for hire in any street..."

Plying for hire. This is not defined in the Act. In the context of the London Hackney Carriage Act 1853, s.7, it has been held that a taxi does not ply for hire while it is in motion, but only when it is standing on a taxi rank or in a street (*Hunt v. Morgan* [1949] 1 K.B. 233); a taxi which is stationary is not necessarily "standing" in a street for the purposes of the London Hackney Carriage Act 1831, s.35 (*Eldridge v. British Airports Authority* [1970] 2 Q.B. 387).

Designated transport facilities

33.—(1) In this section "a franchise agreement" means a contract entered into by the operator of a designated transport facility for the provision by the other party to the contract of hire car services—

(a) for members of the public using any part of the transport facility; and

(b) which involve vehicles entering any part of that facility.

(2) The Secretary of State may by regulations provide for the application of any taxi provision in relation to—

(a) vehicles used for the provision of services under a franchise agreement; or

(b) the drivers of such vehicles.

(3) Any regulations under subsection (2) may apply any taxi provision with such modifications as the Secretary of State considers appropriate.

(4) In this section—

"designated" means designated for the purposes of this section by an order made by the Secretary of State;

"hire car" has such meaning as may be prescribed;

"operator", in relation to a transport facility, means any person who is concerned with the management or operation of the facility;

"taxi provision" means any provision of—

(a) this Act, or

(b) regulations made in pursuance of section 20(2A) of the Civic Government (Scotland) Act 1982,

which applies in relation to taxis or the drivers of taxis; and

"transport facility" means any premises which form part of any port, airport, railway station or bus station.

DEFINITIONS

"designated": subs. (4).

"franchise agreement": subs. (1).

"hire car": subs. (4).

"operator": subs. (4).

"regulations": s.68(1).

"taxi provision": subs. (4).

"transport facility": subs. (4).

GENERAL NOTE

This section allows the accessibility requirements which apply to licensed taxis to be extended to other vehicles in certain limited circumstances. It empowers the Secretary of State to apply some or all of the taxi provisions in this Act to vehicles used for the provision of hire car services under "franchise agreements" (as defined in subs. (1)) entered into by the operators of designated transport facilities, or to the drivers of those vehicles. It is intended to address the practice whereby firms providing private hire car services are granted concessions to operate taxi services from ports, airports, railway stations and bus stations, as is the case at Gatwick Airport. Such arrangements may operate on an exclusive basis, with licensed taxis being denied the opportunity to pick up passengers from within the (privately owned) transport facility. As the 1994 Report of the House of Commons Transport Committee on *Taxis and Private Hire Vehicles* noted, such an arrangement may mean that there are no accessible vehicles available at such locations for disabled travellers. The power in this section to apply the taxi accessibility requirements to private hire vehicles in such circumstances is designed to ensure that a disabled passenger will be confident of finding an accessible taxi at a location where such a franchise agreement is in operation.

New licences conditional on compliance with taxi accessibility regulations

34.—(1) No licensing authority shall grant a licence for a taxi to ply for hire unless the vehicle conforms with those provisions of the taxi accessibility regulations with which it will be required to conform if licensed.

(2) Subsection (1) does not apply if such a licence was in force with respect to the vehicle at any time during the period of 28 days immediately before the day on which the licence is granted.

(3) The Secretary of State may by order provide for subsection (2) to cease to have effect on such date as may be specified in the order.

(4) Separate orders may be made under subsection (3) with respect to different areas or localities.

DEFINITIONS
"licensing authority": s.68(1).
"taxi": s.68(1); s.32(5).
"taxi accessibility regulations": s.68(1); s.32(1).

GENERAL NOTE
This section makes the grant of a license for a taxi to ply for hire by a licensing authority conditional on compliance with the taxi accessibility regulations (subs. (1)). In the first instance this requirement will only apply to vehicles which are newly-licensed as taxis, as subs. (2) allows a non-accessible taxi to be re-licensed where the vehicle in question was previously licensed as a taxi within 28 days of the date of issue of the new license. However, subs. (3) empowers the Secretary of State to set an end-date for this concession beyond which a non-accessible vehicle may not be re-licensed (although subs. (4) gives him the power to make separate provision for different areas or localities). As seen in the General Note to s.32, the cost implications of requiring all licensed taxis to become fully accessible are such that the Secretary of State is expected to allow existing non-accessible vehicles to be re-licensed for at least a 10-year period, to allow those vehicles to reach the end of their useful life. This concession is however unlikely to apply in areas such as London, Manchester, Liverpool and Edinburgh, where earlier target-dates for full accessibility have already been set (Minister for Social Security and Disabled People, *Hansard*, H.C., Standing Committee E, col. 447).

Licensing authority. This means, in relation to the area to which the Metropolitan Public Carriage Act 1869 applies, the Secretary of State, or the holder of any office for the time being designated by him, or in relation to any other area in England and Wales; the authority responsible for licensing taxis in that area: s.68(1).

Exemption from taxi accessibility regulations

35.—(1) The Secretary of State may make regulations ("exemption regulations") for the purpose of enabling any relevant licensing authority to apply to him for an order (an "exemption order") exempting the authority from the requirements of section 34.

(2) Exemption regulations may, in particular, make provision requiring a licensing authority proposing to apply for an exemption order—

(a) to carry out such consultations as may be prescribed;

(b) to publish the proposal in the prescribed manner;

(c) to consider any representations made to it about the proposal, before applying for the order;

(d) to make its application in the prescribed form.

(3) A licensing authority may apply for an exemption order only if it is satisfied—

(a) that, having regard to the circumstances prevailing in its area, it would be inappropriate for the requirements of section 34 to apply; and

(b) that the application of section 34 would result in an unacceptable reduction in the number of taxis in its area.

(4) After considering any application for an exemption order and consulting the Disabled Persons Transport Advisory Committee and such other persons as he considers appropriate, the Secretary of State may—

(a) make an exemption order in the terms of the application;

(b) make an exemption order in such other terms as he considers appropriate; or

(c) refuse to make an exemption order.

(5) The Secretary of State may by regulations ("swivel seat regulations") make provision requiring any exempt taxi plying for hire in an area in respect of which an exemption order is in force to conform with provisions of the regulations as to the fitting and use of swivel seats.

(6) The Secretary of State may by regulations make provision with respect to swivel seat regulations similar to that made by section 34 with respect to taxi accessibility regulations.

(7) In this section—

"exempt taxi" means a taxi in relation to which section 34(1) would apply if the exemption order were not in force;

"relevant licensing authority" means a licensing authority responsible for licensing taxis in any area of England and Wales other than the area to which the Metropolitan Public Carriage Act 1869 applies; and

"swivel seats" has such meaning as may be prescribed.

DEFINITIONS
"exemption order": subs. (1).
"exemption regulations": subs. (1).
"exempt taxi": subs. (7).
"licensing authority": s.68(1).
"prescribed": s.68(1).
"regulations": s.68(1).
"relevant licensing authority": subs. (7).
"swivel seat regulations": subs. (5).
"swivel seats": subs. (7).
"taxi": s.68(1); s.32(5).
"taxi accessibility regulations": s.68(1); s.32(1).

GENERAL NOTE
This section is designed to ensure that the imposition of the accessibility requirements does not jeopardise the viability of the taxi trade in a particular area. It empowers the Secretary of State to make exemption regulations under which he may, on the application of a relevant licensing authority, grant an order exempting that authority from the requirements of s.34. Such an application may only be made by a licensing authority where it is satisfied that, in view of the specific circumstances prevailing in its area, it would be inappropriate for those requirements to apply, and that to apply those requirements would result in an unacceptable reduction in the number of taxis in its area (subs. (3)). It would appear that both these conditions must be satisfied, but unfortunately no guidance is given as to the circumstances in which it might be considered inappropriate for the accessibility requirements to apply.

The exemption regulations may make provision as to the manner and form of an application for an exemption order, and may include a requirement for the licensing authority to carry out consultations and consider representations made to it about the proposals before applying for an order (subs. (2)). Before making a decision on an application for an exemption order, the Secretary of State must consult the Disabled Persons Transport Advisory Committee and such other persons as he considers appropriate (subs. (4)). As a concession to accessibility in areas where an exemption order is in force, the Secretary of State may make swivel seat regulations requiring exempt taxis to conform with any requirements as to the fitting and use of swivel seats (subss. (5) and (6)).

Relevant licensing authority. This is defined in subs. (7) as a licensing authority responsible for licensing taxis in any area of England and Wales, other than the area to which the Metropolitan Public Carriage Act 1869 applies, for which the Secretary of State is the licensing authority (see the note to s.34).

Disabled Persons Transport Advisory Committee. This body was established under the Transport Act 1985, s.125, to advise the Secretary of State on matters relating to the needs of disabled persons in connection with public passenger transport.

Carrying of passengers in wheelchairs

36.—(1) This section imposes duties on the driver of a regulated taxi which has been hired—

(a) by or for a disabled person who is in a wheelchair; or

(b) by a person who wishes such a disabled person to accompany him in the taxi.

(2) In this section—

"carry" means carry in the taxi concerned; and

"the passenger" means the disabled person concerned.

(3) The duties are—

(a) to carry the passenger while he remains in his wheelchair;

(b) not to make any additional charge for doing so;

(c) if the passenger chooses to sit in a passenger seat, to carry the wheelchair;

(d) to take such steps as are necessary to ensure that the passenger is carried in safety and in reasonable comfort;

(e) to give such assistance as may be reasonably required—

(i) to enable the passenger to get into or out of the taxi;

(ii) if the passenger wishes to remain in his wheelchair, to enable him to be conveyed into and out of the taxi while in his wheelchair;

(iii) to load the passenger's luggage into or out of the taxi;

(iv) if the passenger does not wish to remain in his wheelchair, to load the wheelchair into or out of the taxi.

(4) Nothing in this section is to be taken to require the driver of any taxi—

(a) except in the case of a taxi of a prescribed description, to carry more than one person in a wheelchair, or more than one wheelchair, on any one journey; or

(b) to carry any person in circumstances in which it would otherwise be lawful for him to refuse to carry that person.

(5) A driver of a regulated taxi who fails to comply with any duty imposed on him by this section is guilty of an offence and liable, on summary conviction, to a fine not exceeding level 3 on the standard scale.

(6) In any proceedings for an offence under this section, it is a defence for the accused to show that, even though at the time of the alleged offence the taxi conformed with those provisions of the taxi accessibility regulations with which it was required to conform, it would not have been possible for the wheelchair in question to be carried in safety in the taxi.

(7) If the licensing authority is satisfied that it is appropriate to exempt a person from the duties imposed by this section—

(a) on medical grounds, or

(b) on the ground that his physical condition makes it impossible or unreasonably difficult for him to comply with the duties imposed on drivers by this section,

it shall issue him with a certificate of exemption.

(8) A certificate of exemption shall be issued for such period as may be specified in the certificate.

(9) The driver of a regulated taxi is exempt from the duties imposed by this section if—

(a) a certificate of exemption issued to him under this section is in force; and

(b) the prescribed notice of his exemption is exhibited on the taxi in the prescribed manner.

DEFINITIONS

"carry": subs. (2).

"certificate of exemption": subs. (7).

"disabled person": s.1(2).

"licensing authority": s.68(1).

"passenger; the": subs. (2).

"prescribed": s.68(1).

"regulated taxi": s.68(1); s.32(5).

"standard scale": Criminal Justice Act 1982, s.37(2).

"taxi": s.68(1); s.32(5).

"taxi accessibility regulations": s.68(1); s.32(1).

GENERAL NOTE

This section places a series of duties on the driver of a regulated taxi which has been hired by or for a disabled person who is in a wheelchair, or by a person who wishes such a person to accompany him in the taxi. Thus, the driver is under a duty to carry the disabled passenger while he remains in his wheelchair, without making any additional charge for doing so, and to carry the wheelchair if the disabled passenger chooses to sit in a passenger seat. He is also under a duty to ensure that the disabled passenger is carried in safety and in reasonable comfort, and to assist him in getting himself, his luggage and his wheelchair into or out of the taxi. A driver of a regulated taxi who fails to comply with any of these duties commits an offence and is liable on summary conviction to a fine not exceeding level 3 on the standard scale. However, unless the taxi is of a certain prescribed description, drivers are not required to carry more than one person in a wheelchair, or more than one wheelchair, on any one journey, or to carry a person if the circumstances are such that it would otherwise be lawful for the driver to refuse to carry that person. It will also be a defence for a driver to show that it would not have been possible for the wheelchair in question to be carried in safety in the taxi, provided at the time of the alleged offence the taxi conformed with the relevant taxi accessibility regulations. A driver may apply to the licensing authority for exemption from these duties on medical grounds, or on the ground that his physical condition makes it impossible or unreasonably difficult for him to comply. If the licensing authority is satisfied that it is appropriate to exempt a driver on these grounds, it must issue a certificate of exemption for a period specified in the certificate. There is a right of appeal against a refusal by a licensing authority to issue an exemption certificate under this section: see s.38. To enjoy the exemption, the driver must exhibit the prescribed notice of his exemption on his taxi in the prescribed manner. The forgery, alteration or misuse, etc. of an exemption certificate or a notice of exemption under this section is an offence: see the note to s.49.

Regulated taxi. This means a taxi to which the taxi accessibility regulations are expressed to apply: see s.68(1).

Which has been hired. The duties in relation to the carrying of passengers in wheelchairs only apply where a taxi has been hired by or for a disabled person in a wheelchair, or someone wishing to accompany such a person. This section does not place any obligation on a taxi driver to accept a hiring from a disabled passenger, which might at first sight appear to be a significant oversight. However, under the general legislation concerning taxis, it is an offence for the driver of a licensed taxi which is plying for hire to refuse to carry a passenger without reasonable excuse (see in particular the London Hackney Carriage Act 1831, s.35, the London Hackney Carriage Act 1853, s.7, and Town Police Clauses Act 1847, s.53), and the introduction of the new accessibility regulations will make it difficult for the driver of a regulated taxi to claim that it was reasonable for him to refuse to carry a passenger in a wheelchair (although note the defence in subs. (6) where the accused is able to show that it would not have been possible for the wheelchair to be carried in safety in the taxi). It should also be noted that the general duty not to refuse to carry a passenger only applies when the vehicle in question is standing or plying for hire, not when it is in motion (see the note to s.32). It remains to be seen whether the duties contained in this section will make it any easier in future for a disabled person in a wheelchair to hail a moving taxi.

Carrying of guide dogs and hearing dogs

37.—(1) This section imposes duties on the driver of a taxi which has been hired—

    (a) by or for a disabled person who is accompanied by his guide dog or hearing dog, or

    (b) by a person who wishes such a disabled person to accompany him in the taxi.

(2) The disabled person is referred to in this section as "the passenger".

(3) The duties are—

    (a) to carry the passenger's dog and allow it to remain with the passenger; and

    (b) not to make any additional charge for doing so.

(4) A driver of a taxi who fails to comply with any duty imposed on him by this section is guilty of an offence and liable, on summary conviction, to a fine not exceeding level 3 on the standard scale.

(5) If the licensing authority is satisfied that it is appropriate on medical grounds to exempt a person from the duties imposed by this section, it shall issue him with a certificate of exemption.

(6) In determining whether to issue a certificate of exemption, the licensing authority shall, in particular, have regard to the physical characteristics of the taxi which the applicant drives or those of any kind of taxi in relation to which he requires the certificate.

(7) A certificate of exemption shall be issued—
(a) with respect to a specified taxi or a specified kind of taxi; and
(b) for such period as may be specified in the certificate.

(8) The driver of a taxi is exempt from the duties imposed by this section if—
(a) a certificate of exemption issued to him under this section is in force with respect to the taxi; and
(b) the prescribed notice of his exemption is exhibited on the taxi in the prescribed manner.

(9) The Secretary of State may, for the purposes of this section, prescribe any other category of dog trained to assist a disabled person who has a disability of a prescribed kind.

(10) This section applies in relation to any such prescribed category of dog as it applies in relation to guide dogs.

(11) In this section—
"guide dog" means a dog which has been trained to guide a blind person; and
"hearing dog" means a dog which has been trained to assist a deaf person.

DEFINITIONS
"certificate of exemption": subs. (5).
"disabled person": s.1(2).
"guide dog": subs. (11).
"hearing dog": subs. (11).
"licensing authority": s.68(1).
"passenger; the": subs. (2).
"prescribed": s.68(1).
"standard scale": Criminal Justice Act 1982, s.37(2).
"taxi": s.68(1); s.32(5).

GENERAL NOTE
This section places a duty on the driver of a licensed taxi which has been hired by or for a disabled person accompanied by his guide dog or hearing dog, or by a person who wishes such a person to accompany him in the taxi, to carry the passenger's dog and allow it to remain with the passenger, without making any additional charge for doing so. Failure to comply is an offence leading, on summary conviction, to a fine not exceeding level 3 on the standard scale. The Secretary of State may extend this duty to other prescribed categories of dogs trained to assist disabled persons. The duty is subject to an exemption where the licensing authority is satisfied, having regard to the physical characteristics of the taxi which the applicant drives, that it would be appropriate on medical grounds to issue him with a certificate of exemption for a specified period for that taxi, or for a specified kind of taxi. This might apply where for example the applicant has a medical condition such as asthma which is aggravated by dogs. There is a right of appeal against a refusal by a licensing authority to issue an exemption certificate under this section: see s.38. To benefit from the exemption, the driver must exhibit the prescribed notice of exemption on his taxi in the prescribed manner, and the certificate of exemption must relate to that taxi. The forgery, alteration or misuse, etc., of an exemption certificate or a notice of exemption under this section is an offence: see the note to s.49.

Taxi. Unlike the duty to carry passengers in wheelchairs, which is confined to the drivers of *regulated* taxis (see the note to s.36), the duty to carry guide dogs and hearing dogs applies more generally to the drivers of all licensed taxis: see s.68(1), applying for these purposes the definition of "taxi" contained in s.32 (as to which, see the note to s.32).

Which has been hired. See the note to s.36.

Appeal against refusal of exemption certificate

38.—(1) Any person who is aggrieved by the refusal of a licensing authority to issue an exemption certificate under section 36 or 37 may appeal to the appropriate court before the end of the period of 28 days beginning with the date of the refusal.

(2) On an appeal to it under this section, the court may direct the licensing authority concerned to issue the appropriate certificate of exemption to have effect for such period as may be specified in the direction.

(3) "Appropriate court" means the magistrates' court for the petty sessions area in which the licensing authority has its principal office.

DEFINITIONS
"appropriate court": subs. (3).
"licensing authority": s.68(1).

GENERAL NOTE
This section confers a right of appeal against a refusal by a licensing authority to issue an exemption certificate under ss.36 and 37. The appeal is to the local magistrates' court (the usual appeal mechanism for taxi licensing matters). Such an appeal must be brought within 28 days of the date of the refusal of the exemption certificate. On appeal, the court may direct the licensing authority to issue an exemption certificate for the period specified in the direction.

Requirements as to disabled passengers in Scotland

39.—(1) Part II of the Civic Government (Scotland) Act 1982 (licensing and regulation) is amended as follows.

(2) In subsection (4) of section 10 (suitability of vehicle for use as taxi)—
(a) after "authority" insert "—(a)"; and
(b) at the end add "; and
(b) as not being so suitable if it does not so comply."

(3) In section 20 (regulations relating to taxis etc.) after subsection (2) insert—

"(2A) Without prejudice to the generality of subsections (1) and (2) above, regulations under those subsections may make such provision as appears to the Secretary of State to be necessary or expedient in relation to the carrying in taxis of disabled persons (within the meaning of section 1(2) of the Disability Discrimination Act 1995) and such provision may in particular prescribe—
(a) requirements as to the carriage of wheelchairs, guide dogs, hearing dogs and other categories of dog;
(b) a date from which any such provision is to apply and the extent to which it is to apply; and
(c) the circumstances in which an exemption from such provision may be granted in respect of any taxi or taxi driver,
and in this subsection—
"guide dog" means a dog which has been trained to guide a blind person;
"hearing dog" means a dog which has been trained to assist a deaf person; and
"other categories of dog" means such other categories of dog as the Secretary of State may prescribe, trained to assist disabled persons who have disabilities of such kinds as he may prescribe."

DEFINITIONS
"disabled person": s.1(2).

GENERAL NOTE
This section, which amends those parts of the Civic Government (Scotland) Act 1982 (c. 45) which concern the licensing and regulation of taxis, enables the Secretary of State for Scotland to

introduce regulations providing for the carrying of disabled passengers, wheelchairs, guide dogs and hearing dogs in taxis in Scotland.

Public service vehicles

PSV accessibility regulations

40.—(1) The Secretary of State may make regulations ("PSV accessibility regulations") for the purpose of securing that it is possible for disabled persons—

  (a) to get on to and off regulated public service vehicles in safety and without unreasonable difficulty (and, in the case of disabled persons in wheelchairs, to do so while remaining in their wheelchairs); and

  (b) to be carried in such vehicles in safety and in reasonable comfort.

(2) PSV accessibility regulations may, in particular, make provision as to the construction, use and maintenance of regulated public service vehicles including provision as to—

  (a) the fitting of equipment to vehicles;

  (b) equipment to be carried by vehicles;

  (c) the design of equipment to be fitted to, or carried by, vehicles;

  (d) the fitting and use of restraining devices designed to ensure the stability of wheelchairs while vehicles are moving;

  (e) the position in which wheelchairs are to be secured while vehicles are moving.

(3) Any person who—

  (a) contravenes or fails to comply with any provision of the PSV accessibility regulations,

  (b) uses on a road a regulated public service vehicle which does not conform with any provision of the regulations with which it is required to conform, or

  (c) causes or permits to be used on a road such a regulated public service vehicle,

is guilty of an offence.

(4) A person who is guilty of such an offence is liable, on summary conviction, to a fine not exceeding level 4 on the standard scale.

(5) In this section—

  "public service vehicle" means a vehicle which is—

     (a) adapted to carry more than eight passengers; and

     (b) a public service vehicle for the purposes of the Public Passenger Vehicles Act 1981;

  "regulated public service vehicle" means any public service vehicle to which the PSV accessibility regulations are expressed to apply.

(6) Different provision may be made in regulations under this section—

  (a) as respects different classes or descriptions of vehicle;

  (b) as respects the same class or description of vehicle in different circumstances.

(7) Before making any regulations under this section or section 41 or 42 the Secretary of State shall consult the Disabled Persons Transport Advisory Committee and such other representative organisations as he thinks fit.

DEFINITIONS

  "disabled person": s.1(2).

  "PSV accessibility regulations": s.68(1); subs. (1).

  "public service vehicle": subs. (5).

  "regulated public service vehicle": subs. (5).

  "regulations": s.68(1).

  "standard scale": Criminal Justice Act 1982, s.37(2).

GENERAL NOTE

This section empowers the Secretary of State for Transport to make regulations ("PSV accessibility regulations") laying down detailed specifications for the construction, use and maintenance of public service vehicles (PSVs) such as buses and coaches, to ensure that they are fully accessible to disabled persons, whether or not they are travelling in wheelchairs. Subsection (1) provides that accessibility for these purposes means ensuring that it is possible for disabled persons to get on to and off PSVs in safety and without unreasonable difficulty (those in wheelchairs must be able to do so while remaining in their wheelchairs), and to be carried in safety and in reasonable comfort. Significantly, the parallel provisions in s.32 concerning the accessibility of taxis make no reference to the difficulty of access, but simply provide that it must be possible for disabled persons to get into and out of taxis "in safety". Subsection (2) provides that the regulations may make provision as to the construction, use and maintenance of PSVs, including, *inter alia*, the design and fitting of equipment to be fitted to or carried by vehicles, the fitting and use of devices to restrain wheelchairs while the vehicle is moving, and the position in which wheelchairs must be secured. To ensure sufficient flexibility to deal with the wide range of PSVs, subs. (6) provides for different provision to be made for different classes or descriptions of vehicle, and for the same class or description of vehicle in different circumstances. "That will enable us to make regulations making different requirements for different types of vehicle over different time-scales which will ensure a smooth transition towards accessibility." (Minister of State, *Hansard*, H.L., Vol. 565, col. 716). There is also a general power in s.67 to make different provision for different areas or localities. Before making any such regulations, the Secretary of State is required by subs. (7) to consult the Disabled Persons Transport Advisory Committee, and such other "representative organisations" (not defined) as he thinks fit. A public service vehicle to which the PSV accessibility regulations apply must not be used on a road unless an accessibility certificate or an approval certificate has been issued in respect of that vehicle (see the notes to ss.41 and 42).

Failure to comply with any provision of the PSV accessibility regulations, or to use, or to cause or permit to be used, on a road a PSV which does not conform with any relevant provision of the regulations, is an offence leading on summary conviction to a fine not exceeding level 4 on the standard scale (subss. (3) and (4)). Separate provision is made for the liability in certain circumstances of the officers of a body corporate where an offence is committed by the body corporate: see the note to s.48.

The survey conducted in 1986 by the Office of Population Censuses and Surveys revealed that 1.1 million disabled people were unable to use buses, chiefly because of the height of the steps. Some progress has been made in recent years towards improving the accessibility of buses for disabled passengers, and most new buses now incorporate the design features contained in the Bus Specifications drawn up by the Disabled Persons Transport Advisory Committee (*Making Buses More Suitable for Elderly and Ambulant Disabled People*, London, DPTAC, 1988). However, these buses represent only a small proportion of the total number of buses in service, and in any event the DPTAC specifications are primarily aimed at improving access for ambulant disabled people, not for those in wheelchairs. There has however been some experimentation with wheelchair-accessible low-floor buses on urban bus-routes in London, Liverpool and Tyneside, and the Government has confirmed its commitment to ensuring that, as far as is technically feasible, all new buses will be of low-floor construction, although no implementation date has yet been fixed.

Public service vehicle. As defined in subs. (5), this means a vehicle which is adapted to carry more than eight passengers, and is a public service vehicle for the purposes of the Public Passenger Vehicles Act 1981 (c. 14). Section 1(1)(a) of the 1981 Act defines a public service vehicle as "a motor vehicle (other than a tramcar) which, being a vehicle adapted to carry more than eight passengers, is used for carrying passengers for hire or reward"; and s.1(5) of that Act provides for a number of circumstances in which a vehicle is to be treated as carrying passengers for hire or reward. The requirement in subs. (5)(a) of this section that the vehicle be adapted to carry more than eight passengers is designed to exclude PSVs falling within s.1(1)(b) of the 1981 Act (*i.e.* those which are not adapted to carry more than eight passengers) from the scope of the PSV accessibility regulations. It seems clear that in this context "adapted" is intended to mean that the vehicle is fit or suitable to carry more than eight passengers, not that it has been modified or altered to carry more than eight passengers (see *e.g. Herrmann v. Metropolitan Leather Co.* [1942] Ch. 248; *Maddox v. Storer* [1963] 1 Q.B. 451; *Burns v. Currell* [1963] 2 Q.B. 433; *Wurzal v. Addison* [1965] 2 Q.B. 131; but compare *Flower Freight Co. v. Hammond* [1963] 1 Q.B. 275; *Backer v. Secretary of State for the Environment* [1983] 2 All E.R. 1021).

Disabled Persons Transport Advisory Committee. See the note to s.35.

Accessibility certificates

41.—(1) A regulated public service vehicle shall not be used on a road unless—

(a) a vehicle examiner has issued a certificate (an "accessibility certificate") that such provisions of the PSV accessibility regulations as may be prescribed are satisfied in respect of the vehicle; or

(b) an approval certificate has been issued under section 42 in respect of the vehicle.

(2) The Secretary of State may make regulations—

(a) with respect to applications for, and the issue of, accessibility certificates;

(b) providing for the examination of vehicles in respect of which applications have been made;

(c) with respect to the issue of copies of accessibility certificates in place of certificates which have been lost or destroyed.

(3) If a regulated public service vehicle is used in contravention of this section, the operator of the vehicle is guilty of an offence and liable on summary conviction to a fine not exceeding level 4 on the standard scale.

(4) In this section "operator" has the same meaning as in the Public Passenger Vehicles Act 1981.

DEFINITIONS
    "accessibility certificate": s.68(1); s.41(1)(a).
    "approval certificate": s.68(1); s.42(4).
    "operator": subs. (4).
    "PSV accessibility regulations": s.68(1); s.40(1).
    "prescribed": s.68(1).
    "public service vehicle": s.40(5).
    "regulated public service vehicle": s.40(5).
    "regulations": s.68(1).
    "standard scale": Criminal Justice Act 1982, s.37(2).

GENERAL NOTE
This section provides that a public service vehicle to which the PSV accessibility regulations apply must not be used on a road unless a vehicle examiner has issued an "accessibility certificate" in respect of that vehicle, in accordance with regulations made for the purpose by the Secretary of State under subs. (2), or an "approval certificate" has been issued in respect of the vehicle certifying that it conforms to an approved "type vehicle" (see the note to s.42). These provisions parallel the existing certification procedures for the initial fitness of public service vehicles contained in Pt. II of the Public Passenger Vehicles Act 1981, and it is intended that an accessibility certificate will be issued at the same time as a certificate of initial fitness. Regulations may be made under subs. (2) with respect to matters such as the application procedure for accessibility certificates, the examination of vehicles by vehicle examiners and the issue of duplicate certificates. There is a right of appeal to the Secretary of State against the refusal of a vehicle examiner to issue an accessibility certificate: see s.44(3). As to the fees payable in respect of an application for an accessibility certificate or an appeal under s.44, see s.45.

If a regulated PSV is used in contravention of this section, the operator of the vehicle is liable on summary conviction to a fine not exceeding level 4 on the standard scale (subs. (3)). Under the parallel provisions contained in Pt. II of the Public Passenger Vehicles Act 1981 concerning the initial fitness of public service vehicles, the operator has a defence under s.68(3) of that Act if he can prove that he took all reasonable precautions and exercised all due diligence to avoid the commission of an offence. No provision is made for any such defence under this section. The forgery, alteration or misuse, etc., of an accessibility certificate or an approval certificate is an offence, and it is also an offence for a person knowingly to make a false statement for the purpose of obtaining an accessibility certificate or an approval certificate: see the note to s.49.

Public service vehicle. See the note to s.40, above. A "regulated public service vehicle" means any public service vehicle to which the PSV accessibility regulations are expressed to apply: s.40(5).

Vehicle examiner. This refers to an examiner appointed under s.66A of the Road Traffic Act 1988 (c. 52).

Operator. Subsection (4) provides that "operator" has the same meaning as in the Public Passenger Vehicles Act 1981. Section 81(1) of the 1981 Act provides that, except in cases where a vehicle is made available by one holder of a PSV operator's licence to another under a hiring arrangement, the operator of a vehicle is; (i) the driver, if he own the vehicle; and (ii) in any other case, the person for whom the driver works (whether under a contract of employment or any other description of contract personally to do work).

Approval certificates

42.—(1) Where the Secretary of State is satisfied that such provisions of the PSV accessibility regulations as may be prescribed for the purposes of section 41 are satisfied in respect of a particular vehicle he may approve the vehicle for the purposes of this section.

(2) A vehicle which has been so approved is referred to in this section as a "type vehicle".

(3) Subsection (4) applies where a declaration in the prescribed form has been made by an authorised person that a particular vehicle conforms in design, construction and equipment with a type vehicle.

(4) A vehicle examiner may, after examining (if he thinks fit) the vehicle to which the declaration applies, issue a certificate in the prescribed form ("an approval certificate") that it conforms to the type vehicle.

(5) The Secretary of State may make regulations—
  (a) with respect to applications for, and grants of, approval under subsection (1);
  (b) with respect to applications for, and the issue of, approval certificates;
  (c) providing for the examination of vehicles in respect of which applications have been made;
  (d) with respect to the issue of copies of approval certificates in place of certificates which have been lost or destroyed.

(6) The Secretary of State may at any time withdraw his approval of a type vehicle.

(7) Where an approval is withdrawn—
  (a) no further approval certificates shall be issued by reference to the type vehicle; but
  (b) any approval certificate issued by reference to the type vehicle before the withdrawal shall continue to have effect for the purposes of section 41.

(8) In subsection (3) "authorised person" means a person authorised by the Secretary of State for the purposes of that subsection.

DEFINITIONS
"approval certificate": s.68(1); s.42(4).
"authorised person": subs. (8).
"prescribed": s.68(1).
"PSV accessibility regulations": s.68(1); s.40(1).
"regulations": s.68(1).
"type vehicle": subs. (2).
"vehicle examiner": s.68(1).

GENERAL NOTE
This section provides for the issue of an "approval certificate" by a vehicle examiner authorising the use of a public service vehicle on the road, where that vehicle conforms to a "type vehicle" approved by the Secretary of State for Transport under this section. This process, commonly referred to as "type approval", already exists in relation to the initial fitness of public service vehicles under Pt. II of the Public Passenger Vehicles Act 1981. Subsection (1) empowers the Secretary of State to approve a vehicle as a type vehicle where he is satisfied that it meets the relevant provisions of the PSV accessibility regulations. Where a type vehicle has been approved by the Secretary of State under subs. (1), and a declaration in the prescribed form has been made by an "authorised person" that a particular vehicle conforms in design, construction and equipment with a type vehicle (subs. (2)), a vehicle examiner may (after examining that other vehicle,

if he thinks fit) issue an approval certificate that it conforms to the type vehicle (subs. (4)). The Secretary of State may make regulations with respect to applications for type approval and approval certificates, the examination of vehicles and the issue of duplicate certificates (subs. (5)). Approval of a type vehicle may be withdrawn at any time (subs. (6)), but approval certificates previously issued by reference to that type vehicle will continue to be valid (subs. (7)). Where the Secretary of State refuses an application for type approval, the applicant may ask the Secretary of State to review the decision, and in reviewing his decision the Secretary of State is required to consider any written representations made by the applicant: see s.44(1) and (2). There is also a right of appeal to the Secretary of State against the refusal of a vehicle examiner to issue an approval certificate: see s.44(3). The forgery, alteration or misuse, etc., of an approval certificate is an offence, and it is also an offence for a person knowingly to make a false statement for the purpose of obtaining an approval certificate: see the note to s.49. As to the fees payable in respect of applications for type approval or approval certificates under this section, or reviews and appeals under s.44, see s.45.

Authorised person. i.e. authorised by the Secretary of State: see subs. (8).

Special authorisations

43.—(1) The Secretary of State may by order authorise the use on roads of—

(a) any regulated public service vehicle of a class or description specified by the order, or

(b) any regulated public service vehicle which is so specified,

and nothing in section 40, 41 or 42 prevents the use of any vehicle in accordance with the order.

(2) Any such authorisation may be given subject to such restrictions and conditions as may be specified by or under the order.

(3) The Secretary of State may by order make provision for the purpose of securing that, subject to such restrictions and conditions as may be specified by or under the order, provisions of the PSV accessibility regulations apply to regulated public service vehicles of a description specified by the order subject to such modifications or exceptions as may be specified by the order.

DEFINITIONS
"PSV accessibility regulations": s.68(1); s.40(1).
"regulated public service vehicle": s.40(5).

GENERAL NOTE
This section empowers the Secretary of State for Transport to give special authorisation for the use on the road of specified public service vehicles which do not conform with the accessibility regulations and for which no accessibility certificate or approval certificate has been issued (subs. (1)). It also empowers the Secretary of State to modify the provisions of the PSV accessibility regulations as they apply to certain specified descriptions of public service vehicles (subs. (3)). "It provides flexibility to cater for circumstances in which an individual vehicle or class of vehicle cannot reasonably be expected to meet the full requirements of the accessibility regulations." (Minister of State, *Hansard*, H.L., Vol. 565, col. 717). An obvious example might be so-called heritage vehicles. The power to make orders under this section is exercisable by statutory instrument, unless the order applies only to a specified vehicle, or to vehicles of a specified person (see s.67(1) and (6)).

Reviews and appeals

44.—(1) Subsection (2) applies where—

(a) the Secretary of State refuses an application for the approval of a vehicle under section 42(1); and

(b) before the end of the prescribed period, the applicant asks the Secretary of State to review the decision and pays any fee fixed under section 45.

(2) The Secretary of State shall—

(a) review the decision; and

(b) in doing so, consider any representations made to him in writing, before the end of the prescribed period, by the applicant.

(3) A person applying for an accessibility certificate or an approval certificate may appeal to the Secretary of State against the refusal of a vehicle examiner to issue such a certificate.

(4) An appeal must be made within the prescribed time and in the prescribed manner.

(5) Regulations may make provision as to the procedure to be followed in connection with appeals.

(6) On the determination of an appeal, the Secretary of State may—

(a) confirm, vary or reverse the decision appealed against;

(b) give such directions as he thinks fit to the vehicle examiner for giving effect to his decision.

DEFINITIONS
"accessibility certificate": s.68(1); s.41(1)(a).
"approval certificate": s.68(1); s.42(4).
"prescribed": s.68(1).
"regulations": s.68(1).
"vehicle examiner": s.68(1).

GENERAL NOTE
This section provides for (i) a review by the Secretary of State of a decision by him to refuse an application for type approval under s.42(1) and (ii) an appeal to the Secretary of State against the refusal of a vehicle examiner to issue an accessibility certificate or an approval certificate (as to which, see the notes to ss.41 and 42).

Prescribed period; prescribed time; prescribed manner. i.e. prescribed by regulations made under this section and s.67.

Fees

45.—(1) Such fees, payable at such times, as may be prescribed may be charged by the Secretary of State in respect of—

(a) applications for, and grants of, approval under section 42(1);

(b) applications for, and the issue of, accessibility certificates and approval certificates;

(c) copies of such certificates;

(d) reviews and appeals under section 44.

(2) Any such fees received by the Secretary of State shall be paid by him into the Consolidated Fund.

(3) Regulations under subsection (1) may make provision for the repayment of fees, in whole or in part, in such circumstances as may be prescribed.

(4) Before making any regulations under subsection (1) the Secretary of State shall consult such representative organisations as he thinks fit.

DEFINITIONS
"accessibility certificate": s.68(1); s.41(1)(a).
"approval certificate": s.68(1); s.42(4).
"prescribed": s.68(1).
"regulations": s.68(1).

Rail vehicles

Rail vehicle accessibility regulations

46.—(1) The Secretary of State may make regulations ("rail vehicle accessibility regulations") for the purpose of securing that it is possible—

(a) for disabled persons—

(i) to get on to and off regulated rail vehicles in safety and without unreasonable difficulty;

(ii) to be carried in such vehicles in safety and in reasonable comfort; and

(b) for disabled persons in wheelchairs—

(i) to get on to and off such vehicles in safety and without unreasonable difficulty while remaining in their wheelchairs, and

(ii) to be carried in such vehicles in safety and in reasonable comfort while remaining in their wheelchairs.

(2) Rail vehicle accessibility regulations may, in particular, make provision as to the construction, use and maintenance of regulated rail vehicles including provision as to—

(a) the fitting of equipment to vehicles;

(b) equipment to be carried by vehicles;

(c) the design of equipment to be fitted to, or carried by, vehicles;

(d) the use of equipment fitted to, or carried by, vehicles;

(e) the toilet facilities to be provided in vehicles;

(f) the location and floor area of the wheelchair accommodation to be provided in vehicles;

(g) assistance to be given to disabled persons.

(3) If a regulated rail vehicle which does not conform with any provision of the rail vehicle accessibility regulations with which it is required to conform is used for carriage, the operator of the vehicle is guilty of an offence.

(4) A person who is guilty of such an offence is liable, on summary conviction, to a fine not exceeding level 4 on the standard scale.

(5) Different provision may be made in rail vehicle accessibility regulations—

(a) as respects different classes or descriptions of rail vehicle;

(b) as respects the same class or description of rail vehicle in different circumstances;

(c) as respects different networks.

(6) In this section—

"network" means any permanent way or other means of guiding or supporting rail vehicles or any section of it;

"operator", in relation to any rail vehicle, means the person having the management of that vehicle;

"rail vehicle" means a vehicle—

(a) constructed or adapted to carry passengers on any railway, tramway or prescribed system; and

(b) first brought into use, or belonging to a class of vehicle first brought into use, after 31st December 1998;

"regulated rail vehicle" means any rail vehicle to which the rail vehicle accessibility regulations are expressed to apply; and

"wheelchair accommodation" has such meaning as may be prescribed.

(7) In subsection (6)—

"prescribed system" means a system using a prescribed mode of guided transport ("guided transport" having the same meaning as in the Transport and Works Act 1992); and

"railway" and "tramway" have the same meaning as in that Act.

(8) The Secretary of State may by regulations make provision as to the time when a rail vehicle, or a class of rail vehicle, is to be treated, for the purposes of this section, as first brought into use.

(9) Regulations under subsection (8) may include provision for disregarding periods of testing and other prescribed periods of use.

(10) For the purposes of this section and section 47, a person uses a vehicle for carriage if he uses it for the carriage of members of the public for hire or reward at separate fares.

(11) Before making any regulations under subsection (1) or section 47 the Secretary of State shall consult the Disabled Persons Transport Advisory Committee and such other representative organisations as he thinks fit.

DEFINITIONS
   "disabled person": s.1(2).
   "network": subs. (6).
   "operator": subs. (6).
   "prescribed": s.68(1).
   "prescribed system": subs. (7).
   "rail vehicle": s.68(1); subs. (6).
   "rail vehicle accessibility regulations": s.68(1); subs. (1).
   "railway": subs. (7).
   "regulated rail vehicle": s.68(1); subs. (6).
   "regulations": s.68(1).
   "standard scale": Criminal Justice Act 1982, s.37(2).
   "tramway": subs. (7).
   "wheelchair accommodation": s.46(6).

GENERAL NOTE
   This section empowers the Secretary of State for Transport to make regulations ("rail vehicle accessibility regulations") making detailed provision as to the construction, use and maintenance of rail vehicles, to ensure that they are fully accessible to disabled persons, whether or not they are travelling in wheelchairs. The provisions are similar to those concerning the accessibility of public service vehicles contained in s.40 (see the note to that section). Subsection (1) provides that accessibility for these purposes means ensuring that it is possible for disabled persons to get on to and off rail vehicles in safety and without unreasonable difficulty, and to be carried in safety and in reasonable comfort; for disabled persons in wheelchairs, these requirements must be satisfied while they remain in their wheelchairs. The rail vehicle accessibility regulations may make provision as to the construction, use and maintenance of rail vehicles, including, *inter alia*, the design, fitting and use of equipment to be fitted to or carried by vehicles, toilet facilities, the location and floor area of the wheelchair accommodation, and the assistance to be given to disabled persons (subs. (2)). To ensure sufficient flexibility to deal with the wide range of rail vehicles and the various systems on which they operate, subs. (5) provides that different provision may be made for different classes or descriptions of rail vehicle, for the same class or description of vehicle in different circumstances, and for different networks (subs. (5)).
   "That flexibility is important for a number of reasons. For example, we will want to ensure that accessibility regulations do not undermine the historic character of heritage railways ... Equally, it will allow us to look at different parts of, and different vehicles on, the London Underground to ensure that the access requirements are reasonable and practicable for such an old and largely inaccessible system. We need to be able to look at the circumstances of each system to tailor the requirements to the needs of both the industry and disabled consumers." (Minister of State, *Hansard*, H.L., Vol. 565, col. 718).
   In addition, there is a general power in s.67 to make different provision for different areas or localities. Before making any regulations under this section or under s.47 (see below), the Secretary of State is required to consult the Disabled Persons Transport Advisory Committee, and such other "representative organisations" (not defined) as he thinks fit (subs. (11)). The operator of a regulated rail vehicle commits an offence, leading on summary conviction to a fine not exceeding level 4 on the standard scale, if a rail vehicle which does not conform with any provision of the rail vehicle accessibility regulations with which it is required to conform, is used for carriage (subss. (3) and (4)). "Use for carriage" in this context means use for the carriage of members of the public for hire or reward at separate fares (subs. (10)). Provision is also made for the liability in certain circumstances of the officers of a body corporate where an offence is committed by the body corporate: see the note to s.48.
   Difficulty of access to the railway system has been a constant source of complaint on the part of disabled travellers. Some improvement has been made in recent years, and most new trains are now being designed and built to provide improved access and facilities for disabled people (for example, wide-entry doors, automatic doors and wheelchair-accessible toilets), but the overall position is still poor. Accommodation for wheelchair users is often restricted to one space per train, which normally has to be booked 48 hours in advance to ensure that a portable ramp is available, and it is still commonplace for wheelchair users to be relegated to the guard's van. Unstaffed stations are a further obstacle to rail travel, as many disabled people are unable to get on and off trains without assistance. Newer urban transport systems such as the Docklands Light Railway, Manchester Metrolink and Sheffield Supertram have been designed to be accessible to people with disabilities, but older systems such as the London Underground (which banned people in wheelchairs from using below-ground stations until 1993) remain inaccessible for all but the most determined and resourceful disabled travellers.

Until now, such improvements as have been made in the accessibility of rail travel have been achieved without the force of legislation. The Railways Act 1993, s.4(6) places a duty on the Regulator to "have regard" to the interests of disabled users of passenger services and station facilities, and the operators of passenger and station services are under a similar duty as a condition of their licence to operate, but the Government resisted attempts to include in the 1993 Act an obligation to take positive steps to provide access to disabled users. The Regulator has drawn up a Code of Practice, *Meeting the Needs of Disabled Passengers* (in consultation with the Disabled Persons Transport Advisory Committee), as required under s.70 of the 1993 Act, but as the code has no legal force, there is no obligation on passenger or station operators to comply with its recommendations. The measures contained in this section mark a significant break with previous practice, in that they empower the Secretary of State to set a legislative timetable for the introduction of fully accessible rail travel. As the 1995 White Paper observed (para. 5.3), the cost of achieving full accessibility retrospectively would be prohibitively expensive. The rail vehicle accessibility regulations will therefore only apply to new vehicles first brought into use, or belonging to a class of vehicle first brought into use, after December 31, 1998 (subs. (6)). The Secretary of State may determine the time when a rail vehicle is to be treated as first brought into use (subs. (8)), and whether periods of testing, etc., are to be disregarded (subs. (9)).

Railway. This has the same meaning as in the Transport and Works Act 1992 (c. 42), s.67(1), *i.e.*: "a system of transport employing parallel rails which, (a) provide support and guidance for vehicles carried on flanged wheels, and (b) form a track which either is of a gauge of at least 350 millimetres or crosses a carriageway (whether or not on the same level), but does not include a tramway".

Tramway. This has the same meaning as in the Transport and Works Act 1992, s.67(1), *i.e.*: "a system of transport used wholly or mainly for the carriage of passengers and employing parallel rails which, (a) provide support and guidance for vehicles carried on flanged wheels, and (b) are laid wholly or mainly along a street or in any other place to which the public has access (including a place to which the public has access only on making a payment)."

Guided transport. This has the same meaning as in the Transport and Works Act 1992, s.67(1), *i.e.*: "transport by vehicles guided by means external to the vehicles (whether or not the vehicles are also capable of being operated in some other way)."

Disabled Persons Transport Advisory Committee. See the note to s.35.

Exemption from rail vehicle accessibility regulations

47.—(1) The Secretary of State may by order (an "exemption order") authorise the use for carriage of any regulated rail vehicle of a specified description, or in specified circumstances, even though that vehicle does not conform with the provisions of the rail vehicle accessibility regulations with which it is required to conform.

(2) Regulations may make provision with respect to exemption orders including, in particular, provision as to—
   (a) the persons by whom applications for exemption orders may be made;
   (b) the form in which such applications are to be made;
   (c) information to be supplied in connection with such applications;
   (d) the period for which exemption orders are to continue in force;
   (e) the revocation of exemption orders.

(3) After considering any application for an exemption order and consulting the Disabled Persons Transport Advisory Committee and such other persons as he considers appropriate, the Secretary of State may—
   (a) make an exemption order in the terms of the application;
   (b) make an exemption order in such other terms as he considers appropriate;
   (c) refuse to make an exemption order.

(4) An exemption order may be made subject to such restrictions and conditions as may be specified.

(5) In this section "specified" means specified in an exemption order.

DEFINITIONS
   "exemption order": subs. (1).
   "rail vehicle accessibility regulations": s.68(1); s.46(1).

"regulated rail vehicle": s.68(1); s.46(6).
"regulations": s.68(1).
"specified": subs. (5).

GENERAL NOTE
This section empowers the Secretary of State to make an exemption order authorising the use of rail vehicles which do not comply with the rail vehicle accessibility regulations in certain specified circumstances. Before making a decision on an application for an exemption order, the Secretary of State must consult the Disabled Persons Transport Advisory Committee and such other persons as he considers appropriate (subs. (3)). It is apparently not envisaged that this power will be widely used (Minister of State, *Hansard*, H.L., Vol. 565, col. 718).

Disabled Persons Transport Advisory Committee. See the note to s.35.

Supplemental

Offences by bodies corporate etc.

48.—(1) Where an offence under section 40 or 46 committed by a body corporate is committed with the consent or connivance of, or is attributable to any neglect on the part of, a director, manager, secretary or other similar officer of the body, or a person purporting to act in such a capacity, he as well as the body corporate is guilty of the offence.

(2) In subsection (1) "director", in relation to a body corporate whose affairs are managed by its members, means a member of the body corporate.

(3) Where, in Scotland, an offence under section 40 or 46 committed by a partnership or by an unincorporated association other than a partnership is committed with the consent or connivance of, or is attributable to any neglect on the part of, a partner in the partnership or (as the case may be) a person concerned in the management or control of the association, he, as well as the partnership or association, is guilty of the offence.

GENERAL NOTE
This section provides for the liability of certain persons where an offence is committed by a body corporate. In such circumstances, a director, manager, secretary or other similar officer of the body corporate will be guilty of the offence committed by the body corporate, if the offence was committed with his consent or connivance, or is attributable to any neglect on his part.

Consent. "It would seem that where a director consents to the commission of an offence by his company, he is well aware of what is going on and agrees to it" (*Huckerby v. Elliott* [1970] All E.R. 189, 194, per Ashworth J.).

Connivance. This term implies acquiescence in the offence committed, or in a course of conduct reasonably likely to lead to the commission of the offence: "Where [the director] connives at the offence committed by the company he is equally well aware of what is going on but his agreement is tacit, not actively encouraging what happens but letting it continue and saying nothing about it": *Huckerby v. Elliott* (*ibid.*). In *Criminal Law: The General Part*, para. 284, Glanville Williams describes connivance in the criminal law context as requiring "knowledge (including wilful blindness) plus negligent failure to prevent."

Neglect. This term implies "failure to perform a duty which the person knows or ought to know": *Hughes, Re* [1943] Ch. 296, 298, per Simonds J. Some act or neglect on the part of a director must be shown: *Huckerby v. Elliott* (*ibid.*). As to director's duties and the extent to which a director may delegate, see *City Equitable Fire Insurance Co., Re* [1925] Ch. 407.

Other similar officer. See for example *Armour v. Skeen* [1977] IRLR 310.

Person purporting to act in such a capacity. This phrase is intended to meet the situation where the appointment of a director or other officer is defective (as in *Dean v. Hiesler* [1942] 2 All E.R. 340).

Forgery and false statements

49.—(1) In this section "relevant document" means—
(a) a certificate of exemption issued under section 36 or 37;
(b) a notice of a kind mentioned in section 36(9)(b) or 37(8)(b);

(c) an accessibility certificate; or

(d) an approval certificate.

(2) A person is guilty of an offence if, with intent to deceive, he—

(a) forges, alters or uses a relevant document;

(b) lends a relevant document to any other person;

(c) allows a relevant document to be used by any other person; or

(d) makes or has in his possession any document which closely resembles a relevant document.

(3) A person who is guilty of an offence under subsection (2) is liable—

(a) on summary conviction, to a fine not exceeding the statutory maximum;

(b) on conviction on indictment, to imprisonment for a term not exceeding two years or to a fine or to both.

(4) A person who knowingly makes a false statement for the purpose of obtaining an accessibility certificate or an approval certificate is guilty of an offence and liable on summary conviction to a fine not exceeding level 4 on the standard scale.

DEFINITIONS

"accessibility certificate": s.68(1); s.41(1)(a).

"approval certificate": s.68(1); s.42(4).

"relevant document": subs. (1).

"standard scale": Criminal Justice Act 1982, s.37(2).

GENERAL NOTE

This section makes it an offence for a person, with intent to deceive, to forge, alter or use any of the documents listed in subs. (1); to lend such a document to another person; to allow such a document to be used by another person; or to make or have in his possession a document which closely resembles such a document (subs. (2)). It is also an offence for a person knowingly to make a false statement for the purpose of obtaining an accessibility certificate or an approval certificate (subs. (4)).

With intent to deceive. As to proof of criminal intent, see the Criminal Justice Act 1967 (c. 80), s.8.

Knowingly. Mere neglect to ascertain what would have been discovered through reasonable inquiries is not tantamount to knowledge, but deliberately refraining from making inquiries can in certain circumstances constitute actual knowledge: *Roper v. Taylor's Central Garages (Exeter)* (1951) 2 T.L.R. 284, per Devlin J.

PART VI

THE NATIONAL DISABILITY COUNCIL

The National Disability Council

50.—(1) There shall be a body to be known as the National Disability Council (but in this Act referred to as "the Council").

(2) It shall be the duty of the Council to advise the Secretary of State, either on its own initiative or when asked to do so by the Secretary of State—

(a) on matters relevant to the elimination of discrimination against disabled persons and persons who have had a disability;

(b) on measures which are likely to reduce or eliminate such discrimination; and

(c) on matters related to the operation of this Act or of provisions made under this Act.

(3) The Secretary of State may by order confer additional functions on the Council.

(4) The power conferred by subsection (3) does not include power to confer on the Council any functions with respect to the investigation of any complaint which may be the subject of proceedings under this Act.

(5) In discharging its duties under this section, the Council shall in particular have regard to—

(a) the extent and nature of the benefits which would be likely to result from the implementation of any recommendation which it makes; and

(b) the likely cost of implementing any such recommendation.

(6) Where the Council makes any recommendation in the discharge of any of its functions under this section it shall, if it is reasonably practicable to do so, make an assessment of—

(a) the likely cost of implementing the recommendation; and

(b) the likely financial benefits which would result from implementing it.

(7) Where the Council proposes to give the Secretary of State advice on a matter, it shall before doing so—

(a) consult any body—

    (i) established by any enactment or by a Minister of the Crown for the purpose of giving advice in relation to disability, or any aspect of disability; and

    (ii) having functions in relation to the matter to which the advice relates;

(b) consult such other persons as it considers appropriate; and

(c) have regard to any representations made to it as a result of any such consultations.

(8) Schedule 5 makes further provision with respect to the Council, including provision about its membership.

(9) The power conferred on the Council by subsection (2) to give advice on its own initiative does not include power to give advice—

(a) by virtue of paragraph (a) or (b), in respect of any matter which relates to the operation of any provision of or arrangements made under—

    (i) the Disabled Persons (Employment) Acts 1944 and 1958;

    (ii) the Employment and Training Act 1973;

    (iii) the Employment Protection (Consolidation) Act 1978; or

    (iv) section 2(3) of the Enterprise and New Towns (Scotland) Act 1990; or

(b) by virtue of paragraph (c), in respect of any matter arising under Part II or section 53, 54, 56 or 61.

(10) Subsection (9) shall not have effect at any time when there is neither a national advisory council established under section 17(1)(a) of the Disabled Persons (Employment) Act 1944 nor any person appointed to act generally under section 60(1) of this Act.

DEFINITIONS
"Council; the": subs. (1).
"disability": s.1(1).
"disabled person": s.1(2).
"Minister of the Crown": s.68(1).

GENERAL NOTE
This section provides for the establishment of a National Disability Council ("NDC") to advise the Government on general issues relating to discrimination against disabled people. Separate provision is made in Sched. 8, para. 33 for a Northern Ireland Disability Council. The primary duties of the NDC will be to advise the Government: (i) on matters relating to the elimination of discrimination against disabled people; (ii) on measures to reduce or eliminate such discrimination; and (iii) on matters pertaining to the operation of the Act. The NDC also has a duty to draw up codes of practice, albeit only at the request of the Secretary of State (see s.51). However, unlike the Equal Opportunities Commission and the Commission for Racial Equality, the NDC has no power to investigate complaints of discrimination (such activity is specifically excluded by subs. (4)), to provide assistance to individuals in enforcing their rights before the courts and tribunals, or to take strategic enforcement action of its own accord. Nor will it have the responsibility for advising the Government on the employment of disabled people, the giving of advice in that area remaining (for the time being, at least) the preserve of the National Advisory Council on Employment of People with Disabilities (NACEDP), a body established under the Disabled Persons (Employment) Act 1944 (c. 10) to advise Ministers on matters relating to the employment or training of disabled people.

The limited nature of the NDC's remit when compared with bodies such as the EOC and the CRE has been a source of widespread concern among disabled rights campaigners. A number of the organisations which responded to the Government's consultation document on *Measures to Tackle Discrimination Against Disabled People* (July 1994) argued strongly that the new body should have statutory powers of enforcement like the EOC and the CRE. Concern has also been expressed over the split jurisdiction between the NDC and the NACEPD. As the Employers Forum on Disability stated in its response to the consultation document:

"The legislation must send a clear signal to employers that disability discrimination legislation is just as important as race and gender and that they should manage it accordingly. It will be very difficult for such clear messages to be effectively delivered by two sets of civil servants reporting to two different Ministers, advised by two different councils, using two separate drafted codes of practice, enforced by two different legal authorities and supported by two different local advisory arrangements."

The establishment of a statutory disability commission was proposed in the 1982 Report of the Committee on Restrictions Against Disabled People (CORAD), which recommended that there should be "a Commission with powers to investigate, conciliate and if necessary take legal action on individual complaints" (para. 4.53). Sir Peter Large, Chairman of CORAD, described the proposal for the NDC as "... a wheyfaced ghost of what is required. Not only does the proposed advisory council lack teeth but it also lacks a digestive system and a few other essential organs. It enjoys no life of its own. It acts only in response to the summonses of the Secretary of State". The NDC only has the power to advise the Government. It is no part of its function to provide advice, information or guidance on an individual basis to disabled persons, employers or service providers. Instead, s.28 of the Act empowers the Secretary of State to make arrangements for the provision of advice and assistance in relation to Pt. III of the Act (Discrimination in relation to goods, facilities, services and premises), while advice in relation to the employment of people with disabilities will continue to be provided by the Employment Service's Placing, Assessment and Counselling Teams (PACTs) and the Advisory, Conciliation and Arbitration Service (ACAS).

Subs. (7)

It is intended that the NDC will work closely with existing bodies such as the Disabled Persons Transport Advisory Committee, drawing on their expertise in particular areas (White Paper, *Ending Discrimination against Disabled People*, Cm. 2729, para. 7.3). Subs. (7) places a duty on the NDC to consult with such bodies, and to have regard to any representations made to it, before giving advice to the Secretary of State.

Subs. (8)

Schedule 5 makes detailed provision for the constitution and membership of the NDC. The Council is to have a membership of at least 10 but not more than 20 people, appointed by the Secretary of State, and drawn from people who have knowledge or experience of the needs of disabled people, or who are representatives of professional bodies or bodies representing industry or business. In appointing members of the Council, the Secretary of State must try to ensure that at least half the membership are disabled persons, persons who have had a disability, or the parents or guardians of disabled persons (para. 3). Staff are to be provided at the discretion of the Secretary of State (para. 6). Paragraph 7 empowers the Secretary of State to make regulations in relation, *inter alia*, to the commissioning of research to be undertaken on behalf of the Council, and the payment of expenses incurred by the Council.

Subss. (9) and (10)

As discussed in the General Note, the NDC is expressly precluded by subs. (9) from giving advice to the Secretary of State on matters relating to the employment and training of disabled people, the giving of advice in that area remaining the responsibility of the National Advisory Council on Employment of People with Disabilities (NACEDP), until such time as the NACEDP is wound up (see s.60(6)) and the advisory function is transferred to the NDC (subs. (10)). However, where employment matters have an impact on wider issues of discrimination, the NDC will not be precluded from discussing them:

"It is not the Government's intention that the NDC would be precluded from considering the adequacy of anti-discrimination provisions in employment where that is appropriate as an aspect of its broad overview of anti-discrimination measures." (Minister for Social Security and Disabled People, *Hansard*, H.C., Standing Committee E, col. 397).

The Government has undertaken to review the existence and constitution of NACEDP before June 1997, when the terms of office of the current NACEDP members end; if and when the NACEDP is disbanded, its advisory responsibilities will transfer automatically to the NDC by virtue of subs. (10), unless the Secretary of State has in the meantime appointed advisers under s.60(1) to advise him on national employment issues:

"[The Act's] provisions are flexible. They provide for a variety of advisory arrangements, depending on what is appropriate. For example, NACEDP could be retained indefinitely or for a particular period only. If NACEDP were to be abolished, the new advisers could be appointed on national employment issues. If no such advisers were to be appointed, then the NDC would take over that role.".(Minister of State, *Hansard.*, H.L., Vol. 565, col. 690).

Codes of practice prepared by the Council

51.—(1) It shall be the duty of the Council, when asked to do so by the Secretary of State—

    (a) to prepare proposals for a code of practice dealing with the matters to which the Secretary of State's request relates; or

    (b) to review a code and, if it considers it appropriate, propose alterations.

(2) The Secretary of State may, in accordance with the procedural provisions of section 52, issue codes of practice in response to proposals made by the Council under this section.

(3) A failure on the part of any person to observe any provision of a code does not of itself make that person liable to any proceedings.

(4) A code is admissible in evidence in any proceedings under this Act before an industrial tribunal, a county court or a sheriff court.

(5) If any provision of a code appears to a tribunal or court to be relevant to any question arising in any proceedings under this Act, it shall be taken into account in determining that question.

(6) In this section and section 52 "code" means a code issued by the Secretary of State under this section and includes a code which has been altered and re-issued.

DEFINITIONS
    "code": subs. (6).
    "Council; the": s.50(1).

GENERAL NOTE
    This section places a duty on the NDC to prepare or review codes of practice, at the request of the Secretary of State. Unlike the Equal Opportunities Commission, the Commission for Racial Equality and the Advisory, Conciliation and Arbitration Service, all of which have the power to issue codes of practice of their own volition (under the Sex Discrimination Act 1975, s.56A; the Race Relations Act 1976, s.47, and the Trade Union and Labour Relations (Consolidation) Act 1992, s.199, respectively), the NDC may only prepare a proposal for a code of practice when asked to do so by the Secretary of State, who may approve or refuse to approve the proposal, as he thinks fit. The inability of the NDC to issue codes of practice on its own initiative has been a predictable source of criticism. The NDC will be entitled, as part of its general duty to advise on issues relevant to the elimination of discrimination, to advise the Secretary of State that a code of practice on a particular issue would be useful, or that an existing code of practice requires review or update, but in the Government's view, it would be "a shocking waste of time and money" for the Council to undertake detailed preparatory work on codes of practice if they were not then to be taken forward and submitted to Parliament (Minister for Social Security and Disabled People, *Hansard*, H.C., Standing Committee E, col. 412).

Subss. (3), (4) and (5)
    These subsections contain the usual provisions concerning the significance of a failure to observe a provision of a code of practice, and the admissibility of a code of practice in legal proceedings. For the parallel provisions in relation to codes of practice issued by the EOC, CRE and ACAS, see the Sex Discrimination Act 1975, s.56A(10)); the Race Relations Act 1976, s.47(10), and the Trade Union and Labour Relations (Consolidation) Act 1992, s.207, respectively.

In any proceedings under this Act. A code of practice issued by the Secretary of State under this section is stated to be admissible in evidence in any proceedings under this Act, and not in any legal proceedings arising under other legislation in which a disability-related issue might arise.

Further provision about codes issued under section 51

52.—(1) In this section "proposal" means a proposal made by the Council to the Secretary of State under section 51.

(2) In preparing any proposal, the Council shall consult—

(a) such persons (if any) as the Secretary of State has specified in making his request to the Council; and

(b) such other persons (if any) as the Council considers appropriate.

(3) Before making any proposal, the Council shall publish a draft, consider any representations made to it about the draft and, if it thinks it appropriate, modify its proposal in the light of any of those representations.

(4) Where the Council makes any proposal, the Secretary of State may—

(a) approve it;

(b) approve it subject to such modifications as he considers appropriate; or

(c) refuse to approve it.

(5) Where the Secretary of State approves any proposal (with or without modifications), he shall prepare a draft of the proposed code and lay it before each House of Parliament.

(6) If, within the 40-day period, either House resolves not to approve the draft, the Secretary of State shall take no further steps in relation to the proposed code.

(7) If no such resolution is made within the 40-day period, the Secretary of State shall issue the code in the form of his draft.

(8) The code shall come into force on such date as the Secretary of State may appoint by order.

(9) Subsection (6) does not prevent a new draft of the proposed code from being laid before Parliament.

(10) If the Secretary of State refuses to approve a proposal, he shall give the Council a written statement of his reasons for not approving it.

(11) The Secretary of State may by order revoke a code.

(12) In this section "40-day period", in relation to the draft of a proposed code, means—

(a) if the draft is laid before one House on a day later than the day on which it is laid before the other House, the period of 40 days beginning with the later of the two days, and

(b) in any other case, the period of 40 days beginning with the day on which the draft is laid before each House,

no account being taken of any period during which Parliament is dissolved or prorogued or during which both Houses are adjourned for more than four days.

Definitions
   "code": s.51(6).
   "Council; the": s.50(1).
   "proposal": s.52(1).
   "40-day period": s.52(12).

General Note
   This section sets out in detail the procedure for preparing a proposal for a code of practice by the NDC, the consideration of any such proposal by the Secretary of State, and the laying of a draft of the proposed code before both Houses of Parliament under the negative resolution procedure.

PART VII

SUPPLEMENTAL

Codes of practice prepared by the Secretary of State

53.—(1) The Secretary of State may issue codes of practice containing such practical guidance as he considers appropriate with a view to—
(a) eliminating discrimination in the field of employment against disabled persons and persons who have had a disability; or
(b) encouraging good practice in relation to the employment of disabled persons and persons who have had a disability.

(2) The Secretary of State may from time to time revise the whole or any part of a code and re-issue it.

(3) Without prejudice to subsection (1), a code may include practical guidance as to—
(a) the circumstances in which it would be reasonable, having regard in particular to the costs involved, for a person to be expected to make adjustments in favour of a disabled person or a person who has had a disability; or
(b) what steps it is reasonably practicable for employers to take for the purpose of preventing their employees from doing, in the course of their employment, anything which is made unlawful by this Act.

(4) A failure on the part of any person to observe any provision of a code does not of itself make that person liable to any proceedings.

(5) A code is admissible in evidence in any proceedings under this Act before an industrial tribunal, a county court or a sheriff court.

(6) If any provision of a code appears to a tribunal or court to be relevant to any question arising in any proceedings under this Act, it shall be taken into account in determining that question.

(7) In this section and section 54 "code" means a code issued by the Secretary of State under this section and includes a code which has been revised and re-issued.

(8) In subsection (1)(a), "discrimination in the field of employment" includes discrimination of a kind mentioned in section 12 or 13.

(9) In subsections (1)(b) and (3), "employment" includes contract work (as defined by section 12(6)).

DEFINITIONS
"code": subs. (7).
"disability": s.1(1).
"disabled person": s.1(2).
"discrimination in the field of employment": subs. (8).
"employment": subs. (9).

GENERAL NOTE
This section empowers the Secretary of State to issue codes of practice in relation to the employment of disabled people. Separate provision for the issue of such codes by the Secretary of State is necessary because, as discussed in the note to s.50, the NDC is precluded from advising the Secretary of State on matters relating to the employment and training of disabled people, until such time as the National Advisory Council on Employment of People with Disabilities is disbanded.

Subss. (4), (5) and (6)
See the note to s.51, subss. (3), (4) and (5).

Further provision about codes issued under section 53

54.—(1) In preparing a draft of any code under section 53, the Secretary of State shall consult such organisations representing the interests of, employers or of disabled persons in, or seeking, employment as he considers appropriate.

(2) Where the Secretary of State proposes to issue a code, he shall publish a draft of it, consider any representations that are made to him about the draft and, if he thinks it appropriate, modify his proposals in the light of any of those representations.

(3) If the Secretary of State decides to proceed with a proposed code, he shall lay a draft of it before each House of Parliament.

(4) If, within the 40-day period, either House resolves not to approve the draft, the Secretary of State shall take no further steps in relation to the proposed code.

(5) If no such resolution is made within the 40-day period, the Secretary of State shall issue the code in the form of his draft.

(6) The code shall come into force on such date as the Secretary of State may appoint by order.

(7) Subsection (4) does not prevent a new draft of the proposed code from being laid before Parliament.

(8) The Secretary of State may by order revoke a code.

(9) In this section "40-day period", in relation to the draft of a proposed code, means—

(a) if the draft is laid before one House on a day later than the day on which it is laid before the other House, the period of 40 days beginning with the later of the two days, and

(b) in any other case, the period of 40 days beginning with the day on which the draft is laid before each House,

no account being taken of any period during which Parliament is dissolved or prorogued or during which both Houses are adjourned for more than four days.

DEFINITIONS
  "code": s.53(7).
  "disabled person": s.1(2).
  "40-day period": s.54(9).

GENERAL NOTE
The procedure which the Secretary of State is required to follow in order to issue a code of practice under s.53 differs in one important respect from the similar provisions in the Trade Union and Labour Relations (Consolidation) Act 1992 (c. 52), ss.203 *et seq.*, in that under s.204(2) of the 1992 Act, a code of practice issued by the Secretary of State must be approved by an affirmative resolution of each House of Parliament, whereas under this section the negative resolution procedure applies, with consequent reduction in the level of parliamentary scrutiny. The Secretary of State is however still required to consult with representative organisations in preparing a draft of a code, and to consider any representations made to him about the draft.

The existing Code of Good Practice on the Employment of Disabled People, originally issued by the Manpower Services Commission in 1984 and revised by the Employment Service in March 1993, is a non-statutory code, and observance of its recommendations is purely voluntary.

Victimisation

55.—(1) For the purposes of Part II or Part III, a person ("A") discriminates against another person ("B") if—

(a) he treats B less favourably than he treats or would treat other persons whose circumstances are the same as B's; and

(b) he does so for a reason mentioned in subsection (2).

(2) The reasons are that—

(a) B has—

(i) brought proceedings against A or any other person under this Act; or

(ii) given evidence or information in connection with such proceedings brought by any person; or

(iii) otherwise done anything under this Act in relation to A or any other person; or

(iv) alleged that A or any other person has (whether or not the allegation so states) contravened this Act; or

(b) A believes or suspects that B has done or intends to do any of those things.

(3) Where B is a disabled person, or a person who has had a disability, the disability in question shall be disregarded in comparing his circumstances with those of any other person for the purposes of subsection (1)(a).

(4) Subsection (1) does not apply to treatment of a person because of an allegation made by him if the allegation was false and not made in good faith.

DEFINITIONS
"disability": s.1(1).
"disabled person": s.1(2).

GENERAL NOTE
In common with the Sex Discrimination Act 1975, s.4, and the Race Relations Act 1976, s.2, this section makes it unlawful for a person to victimise another person (who need not be disabled) in connection with the exercise of rights conferred by Pts. II and III of the Act. It is unlawful for a person (A) to discriminate against another person (B) by treating B less favourably than he treats or would treat another person whose circumstances are the same as B, for any of the reasons set out in subs. (2), *i.e.*, that B has (i) brought proceedings under the Act against A or any other person; (ii) given evidence or information in connection with any proceedings brought under the Act (iii) done any other thing under the Act in relation to A or any other person; (iv) alleged that A or any other person has contravened the Act (unless that allegation was both false and not made in good faith: see subs. (4)). The provisions apply *mutatis mutandis* where A believes or suspects that B has done or intends to do any of the above.

Where the complaint is of discrimination in relation to employment under Pt. II of the Act, it seems likely that the protection against victimisation afforded by this section will be limited to events occurring during the course of employment, by analogy with *Nagarajan v. Agnew* [1994] I.R.L.R. 61 (a case under the equivalent provisions in the R.R.A.), in which the applicant unsuccessfully alleged that he had been victimised by a bad reference from his ex-manager.

Whose circumstances are the same as B's. In comparing B's circumstances with those of another person, subs. (3) requires any disability which B has, or which he had, to be disregarded.

In *Aziz v. Trinity Street Taxis* [1988] I.R.L.R. 204 (the leading case on the equivalent provisions in the R.R.A.), the Court of Appeal indicated that the correct approach is to compare the treatment of the applicant with the treatment of other persons who have not done any of the acts listed in subs. (2). See also *Cornelius v. University College of Swansea* [1987] I.R.L.R. 141 (a case under the equivalent provisions in the S.D.A.), where the Court of Appeal held that, for a claim of victimisation for bringing proceedings under the 1975 Act to succeed, the applicant would have to show that she would not have been treated in the same way had the proceedings been of an entirely different nature (an interpretation which, if correct, would considerably reduce the scope of the protection).

For a reason mentioned in subsection (2). The applicant must establish the necessary causal connection between the less favourable treatment and the fact that he has done one of the acts referred to in subs. (2). Under the equivalent provisions in the R.R.A., the Court of Appeal has confirmed that to benefit from the statutory protection against victimisation, the applicant must show that the reason for the less favourable treatment is that he has done one of the protected acts, so that if the employer, service provider, etc., can show that there was some other reason for the less favourable treatment, the necessary causal connection will not have been established and the complaint of victimisation will fail: see *Aziz v. Trinity Street Taxis* (above). In *Aziz*, the applicant's complaint failed because the respondent's action was found to have been motivated by the fact that the applicant had made secret tape recordings, and not by the fact that he had made a complaint against the company under the 1976 Act. See also *British Airways Engine Overhaul v. Francis* [1981] I.R.L.R. 9 (a case under the S.D.A.), where the applicant's complaint failed because her actions (she had made statements to the press criticising her union's policy on pursuing equal pay claims) were held by the E.A.T. not to fall within any of the four heads.

For guidance as to the proper approach to be taken in a case under the R.R.A. involving mixed motives, see *Nagarajan v. Agnew* [1994] I.R.L.R. 61:

"Where an Industrial Tribunal finds that there are mixed motives for the doing of an act, one or some but not all of which constitute unlawful discrimination, it is highly desirable for there to be an assessment of the importance from the causative point of view of the unlawful motive or motives. If the Industrial Tribunal finds that the unlawful motive or motives were of sufficient weight in the decision-making process to be treated as a cause, not the sole cause but as a cause, of the act thus motivated, there will be unlawful discrimination" (per Knox J, at p.67).

It seems very likely that a similar approach will be taken to cases involving mixed motives arising under the present Act.

Subs. (2)
Given evidence or information. In *Aziz v. Trinity Street Taxis* (above), the Court of Appeal held that the equivalent head in the R.R.A., s.2(1), applies to the giving of evidence or information by a person who is not a party to the proceedings.

Otherwise done anything under this Act. Quaere whether this would cover an employee victimised by his or her employer for refusing to discriminate against a disabled person? The wording of the present section departs from that of other anti-discrimination Acts in one important respect, in that subs. (2)(a)(iii) refers to B having "otherwise done anything under this Act", whereas the equivalent provisions in the R.R.A. and S.D.A. appear to be broader, in that they refer to the applicant having "otherwise done anything under *or by reference to* this Act" (R.R.A., s.2(1)(c); S.D.A., s.4(1)(c); emphasis added). In *Kirby v. Manpower Services Commission* [1980] I.R.L.R. 229 (a case under the R.R.A.), the applicant was disciplined by his employer for disclosing alleged instances of racial discrimination by other employers to the Commission for Racial Equality. The E.A.T. held that the applicant was not protected by s.2 of the R.R.A. because he had been disciplined for disclosing confidential information, not for making allegations of racial discrimination (see *Aziz*, above, on this point), but more significantly in view of the difference in wording discussed above, the E.A.T. considered that the applicant had not been disciplined for doing something "under" the 1976 Act, because those words imported the existence under that Act of a specific duty to act; the E.A.T. was however prepared to assume that the employee's actions might constitute something done "by reference to" the 1976 Act. The E.A.T. also held that the protection in s.2(1)(d) of the 1976 Act for those alleging a contravention of that Act did not apply on the facts, because the applicant had merely alleged that the employers *might have* contravened the Act. It remains to be seen whether a similarly narrow interpretation will be given to the present section. The point is even more important in the present context, as a person who is victimised for refusing to discriminate against another on racial grounds, and who falls outside the protection of s.2 of the 1976 Act for the reasons explained above, may nevertheless be protected under s.1 of the 1976 Act, which makes it unlawful to discriminate against a person "on racial grounds": see for example *Showboat Entertainment Centre v. Owens* [1984] I.C.R. 65, where a person dismissed for refusing to apply a colour bar was held to have been discriminated against on the grounds of *another's* colour. No such argument is available under the present Act, which makes it unlawful to discriminate against a *disabled person*, not to discriminate against a person *on grounds of disability*.

Help for persons suffering discrimination

56.—(1) For the purposes of this section—
  (a) a person who considers that he may have been discriminated against, in contravention of any provision of Part II, is referred to as "the complainant"; and
  (b) a person against whom the complainant may decide to make, or has made, a complaint under Part II is referred to as "the respondent".

(2) The Secretary of State shall, with a view to helping the complainant to decide whether to make a complaint against the respondent and, if he does so, to formulate and present his case in the most effective manner, by order prescribe–
  (a) forms by which the complainant may question the respondent on his reasons for doing any relevant act, or on any other matter which is or may be relevant; and
  (b) forms by which the respondent may if he so wishes reply to any questions.

(3) Where the complainant questions the respondent in accordance with forms prescribed by an order under subsection (2)—
  (a) the question, and any reply by the respondent (whether in accordance with such an order or not), shall be admissible as evidence in any proceedings under Part II;

(b) if it appears to the tribunal in any such proceedings—
>   (i) that the respondent deliberately, and without reasonable excuse, omitted to reply within a reasonable period, or
>   (ii) that the respondent's reply is evasive or equivocal,
it may draw any inference which it considers it just and equitable to draw, including an inference that the respondent has contravened a provision of Part II.

(4) The Secretary of State may by order prescribe—
(a) the period within which questions must be duly served in order to be admissible under subsection (3)(a); and
(b) the manner in which a question, and any reply by the respondent, may be duly served.

(5) This section is without prejudice to any other enactment or rule of law regulating interlocutory and preliminary matters in proceedings before an industrial tribunal, and has effect subject to any enactment or rule of law regulating the admissibility of evidence in such proceedings.

DEFINITIONS
"complainant; the": subs. (1)(a).
"respondent; the": subs. (1)(b).

GENERAL NOTE
This section requires the Secretary of State to issue forms ("questions and replies" forms) for use by a potential complainant in order to decide whether to bring proceedings under Pt. II of the Act, and for use by the potential respondent in replying. The provisions echo those contained in the Sex Discrimination Act 1975, s.74, and the Race Relations Act 1976, s.65. Subsection (3)(b) makes it clear that a tribunal may draw adverse inferences from a failure to reply; and subs. (5) confirms that these provisions are in addition to the normal power of a tribunal to order discovery under S.I. 1993 No. 2687, Sched. 1, r.4.

Aiding unlawful acts

57.—(1) A person who knowingly aids another person to do an act made unlawful by this Act is to be treated for the purposes of this Act as himself doing the same kind of unlawful act.

(2) For the purposes of subsection (1), an employee or agent for whose act the employer or principal is liable under section 58 (or would be so liable but for section 58(5)) shall be taken to have aided the employer or principal to do the act.

(3) For the purposes of this section, a person does not knowingly aid another to do an unlawful act if—
(a) he acts in reliance on a statement made to him by that other person that, because of any provision of this Act, the act would not be unlawful; and
(b) it is reasonable for him to rely on the statement.

(4) A person who knowingly or recklessly makes such a statement which is false or misleading in a material respect is guilty of an offence.

(5) Any person guilty of an offence under subsection (4) shall be liable on summary conviction to a fine not exceeding level 5 on the standard scale.

DEFINITIONS
"act": s.68(1).
"standard scale": Criminal Justice Act 1982, s.37(2).

GENERAL NOTE
This section provides that a person who knowingly aids another person to do an act which is unlawful under this Act is himself to be treated as having committed the same kind of unlawful act. It mirrors the equivalent provisions in the Sex Discrimination Act 1975, s.42, and the Race Relations Act 1976, s.33. Its effect, when taken together with s.58 (which provides that employers and principals may be vicariously liable for the acts of their employees and agents in certain circumstances), is to enable employees or agents to be held liable for their own acts, even

though the duty not to discriminate under the Act applies only to employers or service providers. This result arises by virtue of subs. (2), which provides that an employee or agent who causes his employer or principal to be vicariously liable is deemed to have aided his employer's or principal's vicarious act. So for example, where an employer is vicariously liable under s.58 for a discriminatory act of one of his employees, the employee responsible for that discriminatory act may himself be held liable under this section for aiding the employer's breach. This will be so even if the employer is able to make out a defence under s.58(5) (*i.e.* that he took such steps as were reasonably practicable to prevent the employee's conduct), by virtue of subs. (2). As has been said in relation to the parallel provisions in the S.D.A.:

"the intriguing result is that the employee may only be liable for aiding and abetting the employer, who in turn is only prima facie liable through being vicariously liable for the employee's acts (which, in themselves, were not directly contrary to the statute), and who may himself be able to make out a defence under s.41(3) [*i.e.* the equivalent of s.58(5)]." (Smith, Wood and Thomas, *Industrial Law*, 5th ed, 1993, at p.205).

A person can avoid liability for aiding under this section if he acts in reliance on a statement by the other person that, because of some provision of the Act, the act would not be unlawful, and it is reasonable for him to rely on that statement (subs. (3)). Anyone who knowingly or recklessly makes such a statement which is false or misleading in a material respect commits an offence, and is liable on summary conviction to a fine not exceeding level 5 on the standard scale (subss. (4) and (5)).

Knowingly. See the note to s.49.

Recklessly. On the meaning of recklessness generally in relation to statutory offences, see *R. v. Caldwell* [1982] A.C. 341. See also *Large v. Mainprize* [1989] Crim.L.R. 213.

Liability of employers and principals

58.—(1) Anything done by a person in the course of his employment shall be treated for the purposes of this Act as also done by his employer, whether or not it was done with the employer's knowledge or approval.

(2) Anything done by a person as agent for another person with the authority of that other person shall be treated for the purposes of this Act as also done by that other person.

(3) Subsection (2) applies whether the authority was—

(a) express or implied; or

(b) given before or after the act in question was done.

(4) Subsections (1) and (2) do not apply in relation to an offence under section 57(4).

(5) In proceedings under this Act against any person in respect of an act alleged to have been done by an employee of his, it shall be a defence for that person to prove that he took such steps as were reasonably practicable to prevent the employee from—

(a) doing that act; or

(b) doing, in the course of his employment, acts of that description.

DEFINITIONS
"act": s.68(1).
"employment": s.68(1).

GENERAL NOTE
This section provides for the vicarious liability of employers for acts done by their employees in the course of their employment, irrespective of whether those acts are done with the employer's knowledge or approval, and also of principals for acts done by their agents with the principal's authority. Like the previous section, it substantially mirrors the equivalent provisions in the Sex Discrimination Act 1975, s.41, and the Race Relations Act 1976, s.32. By virtue of s.57(2), an employee or agent who causes his employer or principal to be vicariously liable under this section is deemed to have aided the employer or principal to do that act, so that *both* parties may in fact be liable for the act in question (as was the case in *Read v. Tiverton District Council* [1977] I.R.L.R. 202, a case under the S.D.A., s.41; see also *Enterprise Glass v. Miles* [1990] I.C.R. 787). The point is discussed more fully in the note to s.57. An employer can however escape liability under subs. (5) if he can show that he took such steps as were reasonably practicable to prevent the employee from doing the act in question, or from doing acts of that description in the course of his employment.

Subs. (1)
In the course of his employment. The meaning of this phrase as it appears in the R.R.A., s.32, was considered in *Irving v. Post Office* [1987] I.R.L.R. 289, where the Court of Appeal held, applying *Heasmans (a firm) v. Clarity Cleaning Co.* [1987] I.R.L.R. 286, that whether an employer is vicariously liable for the unauthorised act of an employee depends on whether the employee's act was merely an unauthorised or prohibited mode of doing an authorised act, or was an act which was outside the sphere of the employee's employment. See also *Tower Boot Co. v. Jones* [1995] I.R.L.R. 529. As with common law vicarious liability, an employer is not to be held liable merely because the wrongful act in question was done during the period of the employee's employment, or because the employee's employment provided the opportunity for it to be done. Note that "employment" for these purposes includes employment of a contract personally to do any work, and is not confined to employment under a contract of service or of apprenticeship: see s.68(1).

Subs. (2)
With the authority of that other person. A principal is liable for the acts of his agent which are done with his authority, whether that authority was express or implied, and whether it was given before or after the act in question was done: see subs. (3). It is unclear whether implied authority covers ostensible authority.

Subs. (5)
Such steps as were reasonably practicable. The question of whether the employer has taken such steps as were reasonably practicable to prevent the discrimination is a question of fact for the tribunal, and the onus is on the employer to establish the defence. The meaning of this phrase as it appears in the S.D.A., s.41, was considered by the E.A.T. in *Balgobin and Francis v. Tower Hamlets London Borough* [1987] I.R.L.R. 401, a case involving allegations of sexual harassment, where the defence was held to be established where the employers had no knowledge of the discriminatory conduct complained of, but were able to show that there had been proper and adequate supervision of the staff, and that they had publicised their policy of equal opportunities (see also *Bracebridge Engineering v. Darby* [1990] I.R.L.R. 3).

Statutory authority and national security etc.

59.—(1) Nothing in this Act makes unlawful any act done—
(a) in pursuance of any enactment; or
(b) in pursuance of any instrument made by a Minister of the Crown under any enactment; or
(c) to comply with any condition or requirement imposed by a Minister of the Crown (whether before or after the passing of this Act) by virtue of any enactment.

(2) In subsection (1) "enactment" includes one passed or made after the date on which this Act is passed and "instrument" includes one made after that date.

(3) Nothing in this Act makes unlawful any act done for the purpose of safeguarding national security.

<small>DEFINITIONS</small>
"enactment": s.68(1); subs. (2).
"instrument": subs. (2).
"Minister of the Crown": s.68(1).

<small>GENERAL NOTE</small>
This section provides that the Act does not apply to acts done under statutory authority, or acts done for the purpose of safeguarding national security.

Subs. (1)
The effect of the provisions concerning statutory authority is to exempt from liability any act done (i) under any enactment (including an Order in Council: see s.68(1)), or (ii) under any instrument made by a Minister of the Crown under any enactment, or (iii) to comply with any condition or requirement imposed by a Minister of the Crown by virtue of any enactment, whether the authority to discriminate arises before or after the passing of the Act. This means that the obligations under the Act not to discriminate against disabled persons are subordinate to other enactments, and to conditions or requirements imposed under such enactments, which might conflict with those obligations. To use the example given by the Minister, if a health and

safety requirement is imposed on an employer to modify equipment to protect the health and safety of employees, but that modification makes that equipment impossible for a disabled employee to operate, the health and safety provisions would take precedence over those in the Act, although the employer would still have a duty under the Act to make a reasonable adjustment to allow a disabled person to continue to work in that post if at all possible (Minister for Social Security and Disabled People, *Hansard*, H.C., Standing Committee E, col. 428).

These provisions are broadly similar to those in the R.R.A., s.41(1); the provisions concerning statutory authority in the S.D.A., s.51, are however significantly different, having been amended by the Employment Act 1989 to comply with E.C. Directive 76/207 (the Equal Treatment Directive). On the position under the S.D.A., see the author's annotations to the Employment Act 1989 (c. 38), ss.1–6, *Current Law Statutes Annotated*, 1989, Vol. 3.

In pursuance of. The meaning of this phrase as it appears in equivalent provisions in the R.R.A., s.41(1)(b), was considered by the House of Lords in *Hampson v. Department of Education and Science* [1990] I.R.L.R. 302. The E.A.T. and a majority of the Court of Appeal (Balcombe L.J. dissenting) had favoured a wide interpretation, covering any act done in the exercise of a power or discretion conferred by an instrument, but the House of Lords overruled the Court of Appeal, and held that the phrase "in pursuance of", while not limited to describing an act which is done "in order" to comply with an enactment, should be interpreted narrowly as authorising only acts done in necessary performance of an express obligation contained in the instrument. Their Lordships considered that a wide interpretation of the statutory language might have undermined the object of the 1976 Act, by conferring virtual immunity on the acts of public authorities acting under statutory powers. As Lord Lowry observed:

"almost every discretionary decision, such as that which is involved in the appointment, promotion and dismissal of individuals in, say, local government, the police, the National Health Service and the public sector of the teaching profession, is taken against a statutory background which imposes a duty on someone." (At p.307).

Condition or requirement imposed by a Minister of the Crown. In any proceedings under s.8 (Employment), or s.25 (Goods, facilities, services and premises), a certificate signed by or on behalf of a Minister of the Crown stating that the conditions or requirements specified in the certificate were imposed by a Minister and were in operation at a specified time is conclusive evidence of the facts stated, and a document purporting to be such a certificate will be deemed to be such unless the contrary is proved (Sched. 3, paras. 4 and 8).

The passing of this Act. The Disability Discrimination Act 1995 received the Royal Assent on November 8, 1995.

Subs. (2)

An act of discrimination done for the purpose of safeguarding national security is lawful. In any proceedings under s.8 (Employment), or s.25 (Goods, facilities, services and premises), a certificate signed by or on behalf of a Minister of the Crown stating that an act was done for the purpose of safeguarding national security is conclusive evidence of that fact, and a document purporting to be such a certificate will be deemed to be such unless the contrary is proved (Sched. 3, paras. 4 and 8).

PART VIII

MISCELLANEOUS

Appointment by Secretary of State of advisers

60.—(1) The Secretary of State may appoint such persons as he thinks fit to advise or assist him in connection with matters relating to the employment of disabled persons and persons who have had a disability.

(2) Persons may be appointed by the Secretary of State to act generally or in relation to a particular area or locality.

(3) The Secretary of State may pay to any person appointed under this section such allowances and compensation for loss of earnings as he considers appropriate.

(4) The approval of the Treasury is required for any payment under this section.

(5) In subsection (1) "employment" includes self-employment.

(6) The Secretary of State may by order—

(a) provide for section 17 of, and Schedule 2 to, the Disabled Persons (Employment) Act 1944 (national advisory council and district advisory committees) to cease to have effect—

    (i) so far as concerns the national advisory council; or

    (ii) so far as concerns district advisory committees; or

(b) repeal that section and Schedule.

(7) At any time before the coming into force of an order under paragraph (b) of subsection (6), section 17 of the Act of 1944 shall have effect as if in subsection (1), after "disabled persons" in each case there were inserted ", and persons who have had a disability," and as if at the end of the section there were added—

"(3) For the purposes of this section—

(a) a person is a disabled person if he is a disabled person for the purposes of the Disability Discrimination Act 1995; and

(b) "disability" has the same meaning as in that Act."

(8) At any time before the coming into force of an order under paragraph (a)(i) or (b) of subsection (6), section 16 of the Chronically Sick and Disabled Persons Act 1970 (which extends the functions of the national advisory council) shall have effect as if after "disabled persons" in each case there were inserted ", and persons who have had a disability," and as if at the end of the section there were added—

"(2) For the purposes of this section—

(a) a person is a disabled person if he is a disabled person for the purposes of the Disability Discrimination Act 1995; and

(b) "disability" has the same meaning as in that Act."

DEFINITIONS
"disability": s.1(1).
"disabled person": s.1(2).
"employment": s.68(1); subs. (5).

GENERAL NOTE
This section empowers the Secretary of State to appoint advisers to advise him on matters concerning the employment and self-employment of disabled persons. It also empowers him to end the current arrangements whereby Ministers are advised and assisted in matters relating to the employment and training of disabled persons by the National Advisory Council on Employment of People with Disabilities (NACEDP), and the 60 district advisory Committees for the Employment of People with Disabilities (CEPDs), established under the Disabled Persons (Employment) Act 1944 (c. 10), s.17 (see the note to s.50). Until such time as those bodies are wound up, subs. (7) and (8) apply the definition of disability contained in s.1 of this Act to s.17 of the 1944 Act and also to s.16 of the Chronically Sick and Disabled Persons Act 1970 (c. 44) (which extended the functions of NACEDP in relation to training).

The power conferred by subs. (1) is designed to give the Secretary of State greater flexibility in the appointment of bodies at national, regional and local level to advise him on employment issues relating to people with disabilities. It gives him the option of retaining the existing advisory arrangements or of bringing them to an end, either in whole or in part, and appointing people to advise him either generally (*i.e.* nationally) or in relation to a particular area or locality (subs. (2)). A further option available to the Secretary of State would of course be to transfer the general advisory function in relation to employment to the National Disability Council, although it is expressly provided in s.50(10) that this may not happen while the NACEDP remains in existence or while there are advisers appointed under subs. (1) to act generally in relation to employment. As to the relationship between NACEDP and the National Disability Council, see the note to s.50.

Subs. (6)
The power is drafted so as to allow NACEDP and the CEDPs to be wound up separately or together. Although both types of body were established under the 1944 Act, they are independent of each other and have different functions: NACEDP advises the Secretary of State on

national employment and training issues relating to people with disabilities, while the CEDPs advise on local employment issues, including matters relating to the registration of disabled persons and the quota scheme under the 1944 Act (see the note to s.61).

Amendment of Disabled Persons (Employment) Act 1944

61.—(1) Section 15 of the Disabled Persons (Employment) Act 1944 (which gives the Secretary of State power to make arrangements for the provision of supported employment) is amended as set out in subsections (2) to (5).

(2) In subsection (1)—

(a) for "persons registered as handicapped by disablement" substitute "disabled persons";

(b) for "their disablement" substitute "their disability"; and

(c) for "are not subject to disablement" substitute "do not have a disability".

(3) In subsection (2), for the words from "any of one or more companies" to "so required and prohibited" substitute "any company, association or body".

(4) After subsection (2) insert—

"(2A) The only kind of company which the Minister himself may form in exercising his powers under this section is a company which is—

(a) required by its constitution to apply its profits, if any, or other income in promoting its objects; and

(b) prohibited by its constitution from paying any dividend to its members."

(5) After subsection (5) insert—

"(5A) For the purposes of this section—

(a) a person is a disabled person if he is a disabled person for the purposes of the Disability Discrimination Act 1995; and

(b) "disability" has the same meaning as in that Act."

(6) The provisions of section 16 (preference to be given under section 15 of that Act to ex-service men and women) shall become subsection (1) of that section and at the end insert—

"and whose disability is due to that service.

(2) For the purposes of subsection (1) of this section, a disabled person's disability shall be treated as due to service of a particular kind only in such circumstances as may be prescribed."

(7) The following provisions of the Act of 1944 shall cease to have effect—

(a) section 1 (definition of "disabled person");

(b) sections 6 to 8 (the register of disabled persons);

(c) sections 9 to 11 (obligations on employers with substantial staffs to employ a quota of registered persons);

(d) section 12 (the designated employment scheme for persons registered as handicapped by disablement);

(e) section 13 (interpretation of provisions repealed by this Act);

(f) section 14 (records to be kept by employers);

(g) section 19 (proceedings in relation to offences); and

(h) section 21 (application as respects place of employment, and nationality).

(8) Any provision of subordinate legislation in which "disabled person" is defined by reference to the Act of 1944 shall be construed as if that expression had the same meaning as in this Act.

(9) Subsection (8) does not prevent the further amendment of any such provision by subordinate legislation.

DEFINITIONS

"disability": s.1(1); subs. (5).

"disabled person": s.1(2); subss. (5) and (8).

"employment": s.68(1).

GENERAL NOTE

This section repeals much of the Disabled Persons (Employment) Act 1944, including the provisions relating to the register of disabled persons, the quota system which obliges employers of a certain size to employ a quota of disabled persons, the designated employment scheme whereby certain types of employment are reserved for disabled employees, and the keeping of records by employers. It also amends a number of the remaining provisions of the 1944 Act; in particular, it extends the powers of the Secretary of State under s.15 of the 1944 Act to make arrangements for the provision of supported employment, by allowing the funding of places in dividend-distributing bodies.

Subss. (1)–(5)

The supported employment programme was set up under s.15 of the 1944 Act to provide employment opportunities for severely disabled people who would otherwise be unlikely to obtain employment. The current criteria for entry to the programme are that severely disabled people should be capable of productivity within the range of 30 per cent to 80 per cent of a non-disabled worker. Around 21,800 severely disabled people are currently in supported employment, at an annual cost of about £153 million. The programme takes a variety of forms, including supported factories such as *Remploy Ltd*, which currently employs over 9,000 people, some 4,600 people in sheltered workshops run by local authorities and voluntary organisations, and over 8,000 people on the supported placement scheme, whereby local authorities and voluntary organisations help to arrange the placement of severely disabled employees in open employment (Minister of State, *Hansard*, H.L., Vol. 565, col. 708). Until now, the 1944 Act has prevented funding for supported employment from being provided to profit-distributing organisations. This is now to change, as subs. (2) allows the Secretary of State to fund supported employment in such bodies. Concern has been expressed that this development represents further evidence of creeping commercialisation in the provision of supported employment, and it has been claimed that the dividend-distributing providers may be reluctant to recruit the most severely disabled (and therefore least productive) employees because of the greater pressure on them to act like commercial enterprises (Lord Gladwin of Clee, *ibid*. col. 700). The Government has reaffirmed its commitment to the supported employment programme, and has undertaken to consult with relevant organisations before exercising the power conferred by this section (Minister of State, *ibid*. col. 708).

Restriction of publicity: industrial tribunals

62.—(1) This section applies to proceedings on a complaint under section 8 in which evidence of a personal nature is likely to be heard by the industrial tribunal hearing the complaint.

(2) The power of the Secretary of State to make regulations with respect to the procedure of industrial tribunals includes power to make provision in relation to proceedings to which this section applies for—

(a) enabling an industrial tribunal, on the application of the complainant or of its own motion, to make a restricted reporting order having effect (if not revoked earlier) until the promulgation of the tribunal's decision; and

(b) where a restricted reporting order is made in relation to a complaint which is being dealt with by the tribunal together with any other proceedings, enabling the tribunal to direct that the order is to apply also in relation to those other proceedings or such part of them as the tribunal may direct.

(3) If any identifying matter is published or included in a relevant programme in contravention of a restricted reporting order—

(a) in the case of publication in a newspaper or periodical, any proprietor, any editor and any publisher of the newspaper or periodical,

(b) in the case of publication in any other form, the person publishing the matter, and

(c) in the case of matter included in a relevant programme—

(i) any body corporate engaged in providing the service in which the programme is included, and

(ii) any person having functions in relation to the programme corresponding to those of an editor of a newspaper,
shall be guilty of an offence and liable on summary conviction to a fine not exceeding level 5 on the standard scale.

(4) Where a person is charged with an offence under subsection (3), it is a defence to prove that at the time of the alleged offence—

(a) he was not aware, and

(b) he neither suspected nor had reason to suspect,
that the publication or programme in question was of, or included, the matter in question.

(5) Where an offence under subsection (3) committed by a body corporate is proved to have been committed with the consent or connivance of, or to be attributable to any neglect on the part of—

(a) a director, manager, secretary or other similar officer of the body corporate, or

(b) a person purporting to act in any such capacity,
he as well as the body corporate is guilty of the offence and liable to be proceeded against and punished accordingly.

(6) In relation to a body corporate whose affairs are managed by its members "director", in subsection (5), means a member of the body corporate.

(7) In this section—

"evidence of a personal nature" means any evidence of a medical, or other intimate, nature which might reasonably be assumed to be likely to cause significant embarrassment to the complainant if reported;

"identifying matter" means any matter likely to lead members of the public to identify the complainant or such other persons (if any) as may be named in the order;

"promulgation" has such meaning as may be prescribed by the regulations;

"relevant programme" means a programme included in a programme service, within the meaning of the Broadcasting Act 1990;

"restricted reporting order" means an order—

(a) made in exercise of the power conferred by regulations made by virtue of this section; and

(b) prohibiting the publication in Great Britain of identifying matter in a written publication available to the public or its inclusion in a relevant programme for reception in Great Britain; and

"written publication" includes a film, a soundtrack and any other record in permanent form but does not include an indictment or other document prepared for use in particular legal proceedings.

DEFINITIONS

"director": subs. (6).

"evidence of a personal nature": subs. (7).

"identifying matter": subs. (7).

"promulgation": subs. (7).

"relevant programme": subs. (7).

"restricted reporting order": subs. (7).

"standard scale": Criminal Justice Act 1982, s.37(2).

"written publication": subs. (7).

GENERAL NOTE

This section gives the Secretary of State power to make regulations enabling an industrial tribunal to make a restricted reporting order in proceedings under s.8 of this Act where "evidence of a personal nature" is likely to be heard by the tribunal hearing the complaint. "Evidence of a personal nature" is defined in subs. (7) as evidence of a medical or other intimate nature which might reasonably be assumed to be likely to cause significant embarrassment to the complainant if reported. The effect of a restricted reporting order is to prohibit the publication in a "written publication" or a "relevant programme" (see below) of anything which would be likely to identify the complainant or any other person named in the order. In all other respects, the freedom of the media to report on the proceedings is unaffected; indeed, the media are free to report the complainant's identity once the tribunal has issued its decision, as the order only remains in force (unless revoked earlier) until the promulgation of the tribunal's decision (subs. (2)(a)). A restricted reporting order may be made on the application of the complainant or by the tribunal of its own motion; where the complaint is being dealt with by the tribunal together with other proceedings, the regulations may permit the tribunal to extend the restricted reporting order to those other proceedings (subs. (2)(b)). There are parallel provisions in s.63 with respect to the E.A.T., but the powers of the E.A.T. to make a restricted reporting order are more limited.

Contravention of a restricted reporting order is an offence punishable on summary conviction by a fine not exceeding level 5 on the standard scale. The offence may be committed, in the case of publication in a newspaper or periodical, by the proprietor, editor and publisher of that newspaper or periodical; in the case of publication in any other form, by the person publishing the material; and in the case of material broadcast in a relevant programme, by the broadcasting company and the editor of the programme (subs. 3). Where an offence by the broadcasting company is committed with the consent or connivance of or through the neglect of a director, manager, secretary or other similar officer of that company, the offence is also committed by that person (subs. (5)). It is a defence for a person charged with an offence under these provisions to show that he was not aware, and neither suspected nor had reason to suspect, that the publication or programme in question included the restricted material (subs. (4)), but it seems that ignorance of the restricted reporting order will not be a defence.

The power to make a restricted reporting order was first introduced for cases involving sexual misconduct by the Trade Union Reform and Employment Rights Act 1993, s.40, following fears that potential complainants might be deterred by the prospect of being subjected to high-profile, intrusive media coverage. Those provisions may be found in the Industrial Tribunals Rules of Procedure 1993, S.I. 1993 No. 2687, r.14, made pursuant to the E.P.(C.)A. 1978, Sched. 9, para. 1(5A). The extension of the power to make a restricted reporting order to cases involving disability discrimination is designed to cover employees with, for example, HIV or AIDS, or a history of mental illness, who might be reluctant to pursue a claim because of fears of publicity. The power to make such an order only applies to proceedings on a complaint under s.8 (*i.e.* in relation to employment); complaints under Pt. III (access to goods, facilities and services) may be dealt with under the small claims arbitration procedure, where hearings are held in private.

Restricted reporting order. This is defined in subs. (7) as an order prohibiting the publication in Great Britain, in a written publication available to the public, or a relevant programme for reception in Great Britain, of any "identifying matter", *i.e.* anything likely to lead the public to identify the complainant or any other person named in the order. It should be noted that such an order does not prohibit all reporting of the case—merely the publication in the media of anything which might identify the complainant or anyone else covered by the order.

Written publication; relevant programme. The definitions of these terms in subs. (7) are also used for the purposes of the Sexual Offences (Amendment) Act 1992 (c. 34), s.6.

Promulgation. The existing rules concerning restricted reporting orders in cases involving sexual misconduct state that "promulgation occurs on the date recorded as being the date on which the document recording the determination of the originating application was sent to the parties" (see the Industrial Tribunals Rules of Procedure 1993, r.14(5)).

Restriction of publicity: Employment Appeal Tribunal

63.—(1) This section applies to proceedings—
   (a) on an appeal against a decision of an industrial tribunal to make, or not to make, a restricted reporting order, or
   (b) on an appeal against any interlocutory decision of an industrial tribunal in proceedings in which the industrial tribunal has made a restricted reporting order which it has not revoked.

(2) The power of the Lord Chancellor to make rules with respect to the procedure of the Employment Appeal Tribunal includes power to make provision in relation to proceedings to which this section applies for—
   (a) enabling the Tribunal, on the application of the complainant or of its own motion, to make a restricted reporting order having effect (if not revoked earlier) until the promulgation of the Tribunal's decision; and

(b) where a restricted reporting order is made in relation to an appeal which is being dealt with by the Tribunal together with any other proceedings, enabling the Tribunal to direct that the order is to apply also in relation to those other proceedings or such part of them as the Tribunal may direct.

(3) Subsections (3) to (6) of section 62 apply in relation to a restricted reporting order made by the Tribunal as they apply in relation to one made by an industrial tribunal.

(4) In subsection (1), "restricted reporting order" means an order which is a restricted reporting order for the purposes of section 62.

(5) In subsection (2), "restricted reporting order" means an order—

(a) made in exercise of the power conferred by rules made by virtue of this section; and

(b) prohibiting the publication in Great Britain of identifying matter in a written publication available to the public or its inclusion in a relevant programme for reception in Great Britain.

(6) In this section—

"complainant" means the person who made the complaint to which the proceedings before the Tribunal relate;

"identifying matter", "written publication" and "relevant programme" have the same meaning as in section 62; and

"promulgation" has such meaning as may be prescribed by the rules.

DEFINITIONS

"complainant": subs. (6).
"identifying matter": s.62(7); subs. (6).
"promulgation": subs. (6).
"relevant programme": s.62(7); subs. (6).
"restricted reporting order": s.62(7); subss. (4) and (5).
"written publication": s.62(7); subs. (6).

GENERAL NOTE

This section allows the Lord Chancellor to amend the Employment Appeal Tribunal Rules to enable the E.A.T. to make a restricted reporting order in the same way and to the same effect as an industrial tribunal (see the note to s.62), but in more limited circumstances. A restricted reporting order may only be made by the E.A.T. under this section in proceedings on an appeal against a decision of an industrial tribunal to make or not to make a restricted reporting order, or on an appeal against an interlocutory decision of an industrial tribunal in a case in which the tribunal made a restricted reporting order which has not been revoked (subs. (1)). The E.A.T. will not be able to make a restricted reporting order on an ordinary appeal from an industrial tribunal, even where the tribunal proceedings were subject to such an order. The thinking behind this is presumably that since the order made by the industrial tribunal would have lapsed once the tribunal issued its decision, the imposition of a further order on appeal would serve no purpose, as the identities of those involved might already have been disclosed.

In other respects, the provisions on restricted reporting orders in relation to the E.A.T. are similar to those which apply to industrial tribunals: an order may be made on the application of the complainant, or by the tribunal of its own motion, and will remain in force until the tribunal's decision is issued, unless revoked earlier (subs. (2)(a)); and where the appeal is being dealt with by the tribunal along with other proceedings, the regulations may permit the tribunal to extend the restricted reporting order to those other proceedings (subs. (2)(b)). Penalties for non-compliance are as in s.62 (see the note to that section).

The E.A.T. already has the power to make a restricted reporting order in cases involving sexual misconduct: see the Employment Appeal Tribunal Rules 1993, S.I. 1993 No. 2854, r.23, made pursuant to the E.P.(C.)A. 1978, Sched. 11, para. 18A. The power to make these rules was introduced by the Trade Union Reform and Employment Rights Act 1993, s.41.

Identifying matter; written publication; relevant programme. See the notes to s.62.

Promulgation. The existing rules concerning restricted reporting orders in cases involving sexual misconduct state that promulgation of the Tribunal's decision "means the date recorded as being the date on which the Appeal Tribunal's order finally disposing of the appeal is sent to the parties" (see the Employment Appeal Tribunal Rules 1993, r.23(9)).

Application to Crown etc.

64.—(1) This Act applies—
(a) to an act done by or for purposes of a Minister of the Crown or government department, or
(b) to an act done on behalf of the Crown by a statutory body, or a person
holding a statutory office,
as it applies to an act done by a private person.
(2) Subject to subsection (5), Part II applies to service—
(a) for purposes of a Minister of the Crown or government department,
other than service of a person holding a statutory office, or
(b) on behalf of the Crown for purposes of a person holding a statutory
office or purposes of a statutory body,
as it applies to employment by a private person.
(3) The provisions of Parts II to IV of the 1947 Act apply to proceedings
against the Crown under this Act as they apply to Crown proceedings in
England and Wales; but section 20 of that Act (removal of proceedings from
county court to High Court) does not apply.
(4) The provisions of Part V of the 1947 Act apply to proceedings against
the Crown under this Act as they apply to proceedings in Scotland which by
virtue of that Part are treated as civil proceedings by or against the Crown;
but the proviso to section 44 of that Act (removal of proceedings from the
sheriff court to the Court of Session) does not apply.
(5) Part II does not apply to service—
(a) as a member of the Ministry of Defence Police, the British Transport
Police, the Royal Parks Constabulary or the United Kingdom Atomic
Energy Authority Constabulary;
(b) as a prison officer; or
(c) for purposes of a Minister of the Crown or government department
having functions with respect to defence as a person who is or may be
required by his terms of service to engage in fire fighting.
(6) Part II does not apply to service as a member of a fire brigade who is or
may be required by his terms of service to engage in fire fighting.
(7) It is hereby declared (for the avoidance of doubt) that Part II does not
apply to service in any of the naval, military or air forces of the Crown.
(8) In this section—
"the 1947 Act" means the Crown Proceedings Act 1947;
"British Transport Police" means the constables appointed, or deemed
to have been appointed, under section 53 of the British Transport
Commission Act 1949;
"Crown proceedings" means proceedings which, by virtue of section 23
of the 1947 Act, are treated for the purposes of Part II of that Act as
civil proceedings by or against the Crown;
"fire brigade" means a fire brigade maintained in pursuance of the Fire
Services Act 1947;
"Ministry of Defence Police" means the force established under section
1 of the Ministry of Defence Police Act 1987;
"prison officer" means a person who is a prison officer within the meaning of section 127 of the Criminal Justice and Public Order Act
1994, apart from those who are custody officers within the meaning
of Part I of that Act;
"Royal Parks Constabulary" means the park constables appointed
under the Parks Regulation Act 1872;
"service for purposes of a Minister of the Crown or government department" does not include service in any office for the time being mentioned in Schedule 2 (Ministerial offices) to the House of Commons
Disqualification Act 1975;

"statutory body" means a body set up by or under an enactment;
"statutory office" means an office so set up; and
"United Kingdom Atomic Energy Authority Constabulary" means the
    special constables appointed under section 3 of the Special Con-
    stables Act 1923 on the nomination of the United Kingdom Atomic
    Energy Authority.

Application to Parliament

65.—(1) This Act applies to an act done by or for purposes of the House of
Lords or the House of Commons as it applies to an act done by a private
person.

(2) For the purposes of the application of Part II in relation to the House of
Commons, the Corporate Officer of that House shall be treated as the
employer of a person who is (or would be) a relevant member of the House of
Commons staff for the purposes of section 139 of the Employment Protection (Consolidation) Act 1978.

(3) Except as provided in subsection (4), for the purposes of the application of sections 19 to 21, the provider of services is—

(a) as respects the House of Lords, the Corporate Officer of that House;
    and

(b) as respects the House of Commons, the Corporate Officer of that
    House.

(4) Where the service in question is access to and use of any place in the
Palace of Westminster which members of the public are permitted to enter,
the Corporate Officers of both Houses jointly are the provider of that service.

(5) Nothing in any rule of law or the law or practice of Parliament prevents
proceedings being instituted before an industrial tribunal under Part II or
before any court under Part III.

Government appointments outside Part II

66.—(1) Subject to regulations under subsection (3), this section applies to
any appointment made by a Minister of the Crown or government department to an office or post where Part II does not apply in relation to the
appointment.

(2) In making the appointment, and in making arrangements for determining to whom the office or post should be offered, the Minister of the Crown or
government department shall not act in a way which would contravene Part
II if he or the department were the employer for the purposes of this Act.

(3) Regulations may provide for this section not to apply to such appoint-
ments as may be prescribed.

Regulations and orders

67.—(1) Any power under this Act to make regulations or orders shall be
exercisable by statutory instrument.

(2) Any such power may be exercised to make different provision for different cases, including different provision for different areas or localities.

(3) Any such power includes power—

(a) to make such incidental, supplemental, consequential or transitional
    provision as appears to the Secretary of State to be expedient; and

(b) to provide for a person to exercise a discretion in dealing with any
    matter.

(4) No order shall be made under section 50(3) unless a draft of the statutory instrument containing the order has been laid before Parliament and
approved by a resolution of each House.

(5) Any other statutory instrument made under this Act, other than one
made under section 3(9), 52(8), 54(6) or 70(3), shall be subject to annulment
in pursuance of a resolution of either House of Parliament.

(6) Subsection (1) does not require an order under section 43 which applies only to a specified vehicle, or to vehicles of a specified person, to be made by statutory instrument but such an order shall be as capable of being amended or revoked as an order which is made by statutory instrument.

(7) Nothing in section 34(4), 40(6) or 46(5) affects the powers conferred by subsections (2) and (3).

Interpretation

68.—(1) In this Act—

"accessibility certificate" means a certificate issued under section 41(1)(a);

"act" includes a deliberate omission;

"approval certificate" means a certificate issued under section 42(4);

"benefits", in Part II, has the meaning given in section 4(4);

"conciliation officer" means a person designated under section 211 of the Trade Union and Labour Relations (Consolidation) Act 1992;

"employment" means, subject to any prescribed provision, employment under a contract of service or of apprenticeship or a contract personally to do any work, and related expressions are to be construed accordingly;

"employment at an establishment in Great Britain" is to be construed in accordance with subsections (2) to (5);

"enactment" includes subordinate legislation and any Order in Council;

"licensing authority" means—

(a) in relation to the area to which the Metropolitan Public Carriage Act 1869 applies, the Secretary of State or the holder of any office for the time being designated by the Secretary of State; or

(b) in relation to any other area in England and Wales, the authority responsible for licensing taxis in that area;

"mental impairment" does not have the same meaning as in the Mental Health Act 1983 or the Mental Health (Scotland) Act 1984 but the fact that an impairment would be a mental impairment for the purposes of either of those Acts does not prevent it from being a mental impairment for the purposes of this Act;

"Minister of the Crown" includes the Treasury;

"occupational pension scheme" has the same meaning as in the Pension Schemes Act 1993;

"premises" includes land of any description;

"prescribed" means prescribed by regulations;

"profession" includes any vocation or occupation;

"provider of services" has the meaning given in section 19(2)(b);

"public service vehicle" and "regulated public service vehicle" have the meaning given in section 40;

"PSV accessibility regulations" means regulations made under section 40(1);

"rail vehicle" and "regulated rail vehicle" have the meaning given in section 46;

"rail vehicle accessibility regulations" means regulations made under section 46(1);

"regulations" means regulations made by the Secretary of State;

"section 6 duty" means any duty imposed by or under section 6;

"section 15 duty" means any duty imposed by or under section 15;

"section 21 duty" means any duty imposed by or under section 21;

"subordinate legislation" has the same meaning as in section 21 of the Interpretation Act 1978;

"taxi" and "regulated taxi" have the meaning given in section 32;

"taxi accessibility regulations" means regulations made under section 32(1);

"trade" includes any business;

"trade organisation" has the meaning given in section 13;

"vehicle examiner" means an examiner appointed under section 66A of the Road Traffic Act 1988.

(2) Where an employee does his work wholly or mainly outside Great Britain, his employment is not to be treated as being work at an establishment in Great Britain even if he does some of his work at such an establishment.

(3) Except in prescribed cases, employment on board a ship, aircraft or hovercraft is to be regarded as not being employment at an establishment in Great Britain.

(4) Employment of a prescribed kind, or in prescribed circumstances, is to be regarded as not being employment at an establishment in Great Britain.

(5) Where work is not done at an establishment it shall be treated as done—

(a) at the establishment from which it is done; or

(b) where it is not done from any establishment, at the establishment with which it has the closest connection.

Financial provisions

69. There shall be paid out of money provided by Parliament—

(a) any expenditure incurred by a Minister of the Crown under this Act;

(b) any increase attributable to this Act in the sums payable out of money so provided under or by virtue of any other enactment.

Short title, commencement, extent etc.

70.—(1) This Act may be cited as the Disability Discrimination Act 1995.

(2) This section (apart from subsections (4), (5) and (7)) comes into force on the passing of this Act.

(3) The other provisions of this Act come into force on such day as the Secretary of State may by order appoint and different days may be appointed for different purposes.

(4) Schedule 6 makes consequential amendments.

(5) The repeals set out in Schedule 7 shall have effect.

(6) This Act extends to Northern Ireland, but in their application to Northern Ireland the provisions of this Act mentioned in Schedule 8 shall have effect subject to the modifications set out in that Schedule.

(7) In Part II of Schedule 1 to the House of Commons Disqualification Act 1975 and in Part II of Schedule 1 to the Northern Ireland Assembly Disqualification Act 1975 (bodies whose members are disqualified) in each case insert at the appropriate places—

"The National Disability Council."

"The Northern Ireland Disability Council."

(8) Consultations which are required by any provision of this Act to be held by the Secretary of State may be held by him before the coming into force of that provision.

SCHEDULES

SCHEDULE 1

PROVISIONS SUPPLEMENTING SECTION 1

Impairment

1.—(1) "Mental impairment" includes an impairment resulting from or consisting of a mental illness only if the illness is a clinically well-recognised illness.

(2) Regulations may make provision, for the purposes of this Act—

(a) for conditions of a prescribed description to be treated as amounting to impairments;

(b) for conditions of a prescribed description to be treated as not amounting to impairments.

(3) Regulations made under sub-paragraph (2) may make provision as to the meaning of "condition" for the purposes of those regulations.

Long-term effects

2.—(1) The effect of an impairment is a long-term effect if—

(a) it has lasted at least 12 months;

(b) the period for which it lasts is likely to be at least 12 months; or

(c) it is likely to last for the rest of the life of the person affected.

(2) Where an impairment ceases to have a substantial adverse effect on a person's ability to carry out normal day-to-day activities, it is to be treated as continuing to have that effect if that effect is likely to recur.

(3) For the purposes of sub-paragraph (2), the likelihood of an effect recurring shall be disregarded in prescribed circumstances.

(4) Regulations may prescribe circumstances in which, for the purposes of this Act—

(a) an effect which would not otherwise be a long-term effect is to be treated as such an effect; or

(b) an effect which would otherwise be a long-term effect is to be treated as not being such an effect.

Severe disfigurement

3.—(1) An impairment which consists of a severe disfigurement is to be treated as having a substantial adverse effect on the ability of the person concerned to carry out normal day-to-day activities.

(2) Regulations may provide that in prescribed circumstances a severe disfigurement is not to be treated as having that effect.

(3) Regulations under sub-paragraph (2) may, in particular, make provision with respect to deliberately acquired disfigurements.

Normal day-to-day activities

4.—(1) An impairment is to be taken to affect the ability of the person concerned to carry out normal day-to-day activities only if it affects one of the following—

(a) mobility;

(b) manual dexterity;

(c) physical co-ordination;

(d) continence;

(e) ability to lift, carry or otherwise move everyday objects;

(f) speech, hearing or eyesight;

(g) memory or ability to concentrate, learn or understand; or

(h) perception of the risk of physical danger.

(2) Regulations may prescribe—

(a) circumstances in which an impairment which does not have an effect falling within sub-paragraph (1) is to be taken to affect the ability of the person concerned to carry out normal day-to-day activities;

(b) circumstances in which an impairment which has an effect falling within sub-paragraph (1) is to be taken not to affect the ability of the person concerned to carry out normal day-to-day activities.

Substantial adverse effects

5. Regulations may make provision for the purposes of this Act—

(a) for an effect of a prescribed kind on the ability of a person to carry out normal day-to-day activities to be treated as a substantial adverse effect;

(b) for an effect of a prescribed kind on the ability of a person to carry out normal day-to-day activities to be treated as not being a substantial adverse effect.

Effect of medical treatment

6.—(1) An impairment which would be likely to have a substantial adverse effect on the ability of the person concerned to carry out normal day-to-day activities, but for the fact that measures are being taken to treat or correct it, is to be treated as having that effect.

(2) In sub-paragraph (1) "measures" includes, in particular, medical treatment and the use of a prosthesis or other aid.

(3) Sub-paragraph (1) does not apply—

(a) in relation to the impairment of a person's sight, to the extent that the impairment is, in his case, correctable by spectacles or contact lenses or in such other ways as may be prescribed; or

(b) in relation to such other impairments as may be prescribed, in such circumstances as may be prescribed.

Persons deemed to be disabled

7.—(1) Sub-paragraph (2) applies to any person whose name is, both on 12th January 1995 and on the date when this paragraph comes into force, in the register of disabled persons maintained under section 6 of the Disabled Persons (Employment) Act 1944.

(2) That person is to be deemed—

(a) during the initial period, to have a disability, and hence to be a disabled person; and

(b) afterwards, to have had a disability and hence to have been a disabled person during that period.

(3) A certificate of registration shall be conclusive evidence, in relation to the person with respect to whom it was issued, of the matters certified.

(4) Unless the contrary is shown, any document purporting to be a certificate of registration shall be taken to be such a certificate and to have been validly issued.

(5) Regulations may provide for prescribed descriptions of person to be deemed to have disabilities, and hence to be disabled persons, for the purposes of this Act.

(6) Regulations may prescribe circumstances in which a person who has been deemed to be a disabled person by the provisions of sub-paragraph (1) or regulations made under sub-paragraph (5) is to be treated as no longer being deemed to be such a person.

(7) In this paragraph—

"certificate of registration" means a certificate issued under regulations made under section 6 of the Act of 1944; and

"initial period" means the period of three years beginning with the date on which this paragraph comes into force.

Progressive conditions

8.—(1) Where—

(a) a person has a progressive condition (such as cancer, multiple sclerosis or muscular dystrophy or infection by the human immunodeficiency virus),

(b) as a result of that condition, he has an impairment which has (or had) an effect on his ability to carry out normal day-to-day activities, but

(c) that effect is not (or was not) a substantial adverse effect,

he shall be taken to have an impairment which has such a substantial adverse effect if the condition is likely to result in his having such an impairment.

(2) Regulations may make provision, for the purposes of this paragraph—

(a) for conditions of a prescribed description to be treated as being progressive;

(b) for conditions of a prescribed description to be treated as not being progressive.

Section 2(2)   SCHEDULE 2

Past Disabilities

1. The modifications referred to in section 2 are as follows.

2. References in Parts II and III to a disabled person are to be read as references to a person who has had a disability.

3. In section 6(1), after "not disabled" insert "and who have not had a disability".

4. In section 6(6), for "has" substitute "has had".

5. For paragraph 2(1) to (3) of Schedule 1, substitute—

"(1) The effect of an impairment is a long-term effect if it has lasted for at least 12 months.

(2) Where an impairment ceases to have a substantial adverse effect on a person's ability to carry out normal day-to-day activities, it is to be treated as continuing to have that effect if that effect recurs.

(3) For the purposes of sub-paragraph (2), the recurrence of an effect shall be disregarded in prescribed circumstances."

SCHEDULE 3

ENFORCEMENT AND PROCEDURE

PART I

EMPLOYMENT

Conciliation

1.—(1) Where a complaint is presented to an industrial tribunal under section 8 and a copy of it is sent to a conciliation officer, he shall—
(a) if requested to do so by the complainant and respondent, or
(b) if he considers that he has a reasonable prospect of success,
try to promote a settlement of the complaint without its being determined by an industrial tribunal.

(2) Where a person is contemplating presenting such a complaint, a conciliation officer shall, if asked to do so by the potential complainant or potential respondent, try to promote a settlement.

(3) The conciliation officer shall, where appropriate, have regard to the desirability of encouraging the use of other procedures available for the settlement of grievances.

(4) Anything communicated to a conciliation officer in a case in which he is acting under this paragraph shall not be admissible in evidence in any proceedings before an industrial tribunal except with the consent of the person who communicated it.

Restriction on proceedings for breach of Part II

2.—(1) Except as provided by section 8, no civil or criminal proceedings may be brought against any person in respect of an act merely because the act is unlawful under Part II.

(2) Sub-paragraph (1) does not prevent the making of an application for judicial review.

Period within which proceedings must be brought

3.—(1) An industrial tribunal shall not consider a complaint under section 8 unless it is presented before the end of the period of three months beginning when the act complained of was done.

(2) A tribunal may consider any such complaint which is out of time if, in all the circumstances of the case, it considers that it is just and equitable to do so.

(3) For the purposes of sub-paragraph (1)—
(a) where an unlawful act of discrimination is attributable to a term in a contract, that act is to be treated as extending throughout the duration of the contract;
(b) any act extending over a period shall be treated as done at the end of that period; and
(c) a deliberate omission shall be treated as done when the person in question decided upon it.

(4) In the absence of evidence establishing the contrary, a person shall be taken for the purposes of this paragraph to decide upon an omission—
(a) when he does an act inconsistent with doing the omitted act; or
(b) if he has done no such inconsistent act, when the period expires within which he might reasonably have been expected to do the omitted act if it was to be done.

Evidence

4.—(1) In any proceedings under section 8, a certificate signed by or on behalf of a Minister of the Crown and certifying—
(a) that any conditions or requirements specified in the certificate were imposed by a Minister of the Crown and were in operation at a time or throughout a time so specified, or
(b) that an act specified in the certificate was done for the purpose of safeguarding national security,
shall be conclusive evidence of the matters certified.

(2) A document purporting to be such a certificate shall be received in evidence and, unless the contrary is proved, be deemed to be such a certificate.

Part II

Discrimination in Other Areas

Restriction on proceedings for breach of Part III

5.—(1) Except as provided by section 25 no civil or criminal proceedings may be brought against any person in respect of an act merely because the act is unlawful under Part III.

(2) Sub-paragraph (1) does not prevent the making of an application for judicial review.

Period within which proceedings must be brought

6.—(1) A county court or a sheriff court shall not consider a claim under section 25 unless proceedings in respect of the claim are instituted before the end of the period of six months beginning when the act complained of was done.

(2) Where, in relation to proceedings or prospective proceedings under section 25, a person appointed in connection with arrangements under section 28 is approached before the end of the period of six months mentioned in sub-paragraph (1), the period allowed by that sub-paragraph shall be extended by two months.

(3) A court may consider any claim under section 25 which is out of time if, in all the circumstances of the case, it considers that it is just and equitable to do so.

(4) For the purposes of sub-paragraph (1)—

(a) where an unlawful act of discrimination is attributable to a term in a contract, that act is to be treated as extending throughout the duration of the contract;

(b) any act extending over a period shall be treated as done at the end of that period; and

(c) a deliberate omission shall be treated as done when the person in question decided upon it.

(5) In the absence of evidence establishing the contrary, a person shall be taken for the purposes of this paragraph to decide upon an omission—

(a) when he does an act inconsistent with doing the omitted act; or

(b) if he has done no such inconsistent act, when the period expires within which he might reasonably have been expected to do the omitted act if it was to be done.

Compensation for injury to feelings

7. In any proceedings under section 25, the amount of any damages awarded as compensation for injury to feelings shall not exceed the prescribed amount.

Evidence

8.—(1) In any proceedings under section 25, a certificate signed by or on behalf of a Minister of the Crown and certifying—

(a) that any conditions or requirements specified in the certificate were imposed by a Minister of the Crown and were in operation at a time or throughout a time so specified, or

(b) that an act specified in the certificate was done for the purpose of safeguarding national security,

shall be conclusive evidence of the matters certified.

(2) A document purporting to be such a certificate shall be received in evidence and, unless the contrary is proved, be deemed to be such a certificate.

Sections 16(5) and 27(5)   SCHEDULE 4

Premises Occupied Under Leases

Part I

Occupation by Employer or Trade Organisation

Failure to obtain consent to alteration

1. If any question arises as to whether the occupier has failed to comply with the section 6 or section 15 duty, by failing to make a particular alteration to the premises, any constraint attribu-

table to the fact that he occupies the premises under a lease is to be ignored unless he has applied to the lessor in writing for consent to the making of the alteration.

Joining lessors in proceedings under section 8

2.—(1) In any proceedings under section 8, in a case to which section 16 applies, the complainant or the occupier may ask the tribunal hearing the complaint to direct that the lessor be joined or sisted as a party to the proceedings.

(2) The request shall be granted if it is made before the hearing of the complaint begins.

(3) The tribunal may refuse the request if it is made after the hearing of the complaint begins.

(4) The request may not be granted if it is made after the tribunal has determined the complaint.

(5) Where a lessor has been so joined or sisted as a party to the proceedings, the tribunal may determine—

(a) whether the lessor has—
  (i) refused consent to the alteration, or
  (ii) consented subject to one or more conditions, and
(b) if so, whether the refusal or any of the conditions was unreasonable,

(6) If, under sub-paragraph (5), the tribunal determines that the refusal or any of the conditions was unreasonable it may take one or more of the following steps—

(a) make such declaration as it considers appropriate;
(b) make an order authorising the occupier to make the alteration specified in the order;
(c) order the lessor to pay compensation to the complainant.

(7) An order under sub-paragraph (6)(b) may require the occupier to comply with conditions specified in the order.

(8) Any step taken by the tribunal under sub-paragraph (6) may be in substitution for, or in addition to, any step taken by the tribunal under section 8(2).

(9) If the tribunal orders the lessor to pay compensation it may not make an order under section 8(2) ordering the occupier to do so.

Regulations

3. Regulations may make provision as to circumstances in which—

(a) a lessor is to be taken, for the purposes of section 16 and this Part of this Schedule to have—
  (i) withheld his consent;
  (ii) withheld his consent unreasonably;
  (iii) acted reasonably in withholding his consent;
(b) a condition subject to which a lessor has given his consent is to be taken to be reasonable;
(c) a condition subject to which a lessor has given his consent is to be taken to be unreasonable.

Sub-leases etc.

4. The Secretary of State may by regulations make provision supplementing, or modifying, the provision made by section 16 or any provision made by or under this Part of this Schedule in relation to cases where the occupier occupies premises under a sub-lease or sub-tenancy.

PART II

OCCUPATION BY PROVIDER OF SERVICES

Failure to obtain consent to alteration

5. If any question arises as to whether the occupier has failed to comply with the section 21 duty, by failing to make a particular alteration to premises, any constraint attributable to the fact that he occupies the premises under a lease is to be ignored unless he has applied to the lessor in writing for consent to the making of the alteration.

Reference to court

6.—(1) If the occupier has applied in writing to the lessor for consent to the alteration and—

(a) that consent has been refused, or
(b) the lessor has made his consent subject to one or more conditions,

the occupier or a disabled person who has an interest in the proposed alteration to the premises being made, may refer the matter to a county court or, in Scotland, to the sheriff.

(2) In the following provisions of this Schedule "court" includes "sheriff".

(3) On such a reference the court shall determine whether the lessor's refusal was unreasonable or (as the case may be) whether the condition is, or any of the conditions are, unreasonable.

(4) If the court determines—

(a) that the lessor's refusal was unreasonable, or

(b) that the condition is, or any of the conditions are, unreasonable,

it may make such declaration as it considers appropriate or an order authorising the occupier to make the alteration specified in the order.

(5) An order under sub-paragraph (4) may require the occupier to comply with conditions specified in the order.

Joining lessors in proceedings under section 25

7.—(1) In any proceedings on a claim under section 25, in a case to which this Part of this Schedule applies, the plaintiff, the pursuer or the occupier concerned may ask the court to direct that the lessor be joined or sisted as a party to the proceedings.

(2) The request shall be granted if it is made before the hearing of the claim begins.

(3) The court may refuse the request if it is made after the hearing of the claim begins.

(4) The request may not be granted if it is made after the court has determined the claim.

(5) Where a lessor has been so joined or sisted as a party to the proceedings, the court may determine—

(a) whether the lessor has—

(i) refused consent to the alteration, or

(ii) consented subject to one or more conditions, and

(b) if so, whether the refusal or any of the conditions was unreasonable.

(6) If, under sub-paragraph (5), the court determines that the refusal or any of the conditions was unreasonable it may take one or more of the following steps—

(a) make such declaration as it considers appropriate;

(b) make an order authorising the occupier to make the alteration specified in the order;

(c) order the lessor to pay compensation to the complainant.

(7) An order under sub-paragraph (6)(b) may require the occupier to comply with conditions specified in the order.

(8) If the court orders the lessor to pay compensation it may not order the occupier to do so.

Regulations

8. Regulations may make provision as to circumstances in which—

(a) a lessor is to be taken, for the purposes of section 27 and this Part of this Schedule to have—

(i) withheld his consent;

(ii) withheld his consent unreasonably;

(iii) acted reasonably in withholding his consent;

(b) a condition subject to which a lessor has given his consent is to be taken to be reasonable;

(c) a condition subject to which a lessor has given his consent is to be taken to be unreasonable.

Sub-leases etc.

9. The Secretary of State may by regulations make provision supplementing, or modifying, the provision made by section 27 or any provision made by or under this Part of this Schedule in relation to cases where the occupier occupies premises under a sub-lease or sub-tenancy.

Section 50(8)   SCHEDULE 5

THE NATIONAL DISABILITY COUNCIL

Status

1.—(1) The Council shall be a body corporate.

(2) The Council is not the servant or agent of the Crown and does not enjoy any status, immunity or privilege of the Crown.

Procedure

2. The Council has power to regulate its own procedure (including power to determine its quorum).

Membership

3.—(1) The Council shall consist of at least 10, but not more than 20, members.

(2) In this Schedule "member", except in sub-paragraph (5)(b), means a member of the Council.

(3) Each member shall be appointed by the Secretary of State.

(4) The Secretary of State shall appoint one member to be chairman of the Council and another member to be its deputy chairman.

(5) The members shall be appointed from among persons who, in the opinion of the Secretary of State—

(a) have knowledge or experience of the needs of disabled persons or the needs of a particular group, or particular groups, of disabled persons;

(b) have knowledge or experience of the needs of persons who have had a disability or the needs of a particular group, or particular groups, of such persons; or

(c) are members of, or otherwise represent, professional bodies or bodies which represent industry or other business interests.

(6) Before appointing any member, the Secretary of State shall consult such persons as he considers appropriate.

(7) In exercising his powers of appointment, the Secretary of State shall try to secure that at all times at least half the membership of the Council consists of disabled persons, persons who have had a disability or the parents or guardians of disabled persons.

Term of office of members

4.—(1) Each member shall be appointed for a term which does not exceed five years but shall otherwise hold and vacate his office in accordance with the terms of his appointment.

(2) A person shall not be prevented from being appointed as a member merely because he has previously been a member.

(3) Any member may at any time resign his office by written notice given to the Secretary of State.

(4) Regulations may make provision for the Secretary of State to remove a member from his office in such circumstances as may be prescribed.

Remuneration

5.—(1) The Secretary of State may pay such remuneration or expenses to any member as he considers appropriate.

(2) The approval of the Treasury is required for any payment made under this paragraph.

Staff

6. The Secretary of State shall provide the Council with such staff as he considers appropriate.

Supplementary regulation-making power

7. The Secretary of State may by regulations make provision—

(a) as to the provision of information to the Council by the Secretary of State;

(b) as to the commissioning by the Secretary of State of research to be undertaken on behalf of the Council;

(c) as to the circumstances in which and conditions subject to which the Council may appoint any person as an adviser;

(d) as to the payment by the Secretary of State, with the approval of the Treasury, of expenses incurred by the Council.

Annual report

8.—(1) As soon as is practicable after the end of each financial year, the Council shall report to the Secretary of State on its activities during the financial year to which the report relates.

(2) The Secretary of State shall lay a copy of every annual report of the Council before each House of Parliament and shall arrange for such further publication of the report as he considers appropriate.

Section 70(4)   SCHEDULE 6

CONSEQUENTIAL AMENDMENTS

Employment and Training Act 1973 (c. 50)

1. In section 12(1) of the Employment and Training Act 1973 (duty of Secretary of State to give preference to ex-service men and women in exercising certain powers in respect of disabled persons)—
   (a) for "persons registered as handicapped by disablement" substitute "disabled persons"; and
   (b) for the words after " "disabled person" " substitute "has the same meaning as in the Disability Discrimination Act 1995."

Employment Protection (Consolidation) Act 1978 (c. 44)

2. In section 136(1) of the Employment Protection (Consolidation) Act 1978 (appeals to Employment Appeal Tribunal), at the end insert—
   "(ff) the Disability Discrimination Act 1995."

3. In paragraph 20 of Schedule 13 to that Act (reinstatement or re-engagement of dismissed employees), in sub-paragraph (3)—
   (a) in the definition of "relevant complaint of dismissal", omit "or" and at the end insert "or a complaint under section 8 of the Disability Discrimination Act 1995 arising out of a dismissal";
   (b) in the definition of "relevant conciliation powers", omit "or" and at the end insert "or paragraph I of Schedule 3 to the Disability Discrimination Act 1995"; and
   (c) in the definition of "relevant compromise contract" for "or section" substitute "section" and at the end insert "or section 9(2) of the Disability Discrimination Act 1995".

Companies Act 1985 (c. 6)

4. In paragraph 9 of Schedule 7 to the Companies Act 1985 (disclosure in directors' report of company policy in relation to disabled persons), in the definition of "disabled person" in sub-paragraph (4)(b), for "Disabled Persons (Employment) Act 1944" substitute "Disability Discrimination Act 1995".

Local Government and Housing Act 1989 (c. 42)

5. In section 7 of the Local Government and Housing Act 1989 (all staff of a local authority etc. to be appointed on merit), in subsection (2)—
   (a) paragraph (a) shall be omitted;
   (b) the word "and" at the end of paragraph (d) shall be omitted; and
   (c) after paragraph (e) insert—
   "; and
         (f) sections 5 and 6 of the Disability Discrimination Act 1995 (meaning of discrimination and duty to make adjustments)."

Enterprise and New Towns (Scotland) Act 1990 (c. 35)

6. In section 16 of the Enterprise and New Towns (Scotland) Act 1990 (duty of certain Scottish bodies to give preference to ex-service men and women in exercising powers to select disabled persons for training), in subsection (2), for "said Act of 1944" substitute "Disability Discrimination Act 1995".

SCHEDULE 7

REPEALS

Chapter	Short title	Extent of repeal
7 & 8 Geo. 6 c. 10.	The Disabled Persons (Employment) Act 1944.	Section 1. Sections 6 to 14. Section 19. Section 21. Section 22(4).
6 & 7 Eliz. 2 c. 33.	The Disabled Persons (Employment) Act 1958.	Section 2.
1970 c. 44.	The Chronically Sick and Disabled Persons Act 1970.	Section 16.
1978 c. 44.	The Employment Protection (Consolidation) Act 1978.	In Schedule 13, in paragraph 20(3), the word "or" in the definitions of "relevant complaint of dismissal" and "relevant conciliation powers".
1989 c. 42.	The Local Government and Housing Act 1989.	In section 7(2), paragraph (a) and the word "and" at the end of paragraph (d).
1993 c. 62.	The Education Act 1993.	In section 161(5), the words from "and in this subsection" to the end.

Section 70(6)   SCHEDULE 8

MODIFICATIONS OF THIS ACT IN ITS APPLICATION TO NORTHERN IRELAND

1. In its application to Northern Ireland this Act shall have effect subject to the following modifications.

2.—(1) In section 3(1) for "Secretary of State" substitute "Department".

(2) In section 3 for subsections (4) to (12) substitute—

"(4) In preparing a draft of any guidance, the Department shall consult such persons as it considers appropriate.

(5) Where the Department proposes to issue any guidance, the Department shall publish a draft of it, consider any representations that are made to the Department about the draft and, if the Department thinks it appropriate, modify its proposals in the light of any of those representations.

(6) If the Department decides to proceed with any proposed guidance the Department shall lay a draft of it before the Assembly.

(7) If, within the statutory period, the Assembly resolves not to approve the draft, the Department shall take no further steps in relation to the proposed guidance.

(8) If no such resolution is made within the statutory period, the Department shall issue the guidance in the form of its draft.

(9) The guidance shall come into force on such date as the Department may by order appoint.

(10) Subsection (7) does not prevent a new draft of the proposed guidance being laid before the Assembly.

(11) The Department may—

(a) from time to time revise the whole or any part of any guidance and re-issue it;

(b) by order revoke any guidance.

(12) In this section—

"the Department" means the Department of Economic Development;

"guidance" means guidance issued by the Department under this section and includes guidance which has been revised and re-issued;

"statutory period" has the meaning assigned to it by section 41(2) of the Interpretation Act (Northern Ireland) 1954."

3. In section 4(6) for "Great Britain" substitute "Northern Ireland".

4.—(1) In section 7(2) for "Secretary of State" substitute "Department of Economic Development".

(2) In section 7(4) to (10) for "Secretary of State" wherever it occurs substitute "Department of Economic Development", for "he" and "him" wherever they occur substitute "it" and for "his" wherever it occurs substitute "its".

(3) In section 7(9) for "Parliament" substitute "the Assembly".

5.—(1) In section 8(3) omit "or (in Scotland) in reparation".

(2) In section 8(7) for "paragraph 6A of Schedule 9 to the Employment Protection (Consolidation) Act 1978" substitute "Article 61(3) of the Industrial Relations (Northern Ireland) Order 1976".

6.—(1) In section 9(2)(a) for "a conciliation officer" substitute "the Agency".

(2) In section 9(4) in the definition of "qualified lawyer" for the words from "means" to the end substitute "means a barrister (whether in practice as such or employed to give legal advice) or a solicitor of the Supreme Court who holds a practising certificate.".

7.—(1) In section 10(1)(b) omit "or recognised body".

(2) In section 10(2)(b) for "Secretary of State" substitute "Department of Economic Development".

(3) In section 10(3) in the definition of "charity" for "1993" substitute "(Northern Ireland) 1964", omit the definition of "recognised body" and in the definition of "supported employment" for "Act 1944" substitute "Act (Northern Ireland) 1945".

(4) In section 10(4) for "England and Wales" where it twice occurs substitute "Northern Ireland".

(5) Omit section 10(5).

8.—In section 12(5) for "Great Britain" where it twice occurs substitute "Northern Ireland".

9.—(1) In section 19(3)(g) for "section 2 of the Employment and Training Act 1973" substitute "sections 1 and 2 of the Employment and Training Act (Northern Ireland) 1950".

(2) In section 19(5) for paragraph (a) substitute—

"(a) education which is funded, or secured, by a relevant body or provided at—
(i) an establishment which is funded by such a body or by the Department of Education for Northern Ireland; or
(ii) any other establishment which is a school within the meaning of the Education and Libraries (Northern Ireland) Order 1986;".

(3) For section 19(6) substitute—
"(6) In subsection (5) "relevant body" means—
(a) an education and library board;
(b) a voluntary organisation; or
(c) a body of a prescribed kind.".

10. In section 20(7) for paragraphs (b) and (c) substitute "; or
(b) functions conferred by or under Part VIII of the Mental Health (Northern Ireland) Order 1986 are exercisable in relation to a disabled person's property or affairs.".

11. In section 22(4) and (6) omit "or (in Scotland) the subject of".

12.—(1) In section 25(1) omit "or (in Scotland) in reparation".

(2) In section 25(3) for "England and Wales" substitute "Northern Ireland".

(3) Omit section 25(4).

(4) In section 25(5) omit the words from "or" to the end.

13. In section 26(3) omit "or a sheriff court".

14.—(1) In section 28 for "Secretary of State" wherever it occurs substitute "Department of Health and Social Services".

(2) In section 28(3) and (4) for "he" substitute "it".

(3) In section 28(5) for "Treasury" substitute "Department of Finance and Personnel in Northern Ireland".

15. Omit sections 29, 30 and 31.

16.—(1) In section 32(1) for "Secretary of State" substitute "Department of the Environment".

(2) In section 32(5) for the definition of "taxi" substitute—
" "taxi" means a vehicle which—
(a) is licensed under Article 61 of the Road Traffic (Northern Ireland) Order 1981 to stand or ply for hire; and
(b) seats not more than 8 passengers in addition to the driver".

17. In section 33, for "Secretary of State", wherever it occurs, substitute "Department of the Environment".

18. For section 34 substitute—

"New licences conditional on compliance with accessibility tax regulations
34.—(1) The Department of the Environment shall not grant a public service vehicle licence under Article 61 of the Road Traffic (Northern Ireland) Order 1981 for a taxi unless

the vehicle conforms with those provisions of the taxi accessibility regulations with which it will be required to conform if licensed.

(2) Subsection (1) does not apply if such a licence was in force with respect to the vehicle at any time during the period of 28 days immediately before the day on which the licence is granted.

(3) The Department of the Environment may by order provide for subsection (2) to cease to have effect on such date as may be specified in the order.".

19. Omit section 35.

20. In section 36(7) for "licensing authority" substitute "Department of the Environment".

21.—(1) In section 37(5) and (6) for "licensing authority" substitute "Department of the Environment".

(2) In section 37(9) for "Secretary of State" substitute "Department of the Environment".

22.—(1) In section 38(1) for "a licensing authority" substitute "the Department of the Environment".

(2) In section 38(2) for "licensing authority concerned" substitute "Department of the Environment".

(3) In section 38(3) for the words from "the magistrates' court" to the end substitute "a court of summary jurisdiction acting for the petty sessions district in which the aggrieved person resides".

23. Omit section 39.

24.—(1) In section 40 for "Secretary of State" wherever it occurs substitute "Department of the Environment".

(2) In section 40(5) for the definition of "public service vehicle" substitute—

" "public service vehicle" means a vehicle which—

(a) seats more than 8 passengers in addition to the driver; and

(b) is a public service vehicle for the purposes of the Road Traffic (Northern Ireland) Order 1981;".

(3) In section 40(7) for the words from "the Disabled" to the end substitute "such representative organisations as it thinks fit".

25.—(1) In section 41(2) for "Secretary of State" substitute "Department of the Environment".

(2) In section 41 for subsections (3) and (4) substitute—

"(3) Any person who uses a regulated public service vehicle in contravention of this section is guilty of an offence and liable on summary conviction to a fine not exceeding level 4 on the standard scale.".

26.—(1) In section 42 for "Secretary of State" wherever it occurs substitute "Department of the Environment".

(2) In section 42(1) for "he" substitute "it".

(3) In section 42(6) for "his" substitute "its".

27. In section 43 for "Secretary of State" wherever it occurs substitute "Department of the Environment".

28.—(1) In section 44 for "Secretary of State" wherever it occurs substitute "Department of the Environment".

(2) In section 44(2) for "him" substitute "it".

(3) In section 44(6) for "he" substitute "it" and for "his" substitute "its".

29.—(1) In section 45 for "Secretary of State" wherever it occurs substitute "Department of the Environment".

(2) In section 45(2) for "him" substitute "it" and at the end add "of Northern Ireland".

(3) In section 45(4) for "he" substitute "it".

30.—(1) In section 46 for "Secretary of State" wherever it occurs substitute "Department of the Environment".

(2) In section 46(6) in the definition of "rail vehicle" for the words "on any railway, tramway or prescribed system" substitute "by rail".

(3) Omit section 46(7).

(4) In section 46(11) for the words from "the Disabled" to the end substitute "such representative organisations as it thinks fit".

31.—(1) In section 47 for "Secretary of State" wherever it occurs substitute "Department of the Environment".

(2) In section 47(3) for the words "the Disabled Persons Transport Advisory Committee and such other persons as he" substitute "such persons as it" and for "he" substitute "it".

32. Omit section 48(3).

33.—(1) In the heading to Part VI of this Act and in section 50(1) for "National Disability Council" substitute "Northern Ireland Disability Council".

(2) In section 50(2) for "the Secretary of State" in the first place where it occurs substitute "a

Northern Ireland department" and in the other place where it occurs substitute "that department".

(3) In section 50(3) for "Secretary of State" substitute "Department of Health and Social Services".

(4) In section 50(7) for "the Secretary of State" substitute "a Northern Ireland department" and after "Crown" insert "or a Northern Ireland department".

(5) In section 50(9)(a) for sub-paragraphs (i) to (iv) substitute—

"(i) the Disabled Persons (Employment) Act (Northern Ireland) 1945;

(ii) the Contracts of Employment and Redundancy Payments Act (Northern Ireland) 1965;

(iii) the Employment and Training Act (Northern Ireland) 1950;

(iv) the Industrial Relations (Northern Ireland) Orders 1976; or".

(6) In section 50(10) for the words from "time when" to the end substitute "time when—

(a) there are no committees in existence under section 17 of the Disabled Persons (Employment) Act (Northern Ireland) 1945; and

(b) there is no person appointed to act generally under section 60(1) of this Act.".

34.—(1) In section 51(1) for "the Secretary of State" substitute "any Northern Ireland department" and for "the Secretary of State's" substitute "that department's".

(2) In section 51(2) for "The Secretary of State" substitute "A Northern Ireland department".

(3) In section 51(4) for "a county court or a sheriff court" substitute "or a county court".

(4) In section 51(6) for "the Secretary of State" substitute "a Northern Ireland department".

35. For section 52 substitute—

"Further provisions about codes issued under section 51

52.—(1) In this section—

"proposal" means a proposal made by the Council to a Northern Ireland department under section 51;

"responsible department"—

(a) in relation to a proposal, means the Northern Ireland department to which the proposal is made,

(b) in relation to a code, means the Northern Ireland department by which the code is issued; and

"statutory period" has the meaning assigned to it by section 41(2) of the Interpretation Act (Northern Ireland) 1954.

(2) In preparing any proposal, the Council shall consult—

(a) such persons (if any) as the responsible department has specified in making its request to the Council; and

(b) such other persons (if any) as the Council considers appropriate.

(3) Before making any proposal the Council shall publish a draft, consider any representations made to it about the draft and, if it thinks it appropriate, modify its proposal in the light of any of those representations.

(4) Where the Council makes any proposal, the responsible department may—

(a) approve it;

(b) approve it subject to such modifications as that department thinks appropriate; or

(c) refuse to approve it.

(5) Where the responsible department approves any proposal (with or without modifications) that department shall prepare a draft of the proposed code and lay it before the Assembly.

(6) If, within the statutory period, the Assembly resolves not to approve the draft, the responsible department shall take no further steps in relation to the proposed code.

(7) If no such resolution is made within the statutory period, the responsible department shall issue the code in the form of its draft.

(8) The code shall come into force on such date as the responsible department may appoint by order.

(9) Subsection (6) does not prevent a new draft of the proposed code from being laid before the Assembly.

(10) If the responsible department refuses to approve a proposal, that department shall give the Council a written statement of the department's reasons for not approving it.

(11) The responsible department may by order revoke a code.".

36.—(1) In section 53 for "Secretary of State" wherever it occurs substitute "Department of Economic Development".

(2) In section 53(1) for "he" substitute "it".

(3) In section 53(5) for "a county court or a sheriff court" substitute "or a county court".

37. For section 54 substitute—

"Further provisions about codes issued under section 53

54.—(1) In preparing a draft of any code under section 53, the Department shall consult such organisations representing the interests of employers or of disabled persons in, or seeking, employment as the Department considers appropriate.

(2) Where the Department proposes to issue a code, the Department shall publish a draft of the code, consider any representations that are made to the Department about the draft and, if the Department thinks it appropriate, modify its proposals in the light of any of those representations.

(3) If the Department decides to proceed with the code, the Department shall lay a draft of it before the Assembly.

(4) If, within the statutory period, the Assembly resolves not to approve the draft, the Department shall take no further steps in relation to the proposed code.

(5) If no such resolution is made within the statutory period, the Department shall issue the code in the form of its draft.

(6) The code shall come into force on such date as the Department may appoint by order.

(7) Subsection (4) does not prevent a new draft of the proposed code from being laid before the Assembly.

(8) The Department may by order revoke a code.

(9) In this section—

"the Department" means the Department of Economic Development; and

"statutory period" has the meaning assigned to it by section 41(2) of the Interpretation Act (Northern Ireland) 1954.".

38. In section 56(2) and (4) for "Secretary of State" substitute "Department of Economic Development".

39. In section 59(1) after "Crown" where it twice occurs insert "or a Northern Ireland department".

40.—(1) In section 60(1) to (3) for "Secretary of State" wherever it occurs substitute "Department of Economic Development" and for "he" and "him" wherever they occur substitute "it".

(2) In section 60(4) for "Treasury" substitute "Department of Finance and Personnel in Northern Ireland".

(3) For section 60(6) substitute—

"(6) The Department of Economic Development may by order repeal section 17 of, and Schedule 2 to, the Disabled Persons (Employment) Act (Northern Ireland) 1945 (district advisory committees).".

(4) In section 60(7) omit "paragraph (b) of", for "1944" substitute " 1945" and omit "in each case".

(5) In section 60, omit subsection (8).

41. For section 61 substitute—

"Amendments of Disabled Persons (Employment) Act (Northern Ireland) 1945

61.—(1) Section 15 of the Disabled Persons (Employment) Act (Northern Ireland) 1945 (which gives the Department of Economic Development power to make arrangements for the provision of supported employment) is amended as set out in subsections (2) to (5).

(2) In subsection (1)—

(a) for "persons registered as handicapped by disablement" substitute "disabled persons";

(b) for "their disablement" substitute "their disability"; and

(c) for "are not subject to disablement" substitute "do not have a disability".

(3) In subsection (2) for the words from "any of one or more companies" to "so required and prohibited" substitute "any company, association or body".

(4) After subsection (2) insert—

"(2A) The only kind of company which the Department itself may form in exercising its powers under this section is a company which is—

(a) required by its constitution to apply its profits, if any, or other income in promoting its objects; and

(b) prohibited by its constitution from paying any dividend to its members.".

(5) After subsection (5) insert—

"(5A) For the purposes of this section—

(a) a person is a disabled person if he is a disabled person for the purposes of the Disability Discrimination Act 1995; and

(b) "disability" has the same meaning as in that Act.".

(6) The provisions of section 16 of the Act of 1945 (preference to be given under section 15 of that Act to ex-service men and women) shall become subsection (1) of that section and at the end insert—

"and whose disability is due to that service.

    (2) For the purposes of subsection (1) of this section, a disabled person's disability shall be treated as due to service of a particular kind only in such circumstances as may be prescribed."

(7) The following provisions of the Act of 1945 shall cease to have effect—

(a) section 1 (definition of "disabled person");

(b) sections 2 to 4 (training for disabled persons);

(c) sections 6 to 8 (the register of disabled persons);

(d) sections 9 to 11 (obligations on employers with substantial staffs to employ quota of registered persons);

(e) section 12 (the designated employment scheme for persons registered as handicapped by disablement);

(f) section 13 (interpretation of provisions repealed by this Act);

(g) section 14 (records to be kept by employer);

(h) section 19 (proceedings in relation to offences);

(j) sections 21 and 22 (supplementary).

(8) Any statutory provision in which "disabled person" is defined by reference to the Act of 1945 shall be construed as if that expression had the same meaning as in this Act.".

42.—(1) In section 62(2) for "Secretary of State" substitute "Department of Economic Development".

(2) In section 62(7) for "Great Britain" where it twice occurs substitute "Northern Ireland".

43. Omit section 63.

44.—(1) In section 64(3) for "England and Wales" substitute "Northern Ireland".

(2) Omit section 64(4).

(3) In section 64(5)(a) omit the words from ", the British" to the end.

(4) In section 64(8)—

(a) omit the definitions of "British Transport Police", "Royal Parks Constabulary" and "United Kingdom Atomic Energy Authority Constabulary";

(b) in the definition of "the 1947 Act" at the end add "as it applies both in relation to the Crown in right of Her Majesty's Government in Northern Ireland and in relation to the Crown in right of Her Majesty's Government in the United Kingdom";

(c) in the definition of "fire brigade" for the words from "means" to the end substitute "has the same meaning as in the Fire Services (Northern Ireland) Order 1984";

(d) in the definition of "prison officer" for the words from "means" to the end substitute "means any individual who holds any post, otherwise than as a medical officer, to which he has been appointed under section 2(2) of the Prison Act (Northern Ireland) 1953 or who is a prison custody officer within the meaning of Chapter III of Part VIII of the Criminal Justice and Public Order Act 1994";

(e) in the definition of "service for purposes of a Minister of the Crown or government department" at the end add "or service as the head of a Northern Ireland department".

45. Omit section 65.

46. For section 67 substitute—

"Regulations and orders etc.

    67.—(1) Any power under this Act to make regulations or orders shall be exercisable by statutory rule for the purposes of the Statutory Rules (Northern Ireland) Order 1979.

    (2) Any such power may be exercised to make different provision for different cases, including different provision for different areas or localities.

    (3) Any such power, includes power—

(a) to make such incidental, supplementary, consequential or transitional provision as appears to the Northern Ireland department exercising the power to be expedient; and

(b) to provide for a person to exercise a discretion in dealing with any matter.

    (4) No order shall be made under section 50(3) unless a draft of the order has been laid before and approved by a resolution of the Assembly.

    (5) Any other order made under this Act, other than an order under section 3(9), 52(8), 54(6) or 70(3), and any regulations made under this Act shall be subject to negative resolution within the meaning of section 41(6) of the Interpretation Act (Northern Ireland) 1954 as if they were statutory instruments within the meaning of that Act.

    (6) Section 41(3) of the Interpretation Act (Northern Ireland) 1954 shall apply in relation to any instrument or document which by virtue of this Act is required to be laid before the Assembly as if it were a statutory instrument or statutory document within the meaning of that Act.

    (7) Subsection (1) does not require an order under section 43 which applies only to a specified vehicle, or to vehicles of a specified person, to be made by statutory rule.

(8) Nothing in section 40(6) or 46(5) affects the powers conferred by subsections (2) and (3)."

47.—(1) For section 68(1) substitute—

"(1) In this Act—

"accessibility certificate" means a certificate issued under section 41(1)(a);

"act" includes a deliberate omission;

"the Agency" means the Labour Relations Agency;

"approval certificate" means a certificate issued under section 42(4);

"the Assembly" means the Northern Ireland Assembly;

"benefits", in Part II, has the meaning given in section 4(4);

"the Department of Economic Development" means the Department of Economic Development in Northern Ireland;

"the Department of the Environment" means the Department of the Environment for Northern Ireland;

"the Department of Health and Social Services" means the Department of Health and Social Services for Northern Ireland;

"employment" means, subject to any prescribed provision, employment under a contract of service or of apprenticeship or a contract personally to do work and related expressions are to be construed accordingly;

"employment at an establishment in Northern Ireland" is to be construed in accordance with subsections (2) to (5);

"enactment" means any statutory provision within the meaning of section 1(f) of the Interpretation Act (Northern Ireland) 1954;

"government department" means a Northern Ireland department or a department of the Government of the United Kingdom;

"Minister of the Crown" includes the Treasury;

"Northern Ireland department" includes (except in sections 51 and 52) the head of a Northern Ireland department;

"occupational pension scheme" has the same meaning as in the Pension Schemes (Northern Ireland) Act 1993;

"premises", includes land of any description;

"prescribed" means prescribed by regulations;

"profession" includes any vocation or occupation;

"provider of services" has the meaning given in section 19(2)(b);

"public service vehicle" and "regulated public service vehicle" have the meaning given in section 40;

"PSV accessibility regulations" means regulations made under section 40(1);

"rail vehicle" and "regulated rail vehicle" have the meaning given in section 46;

"rail vehicle accessibility regulations" means regulations made under section 46(1);

"regulations" means—

(a) in Parts I and II of this Act, section 66, the definition of "employment" above and subsections (3) and (4) below, regulations made by the Department of Economic Development;

(b) in Part V of this Act, regulations made by the Department of the Environment;

(c) in any other provision of this Act, regulations made by the Department of Health and Social Services.

"section 6 duty" means any duty imposed by or under section 6;

"section 15 duty" means any duty imposed by or under section 15;

"section 21 duty" means any duty imposed by or under section 21;

"taxi" and "regulated taxi" have the meaning given in section 32;

"taxi accessibility regulations" means regulations made under section 32(1);

"trade" includes any business;

"trade organisation" has the meaning given in section 13;

"vehicle examiner" means an officer of the Department of the Environment authorised by that Department for the purposes of sections 41 and 42.".

(2) In section 68(2) to (4) for "Great Britain" wherever it occurs substitute "Northern Ireland".

48.—(1) In section 70(3) for "Secretary of State" substitute "Department of Health and Social Services".

(2) In section 70(8) for "the Secretary of State" substitute "a Northern Ireland department" and for "him" substitute "it".

49.—(1) In Schedule 1 in paragraph 7(1) for "Act 1944" substitute "Act (Northern Ireland) 1945".

(2) In Schedule 1 in paragraph 7(7) for "1944" substitute "1945".

50.—(1) In Schedule 3 in paragraph 1—
(a) for "a conciliation officer" wherever it occurs substitute "the Agency";
(b) in sub-paragraphs (1) and (4) for "he" substitute "it";
(c) in sub-paragraph (3) for "the conciliation officer" substitute "the Agency".
(2) In Schedule 3 for paragraph 4(1) substitute—
    "(1) In any proceedings under section 8—
    (a) a certificate signed by or on behalf of a Minister of the Crown or a Northern Ireland
        department and certifying that any conditions or requirements specified in the cer-
        tificate were imposed by that Minister or that department (as the case may be) and
        were in operation at a time or throughout a time so specified; or
    (b) a certificate signed by or on behalf of the Secretary of State and certifying that an act
        specified in the certificate was done for the purpose of safeguarding national security,
    shall be conclusive evidence of the matters certified.".
(3) In Schedule 3 in paragraph 6(1) omit "or a sheriff court".
(4) In Schedule 3 for paragraph 8(1) substitute—
    "(1) In any proceedings under section 25—
    (a) a certificate signed by or on behalf of a Minister of the Crown or a Northern Ireland
        department and certifying that any conditions or requirements specified in the cer-
        tificate were imposed by that Minister or that department (as the case may be) and
        were in operation at a time or throughout a time so specified; or
    (b) a certificate signed by or on behalf of the Secretary of State and certifying that an act
        specified in the certificate was done for the purpose of safeguarding national security,
    shall be conclusive evidence of the matters certified.".
51.—(1) In Schedule 4 in paragraphs 2(1) and (5) and 7(1) and (5) omit "or sisted".
(2) In Schedule 4 in paragraph 4 for "Secretary of State" substitute "Department of Economic
Development".
(3) In Schedule 4 in paragraph 6(1) omit "or, in Scotland, to the sheriff".
(4) In Schedule 4 omit paragraph 6(2).
(5) In Schedule 4 in paragraph 9 for "Secretary of State" substitute "Department of Health
and Social Services".
52.—(1) In Schedule 5 in the heading for "National" substitute "Northern Ireland".
(2) In Schedule 5 for "Secretary of State" wherever it occurs substitute "Department of
Health and Social Services".
(3) In Schedule 5 in paragraphs 3(6), 5(1), 6 and 8(2) for "he" substitute "it" and in paragraph
3(7) for "his" substitute "its".
(4) In Schedule 5 in paragraphs 5(2) and 7(d) for "Treasury" substitute "Department of
Finance and Personnel in Northern Ireland".
(5) In Schedule 5 in paragraph 8(2) for "each House of Parliament" substitute "the
Assembly".
53. For Schedules 6 and 7 substitute—

"SCHEDULE 6

CONSEQUENTIAL AMENDMENTS

The Industrial Relations (Northern Ireland) Order 1976 (NI 16)

1. In Article 68(6) of the Industrial Relations (Northern Ireland) Order 1976 (reinstatement or re-engagement of dismissed employees)—
    (a) in the definition of "relevant complaint of dismissal", omit "or" and at the end insert
        "or a complaint under section 8 of the Disability Discrimination Act 1995 arising out
        of a dismissal";
    (b) in the definition of "relevant conciliation powers", omit "or" and at the end insert "or
        paragraph 1 of Schedule 3 to the Disability Discrimination Act 1995";
    (c) in the definition of "relevant compromise contract" for "or Article" substitute "Arti-
        cle" and at the end insert "or section 9(2) of the Disability Discrimination Act 1995".

The Companies (Northern Ireland) Order 1986 (NI 6)

3. In paragraph 9 of Schedule 7 to the Companies (Northern Ireland) Order 1986 (disclosure in directors' report of company policy in relation to disabled persons) in the definition of "disabled person" in sub-paragraph (4)(b) for "Disabled Persons (Employment)
Act (Northern Ireland) 1945" substitute "Disability Discrimination Act 1995".

SCHEDULE 7

REPEALS

Chapter	Short title	Extent of repeal
1945 c. 6 (N.I.)	The Disabled Persons (Employment) Act (Northern Ireland) 1945.	Sections 1 to 4. Sections 6 to 14. In section 16 the words "vocational training and industrial rehabilitation courses and", the words "courses and" and the words from "and in selecting" to "engagement". Section 19. Section 21. Section 22.
1960 c. 4 (N.I.)	The Disabled Persons (Employment) Act (Northern Ireland) 1960.	The whole Act.
1976 N.I. 16	The Industrial Relations (Northern Ireland) Order 1976.	In Article 68(6) the word "or" in the definitions of "relevant complaint of dismissal" and "relevant conciliation powers".".

APPENDIX 1

THE DISABILITY DISCRIMINATION ACT, 1995

Code of Practice for the elimination of discrimination in the field of employment against disabled persons or persons who have had a disability.

GENERAL NOTE

This Code of Practice is issued under s. 53 of the 1995 Act. It does not itself impose legal obligations, nor is it an authoritative statement of the law, but it is admissible in evidence in any proceedings under the Act before an industrial tribunal or court, and it must be taken into account in any such proceedings where it appears to the tribunal or court to be relevant: see the note to s. 53 of the 1995 Act.

Chapter 2 of the Code of Practice confirms that the Act does not prohibit an employer from appointing the best person for the job, nor does it prevent employers from treating disabled people more favourably than those without a disability (para. 2.2).

Chapter 3 gives general guidance to help avoid disability, and emphasises that many ways of avoiding discrimination will cost little or nothing (para. 3.1); in particular, it stresses the advantages of planning ahead by considering the needs of possible future disabled employees and applicants when planning for change (para. 3.4), and of extending equal opportunities policies to cover disability issues (para. 3.5).

Chapter 4 explains the main employment provisions of the Act and contains some useful illustrations of the scope of the justification defence (paras. 4.6 and 4.7) and of the duty to make reasonable adjustments (para. 4.20). Paragraphs 4.21 to 4.31 explain the factors listed in s. 6(4) of the Act which must be taken into account in determining whether it will be reasonable for an employer to have to make a particular adjustment. Paragraphs 4.35 to 4.48 explain the position regarding building regulations, listed buildings and leases (on which see the note to the Employment Regulations 1996, S.I. 1996 No. 1456, regs. 11 to 15). Paragraphs 4.55 to 4.64 contain guidance for employers on setting up management systems to help avoid discrimination (or more accurately, perhaps, to help avoid *liability* for discrimination). Paragraph 4.56 suggests a number of ways in which employers may seek to reduce the chances of being held vicariously liable for the actions of their employees and agents under s. 58 of the Act, *e.g.* by communicating to their employees and agents any policy on disability and related matters, by heightening awareness of the anti-discrimination legislation, and by providing guidance on non-discriminatory practices. Paragraphs 4.57 to 4.61 address the difficult question of the extent to which an employer is entitled to disclose information about an employee's disability to other employees, particularly when the information was obtained in confidence. The duty to make reasonable adjustments does not arise if the employer does not know, and could not reasonably be expected to know, that the employee has a disability which is likely to place him or her at a substantial disadvantage (see the note to s. 6 of the 1995 Act). Paragraph 4.62 confirms that an employer will be imputed with knowledge of an employee's disability which is gained by an employee or agent of the employer acting on the employer's behalf, thus preventing the employer from claiming to be excluded from the duty to make a reasonable adjustment. In contrast, information gained by a person providing services to employees independently of the employer (*e.g.* an independent counselling service) will not be imputed to the employer, even if the employer has arranged for those services to be provided (para. 4.63).

Chapter 5 gives guidance on the recruitment of staff, in particular on matters such as the drawing up of a job specification, the advertising of vacancies, the selection process and the terms and conditions on which a job is offered. Paragraph 5.3 warns against the inclusion of unnecessary or marginal requirements, while para. 5.4 points out that blanket exclusions which do not take account of individual circumstances (*e.g.* the exclusion of those with a particular impairment) may lead to discrimination. Even where a requirement is *prima facie* justified (*e.g.* a health requirement), the employer may have to show that it would not be reasonable for him to have to waive it in an individual case (para. 5.5). The same reasoning applies to the statement of preferences where the characteristic in question is not necessary for the performance of the job (para. 5.6). It may be a reasonable adjustment for an employer to have to provide information about jobs in an alternative format (para. 5.9), or to change the interview arrangements to suit a disabled candidate (para. 5.17), but only where the employer knows or could reasonably be expected to know that the particular applicant has a disability which is likely to place him or her at a substantial disadvantage (para. 5.12). In shortlisting candidates for interview, para. 5.14 recommends that the employer should consider whether there is any reasonable adjustment which would bring a disabled candidate within the field of applicants to be considered. The Code emphasises that while the Act does not prohibit an employer from seeking information about a disability, the employer should only ask about a disability if it is, or may be, relevant to the person's ability to do the job (para. 5.20). Employers should also ensure that the routine use of aptitude or other tests in the recruitment process does not discriminate against disabled candidates (para. 5.21). Where an employer specifies that applicants for a job must have a certain qualification, the employer will have to justify the rejection of a disabled candidate who lacks that qualification if the reason for the rejection (*i.e.* the lack of the qualification) is connected with his or her disability (para. 5.22). Insisting on a medical check for a disabled candidate but not for other, non-disabled candidates is probably unlawful discrimination, unless it can be justified on the grounds that the disability is relevant to the person's ability to do the job, or to the environment in which that job is done (para. 5.23). The Code of Practice confirms that the Act does not require an employer to discriminate positively in favour of a disabled candidate. If, after allowing for any reasonable adjustments, a disabled candidate is not the best person for the job, the employer would not have to recruit that person (para. 5.26). Paragraph 5.28 states that an employer, in certain circumstances, may be justified in offering a disabled person a less favourable contract, and para. 5.29 confirms that the Act does not prevent an employer from operating a performance-related pay scheme (see the note to the Employment Regulations 1996, reg. 3).

Chapter 6 gives guidance on discrimination against employees. Paragraph 6.5 stresses the importance of reviewing promotion and transfer arrangements to ensure that they do not discriminate against disabled people (*e.g.* by imposing criteria which a disabled person who would be capable of performing well in the job might be unable to meet because of his or her disability). Paragraphs 6.9 to 6.18 explain the provisions of the Act concerning occupational pension schemes and insurance (see the notes to ss. 17 and 18 of the 1995 Act, and to the Employment Regulations 1996, regs. 4 and 5). Paragraphs 6.19 and 6.20 consider the position of an employee who becomes disabled or who has a disability which worsens, and suggest some adjustments which it may be reasonable for the employer to make, and para. 6.21 confirms that the dismissal or compulsory early retirement of a disabled employee for a reason relating to his or her disability must be justified, and the reason must be one which cannot be removed by any reasonable adjustment. Paragraph 6.22 confirms that harassment of a disabled person on account of his or her disability will almost always amount to a detriment within the meaning of s. 4(2) of the Act, and para. 6.23 states that an employer will be responsible for acts of harassment by employees in the course of their employment unless the employer took such steps as were reasonably practical to prevent it.

Chapter 7 clarifies the position regarding contract workers and trade organisations. In particular, para. 7.6 considers the extent of the duty of the principal and of the sending employer to make reasonable adjustments and para. 7.7 examines the position of contract workers in small firms.

Finally Chapter 8 suggests the use of internal grievance procedures for the resolution of disputes and suggests that existing grievance and disciplinary procedures be reviewed to ensure that they do not discriminate against disabled employees.

1. INTRODUCTION

Purpose and status of the Code

1.1 Pages [118 to 154] are a Code of Practice issued by the Secretary of State for Education and Employment under section 53(1)(a) of the Disability Discrimination Act 1995 ("the Act"). The Code comes into effect on 2 December 1996.

1.2 The employment provisions of the Act and the Disability Discrimination (Employment) Regulations 1996 protect disabled people, and people who have been disabled, from discrimination in the field of employment. Although the Code is written in terms of "disabled" people, it also applies to people who no longer have a disability but have had one in the past. The date from which the employment provision take effect is 2 December 1996 (but see paragraph 7.12). The Code of Practice gives practical guidance to help employers and others—including trade organisations and people who hire staff from employment businesses—in eliminating discrimination and should assist in avoiding complaints to industrial tribunals.

1.3 The Code applies in England, Scotland and Wales. It does not itself impose legal obligations and is not an authoritative statement of the law. Authoritative interpretation of the Act and regulations is for the tribunals and courts. However, the Code is admissible in evidence in any proceedings under the Act before an industrial tribunal or court. If any provision in the

Code appears to the tribunal or court to be relevant to a question arising in the proceedings, it must be taken into account in determining that question.

Using the Code

1.4 The Code describes—and gives general guidance on—the main employment provisions of the Act in paragraphs 4.1 to 4.66. More specific guidance on how these provisions operate in different situations is in later paragraphs but it may be necessary to refer back to the general guidance occasionally. For example, someone thinking of recruiting new staff will need to read paragraphs 5.1 to 5.29 and also, unless already familiar with it, the general guidance on the provisions in paragraphs 4.1 to 4.66. Someone dealing with a new or existing employee should read paragraphs 6.1 to 6.23, again with reference to the general guidance as necessary. Examples of how the Act is likely to work in practice are given in boxes (see also paragraph 3.1). Annexes 1–3 are not part of the Code but include information on related subjects.

1.5 References to the legal provisions relevant to the guidance in the Code are generally just on the first, or only, main mention of a provision. For example, "S5(1)" means Section 5, subsection (1) of the Act. "Sch. 1 Para. 1(1)" means Schedule 1, paragraph 1 subparagraph (1) of the Act.

1.6 References in footnotes to "Employment Regulations" means The Disability Discrimination (Employment) Regulations 1996 and to "Definition Regulations" mean The Disability Discrimination (Meaning of Disability) Regulations 1996.

1.7 In the examples, references to male and female individual disabled people are given for realism. All other references are masculine for simplicity but could, of course apply to either sex.

2. WHO IS, AND WHO IS NOT, COVERED BY THE EMPLOYMENT PROVISIONS

What is the main purpose of the employment provisions of the Act?

2.1 The Act protects disabled people from discrimination in the field of employment. As part of this protection employers may have to make "reasonable adjustments" if their employment arrangements or premises place disabled people at a substantial disadvantage compared with non-disabled people. These provisions replace the quota scheme, the designated employment scheme and registration as a disabled person *(S61(7))*.

2.2 The Act does not prohibit an employer from appointing the best person for the job. Nor does it prevent employers from treating disabled people more favourably than those without a disability.

Who has rights or obligations under the Act?

2.3 Disabled people have rights under the Act, as do people who have had disabilities but have fully or largely recovered. The Act defines a disabled person as someone with a physical or mental impairment which has a substantial and long-term adverse effect on his ability to carry out normal day-to-day activities *(S1 and Sch. 1)*. (See Annex 1).

2.4 The following people and organisations may have obligations under the Act:
— employers;
— the Crown (including Government Departments and Agencies) *(S64)*;
— employees and agents of an employer;
— landlords of premises occupied by employers;
— people who hire contract workers;
— trustees or managers of occupational pension schemes;

— people who provide group insurance schemes for an employer's employees;
— trade organisations.

2.5 This Act does not confer rights on people who do not have—and have not had—a disability, with the exception of the provisions covering victimisation (see paragraphs 4.53 and 4.54).

Who does not have obligations or rights under the Act?

2.6 The employment provisions do not apply to employers with fewer than 20 employees *(S7)*. The Act applies when an employer has 20 or more employees in total, regardless of the size of individual workplaces or branches. However, if the number of employees falls below 20 the employer will be exempted for as long as there are fewer than 20 employees. Independent franchise holders are exempt if they employ fewer than 20 people even if the franchise network has 20 or more employees. The Government must carry out a review of the threshold for the exclusion of small firms within 5 years of the employment provisions coming into force.

2.7 The employment provisions do not apply to:
— members of the Armed Forces *(S64(7))*;
— prison officers *(S64(5)(b))*;
— firefighters *(S64(5)(c) and (6))*;
— employees who work wholly or mainly outside Great Britain *(S68(2))*;
— employees who work on board ships, aircraft or hovercraft *(S68(3))*;
— members of the Ministry of Defence Police, the British Transport Police, the Royal Parks Constabulary and the United Kingdom Atomic Energy Authority Constabulary *(S68(5)(a))*; and
— other police officers who are in any event not employees as defined in *S68(1)*.

Who counts as an employee under the Act?

2.8 "Employment" means employment under a contract of service or of apprenticeship, or a contract personally to do any work *(S68)*. The last category covers persons who are self-employed and agree to perform the work personally. "Employee" means anyone whose contract is within that definition of employment, whether or not, for example, he works full-time.

3. GENERAL GUIDANCE TO HELP AVOID DISCRIMINATION

Be flexible

3.1 There may be several ways to avoid discrimination in any one situation. Examples in this Code are *illustrative only*, to indicate what should or should not be done in those and other broadly similar types of situations. They cannot cover every possibility, so it is important to consider carefully how the guidance applies in any specific circumstances. **Many ways of avoiding discrimination will cost little or nothing.** The Code should not be read narrowly; for instance, its guidance on recruitment might help avoid discrimination when promoting employees.

Do not make assumptions

3.2 It will probably be helpful to talk to each disabled person about what the real effects of the disability might be or what might help. There is less chance of a dispute where the person is involved from the start. Such discussions should not, of course, be conducted in a way which would itself give the disabled person any reason to believe that he was being discriminated against.

Consider whether expert advice is needed

3.3 It is possible to avoid discrimination using personal, or in-house knowledge and expertise, particularly if the views of the disabled person are sought. The Act does not oblige anyone to get expert advice but it could help in some circumstances to seek independent advice on the extent of a disabled person's capabilities. This might be particularly appropriate where a person is newly disabled or the effects of someone's disability become more marked. It may also help to get advice on what might be done to change premises or working arrangements, especially if discussions with the disabled person to not lead to a satisfactory solution. Annex 2 gives information about getting advice or help.

Plan ahead

3.4 Although the Act does not require an employer to make changes in anticipation of ever having a disabled applicant or employee, nevertheless when planning for change it could be cost-effective to consider the needs of a range of possible future disabled employees and applicants. There may be helpful improvements that could be built into plans. For example, a new telecommunications system might be made accessible to deaf people even if there are currently no deaf employees.

Promote equal opportunities

3.5 If an employer has an equal opportunities policy or is thinking of introducing one, it would probably help to avoid a breach of the Act if that policy covered disability issues. Employers who have, and follow, a good policy—including monitoring its effectiveness—are likely to have that counted in their favour by a tribunal if a complaint is made. But employers should remember that treating people equally will not always avoid a breach of the Act. An employer may be under a duty to make a reasonable adjustment. This could apply at any time in the recruitment process or in the course of a disabled person's employment.

4. THE MAIN EMPLOYMENT PROVISIONS OF THE ACT

Discrimination

What does the Act say about discrimination?

4.1 *The Act makes it unlawful* for an employer to discriminate against a disabled person in the field of employment *(S4)*. *The Act says* "discrimination" occurs in two ways.

4.2 One way in which discrimination occurs is when:
- for a reason which relates to a disabled person's disability, the employer treats that disabled person less favourably than the employer treats or would treat others to whom the reason does not or would not apply; *and*
- the employer cannot show that this treatment is justified *(S5(1))*.

A woman with a disability which requires use of a wheelchair applies for a job. She can do the job but the employer thinks the wheelchair will get in the way in the office. He gives the job to a person who is no more suitable for the job but who does not use a wheelchair. The employer has therefore treated the woman *less favourably* than the other person because he did not give her the job. The treatment was *for a reason related to the disability*—the fact that she used a wheelchair. And the reason for treating her less favourably *did not apply to the other person* because that person did not use a wheelchair.

If the employer could not justify his treatment of the disabled woman then he would have unlawfully discriminated against her.

An employer decides to close down a factory and makes all the employees redundant, including a disabled person who works there. This is not discrimination as the disabled employee is not being dismissed for a reason which relates to the disability.

4.3 A disabled person may not be able to point to other people who were actually treated more favourably. However, it is still "less favourable treatment" if the employer would give better treatment to someone else to whom the reason for the treatment of the disabled person did not apply. This comparison can also be made with other disabled people, not just non-disabled people. For example, an employer might be discriminating by treating a person with a mental illness less favourably than he treats or would treat a physically disabled person.

4.4 The other way *the Act says* that discrimination occurs is when:
— an employer fails to comply with a duty of reasonable adjustment imposed on him by section 6 in relation to the disabled person; *and*
— he cannot show that this failure is justified *(S5(2))*.

4.5 The relationship between the duty of reasonable adjustment and the need to justify less favourable treatment is described in paragraphs 4.7–4.9. The duty itself is described from paragraph 4.12 onwards and the need to justify a failure to comply with it is described in paragraph 4.34.

What will, and what will not, be justified treatment?

4.6 *The Act says* that less favourable treatment of a disabled person will be justified only if the reason for it is both material to the circumstances of the particular case *and* substantial *(S5(3))*. This means that the reason has to relate to the individual circumstances in question and not just be trivial or minor.

Someone who is blind is not shortlisted for a job involving computers because the employer thinks blind people cannot use them. The employer makes no effort to look at the individual circumstances. A general assumption that blind people cannot use computers would not in itself be a material reason—it is not related to the particular circumstances.

A factory worker with a mental illness is sometimes away from work due to his disability. Because of that he is dismissed. However, the amount of time off is very little more than the employer accepts as sick leave for other employees and so is very unlikely to be a substantial reason.

A clerical worker with a learning disability cannot sort papers quite as quickly as some of his colleagues. There is very little difference in productivity but he is dismissed. That is very unlikely to be a substantial reason.

An employer seeking a clerical worker turns down an applicant with a severe facial disfigurement solely on the ground that other employees would be uncomfortable working alongside him. This will be unlawful because such a reaction by other employees will not in itself justify less favourable treatment of this sort—it is not substantial. The same would apply if it were thought that a customer would feel uncomfortable.

An employer moves someone with a mental illness to a different workplace solely because he mutters to himself while he works. If the employer accepts similar levels of noise from other people, the treatment of the disabled person would probably be unjustified— that level of noise is unlikely to be a substantial reason.

Someone who has psoriasis (a skin condition) is rejected for a job involving modelling cosmetics on a part of the body which in his case is severely disfigured by the condition. That would be lawful if his appearance would be incompatible with the purpose of the work. This is a substantial reason which is clearly related—material—to the individual circumstance.

4.7 *The Act says* that less favourable treatment cannot be justified where the employer is under a duty to make a reasonable adjustment but fails (without justification) to do so, *unless* the treatment would have been justified even after that adjustment *(S5(5))*.

An employee who uses a wheelchair is not promoted, solely because the work station for the higher post is inaccessible to wheelchairs—though it could readily be made so by rearrangement of the furniture. If the furniture had been rearranged, the reason for refusing promotion would not have applied. The refusal of promotion would therefore not be justified.

An applicant for a typing job is not the best person on the face of it, but only because her typing speed is too slow due to arthritis in her hands. If a reasonable adjustment—perhaps an adapted keyboard—would overcome this, her typing speed would not in itself be a substantial reason for not employing her. Therefore the employer would be unlawfully discriminating if on account of her typing speed he did not employ her and provide the adjustment.

An employer refuses a training course for an employee with an illness which is very likely to be terminal within a year because, even with a reasonable adjustment to help in the job after the course, the benefits of the course could not be adequately realised. This is very likely to be a substantial reason. It is clearly material to the circumstances. The refusal of training would therefore very likely be justified.

Someone who is blind applies for a job which requires a significant amount of driving. If it is not reasonable for the employer to adjust the job so that the driving duties are given to someone else, the employer's need for a driver might well be a substantial reason for not employing the blind person. It is clearly material to the particular circumstances. The non-appointment could therefore be justified.

How does an employer avoid unlawful discrimination?

4.8 An employer should not treat a disabled employee or disabled job applicant less favourably, for a reason relating to the disability, than others to whom that reason does not apply, unless that reason is material to the particular circumstances and substantial. If the reason is material and substantial, the employer may have to make a reasonable adjustment to remove it or make it less than substantial *(S5(3) and (5))*.

4.9 Less favourable treatment is therefore justified if the disabled person cannot do the job concerned, and no adjustment which would enable the person to do the job (or another vacant job) is practicable *(S5(3) and (5))*. (See paragraph 4.20 for examples of adjustments which employers may have to make.)

4.10 *The Act says* that some charities (and Government-funded supported employment) are allowed to treat some groups of disabled people more favourably than others. But they can do this only if the group being treated more favourably is one with whom the charitable purposes of the charity are connected and the more favourable treatment is in pursuance of those purposes (or, in the case of supported employment, those treated more favourably are severely disabled people whom the programme aims to help) *(S10)*.

What does the Act say about helping others to discriminate?

4.11 *The Act says* that a person who knowingly helps another to do something made unlawful by the Act will also be treated as having done the same kind of unlawful act *(S57(1))*.

A recruitment consultant engaged by an engineering company refuses to consider a disabled applicant for a vacancy, because the employer has told the consultant that he does not want the post filled by someone who is "handicapped". Under the Act the consultant could be liable for aiding the company.

Reasonable adjustment

What does the Act say about the duty of "reasonable adjustment"?

4.12 *The Act says* that the duty applies where any physical feature of premises occupied by the employer, or any arrangements made by or on behalf of the employer, cause a substantial disadvantage to a disabled person compared with non-disabled people. An employer has to take such steps as it is reasonable for him to have in all the circumstances to prevent that disadvantage—in other words the employer has to make a "reasonable adjustment" *(S6(1))*.

A man who is disabled by dyslexia applies for a job which involves writing letters within fairly long deadlines. The employer gives all applicants a test of their letter-writing ability. The man can generally write letters very well but finds it difficult to do so in stressful situations. The *employer's arrangements* would mean he had to begin his test immediately on arrival and to do it in a short time. He would be *substantially disadvantaged compared to non-disabled people* who would not find such arrangements stressful or, if they did, would not be so affected by them. The employer therefore gives him a little time to settle in and longer to write the letter. These new arrangements do not inconvenience the employer very much and only briefly delay the decision on an appointment. These are *steps that it is reasonable for the employer to have to take in the circumstances to prevent the disadvantage*—a "reasonable adjustment".

4.13 If a disabled person cannot point to an existing non-disabled person compared with whom he is at a substantial disadvantage, then the comparison should be made with how the employer would have treated a non-disabled person.

4.14 How to comply with this duty in recruitment and during employment is explained in paragraphs 5.1–5.29 and 6.1–6.21. The following paragraphs explain how to satisfy this duty more generally.

What "physical features" and "arrangements" are covered by the duty?

4.15 *Regulations define* the term "physical features" to include anything on the premises arising from a building's design or construction or from an approach to, exit from or access to such a building; fixtures, fittings, furnishings, furniture, equipment or materials; and any other physical element or quality of land in the premises. All of these are covered whether temporary or permanent (Employment Regulations: see para. 1.6).

4.16 *The Act says* that the duty applies to "arrangements" for determining to whom employment should be offered and any term, condition or arrangement on which employment, promotion, transfer, training or any other benefit is offered or afforded *(S6(2))*. The duty applies in recruitment and during employment; for example, selection and interview procedures and the arrangements for using premises for such procedures as well as job offers, contractual arrangements, and working conditions.

> The design of a particular workplace makes it difficult for someone with a hearing impairment to hear. That is a disadvantage caused by the *physical features*. There may be nothing that can reasonably be done in the circumstances to change these features. However, requiring someone to work in such a workplace is an *arrangement made by the employer* and it might be reasonable to overcome the disadvantage by a transfer to another workplace or by ensuring that the supervisor gives instructions in an office rather than in the working area.

What "disadvantages" give rise to the duty?

4.17 *The Act says* that only substantial disadvantages give rise to the duty *(S6(1))*. Substantial disadvantages are those which are not minor or trivial.

> An employer is unlikely to be required to widen a particular doorway to enable passage by an employee using a wheelchair if there is an easy alternative route to the same destination.

4.18 An employer cannot be required to prevent a disadvantage caused by premises or by non-pay arrangements by increasing the disabled person's pay. (See paragraph 5.29).

4.19 The duty of reasonable adjustment does not apply in relation to benefits under occupational pension schemes or certain benefits under other employment-related benefit schemes although there is a duty not to discriminate in relation to such benefits (see paragraphs 6.9–6.16).

What adjustments might an employer have to make?

4.20 *The Act gives* a number of examples of "steps" which employers may have to take, if it is reasonable for them to have to do so in all the circumstances of the case *(S6(3))*. Steps other than those listed here, or a combination of steps, will sometimes have to be taken. The steps in the Act are:

— *making adjustments to premises*

> An employer might have to make structural or other physical changes such as: widening a doorway, providing a ramp or moving furniture for a wheelchair user; relocating light switches, door handles or shelves for someone who has difficulty in reaching; providing appropriate contrast in decor to help the safe mobility of a visually impaired person.

— *allocating some of the disabled person's duties to another person*
Minor or subsidiary duties might be reallocated to another employee if the disabled person has difficulty in doing them because of the disability. For example, if a job occasionally involves going onto the open roof of a building an employer might have to transfer this work away from an employee whose disability involves severe vertigo.

— *transferring the person to fill an existing vacancy*
If an employee becomes disabled, or has a disability which worsens so she cannot work in the same place or under the same arrangements and there is no reasonable adjustment which would enable the employee to continue doing the current job, then she might have to be considered for any suitable alternative posts which are available. (Such a case might also involve retraining.)

— *altering the person's working hours*
This could include allowing the disabled person to work flexible hours to enable additional breaks to overcome fatigue arising from the disability, or changing the disabled person's hours to fit with the availability of a carer.

— *assigning the person to a different place of work*
This could mean transferring a wheelchair user's work station from an inaccessible third floor office to an accessible one on the ground floor. It could mean moving the person to other premises of the same employer if the first building is inaccessible.

— *allowing the person to be absent during working hours for rehabilitation, assessment or treatment*
For example, if a person were to become disabled, the employer might have to allow the person more time off during work, than would be allowed to non-disabled employees, to receive physiotherapy or psychoanalysis or undertake employment rehabilitation. A similar adjustment might be appropriate if a disability worsens or if a disabled person needs occasional treatment anyway.

— *giving the person, or arranging for him to be given, training*
This could be training in the use of particular pieces of equipment unique to the disabled person, or training appropriate for all employees but which needs altering for the disabled person because of the disability. For example, all employees might need to be trained in the use of a particular machine but an employer might have to provide slightly different or longer training for an employee with restricted hand or arm movements, or training in additional software for a visually impaired person so that he can use a computer with speech output.

— *acquiring or modifying equipment*
An employer might have to provide special equipment (such as an adapted keyboard for a visually impaired person or someone with arthritis), or an adapted telephone for someone with a hearing impairment or modified equipment (such as longer handles on a machine). There is no requirement to provide or modify equipment for personal purposes unconnected with work, such as providing a wheelchair if a person needs one in any event but does not have one: the disadvantage in such a case does not flow from the employer's arrangements or premises.

— *modifying instructions or reference manuals*
The way instruction is normally given to employees might need to be revised when telling a disabled person how to do a task. The format of instructions or manuals may need to be modified (*e.g.* produced in braille or on audio tape) and instructions for people with learning disabilities may need to be conveyed orally with individual demonstration.

— *modifying procedures for testing or assessment*
This could involve ensuring that particular tests do not adversely affect people with particular types of disability. For example, a person with restricted manual dexterity might be disadvantages by a written test, so an employer might have to give that person an oral test.

— *providing a reader or interpreter*
This could involve a colleague reading mail to a person with a visual impairment at particular times during the working day or, in appropriate circumstances, the hiring of a reader or sign language interpreter.

— *providing supervision*
This could involve the provision of a support worker, or help from a colleague, in appropriate circumstances, for someone whose disability leads to uncertainty or lack of confidence.

When is it "reasonable" for an employer to have to make an adjustment?

4.21 Effective and practicable adjustments for disabled people often involve little or no cost or disruption and are therefore very likely to be reasonable for an employer to have to make. *The Act lists* a number of factors which may, in particular, have a bearing on whether it will be reasonable for the employer to have to make a particular adjustment *(S6(4))*. These factors make a useful checklist, particularly when considering more substantial adjustments. The effectiveness and practicability of a particular adjustment might be considered first. If it is practicable and effective, the financial aspects might be looked at as a whole—cost of the adjustment and resources available to fund it. Other factors might also have a bearing. The factors in the Act are listed below.

The effectiveness of the step in preventing the disadvantage

4.22 It is unlikely to be reasonable for an employer to have to make an adjustment involving little benefit to the disabled employee.

A disabled person is significantly less productive than his colleagues and so is paid less. A particular adjustment would improve his output and thus his pay. It is more likely to be reasonable for the employer to have to make that adjustment if it would significantly improve his pay, than if the adjustment would make only a relatively small improvement.

The practicability of the step

4.23 It is more likely to be reasonable for an employer to have to take a step which is easy to take than one which is difficult.

It might be impracticable for an employer who needs to appoint an employee urgently to have to wait for an adjustment to be made to an entrance. How long it might be reasonable for the employer to have to wait would depend on the circumstances. However, it might be possible to make a temporary adjustment in the meantime, such as using another, less convenient entrance.

The financial and other costs of the adjustment and the extent of any disruption caused

4.24 If an adjustment costs little or nothing and is not disruptive, it would be reasonable unless some other factor (such as practicability or effectiveness) made it unreasonable. The costs to be taken into account include staff and other resource costs. The significance of the cost of a step may depend in part on what the employer might otherwise spend in the circumstances.

It would be reasonable for an employer to have to spend at least as much on an adjustment to enable the retention of a disabled person—including any retraining—as might be spent on recruiting and training a replacement.

4.25 The significance of the cost of a step may also depend in part on the value of the employee's experience and expertise to the employer.

Examples of the factors that might be considered as relating to the value of an employee would include:

— the amount of resources (such as training) invested in the individual by the employer;
— the employee's length of service;
— the employee's level of skill and knowledge;
— the employee's quality of relationships with clients;
— the level of the employee's pay.

4.26 It is more likely to be reasonable for an employer to have to make an adjustment with significant costs for an employee who is likely to be in the job for some time than for a temporary employee.

4.27 An employer is more likely to have to make an adjustment which might cause only minor inconvenience to other employees or the employer than one which might unavoidably prevent other employees from doing their job, or cause other significant disruption.

The extent of the employer's financial or other resources

4.28 It is more likely to be reasonable for an employer with substantial financial resources to have to make an adjustment with a significant cost, than for an employer with fewer resources. The resources in practice available to the employer as a whole should be taken into account as well as other calls on those resources. The reasonableness of an adjustment will depend, however, not only on the resources in practice available for the adjustment but also on all other relevant factors (such as effectiveness and practicability).

4.29 Where the resources of the employer are spread across more than one "business unit" or "profit centre" the calls on them should also be taken into account in assessing reasonableness.

A large retailer probably could not show that the limited resources for which an individual shop manager is responsible meant it was not reasonable for the retailer to have to make an adjustment at that shop. Such an employer may, however, have a number—perhaps a large number—of other disabled employees in other shops. The employer's expenditure on other adjustments, or his potential expenditure on similar adjustments for other existing disabled employees, might then be taken into account in assessing the reasonableness of having to make a new adjustment for the disabled employee in question.

4.30 It is more likely to be reasonable for an employer with a substantial number of staff to have to make certain adjustments, than for a smaller employer.

It would generally be reasonable for an employer with many staff to have to make significant efforts to reallocate duties, identify a suitable alternative post or provide supervision from existing staff. It could also be reasonable for a small company covered by the Act to have to make any of these adjustments but not if it involved disproportionate effort.

The availability to the employer of financial or other assistance to help make an adjustment.

4.31 The availability of outside help may well be a relevant factor.

An employer, in recruiting a disabled person, finds that the only feasible adjustment is too costly for him alone. However, if assistance is available *e.g.* from a Government programme or voluntary body, it may well be reasonable for him to have to make the adjustment after all.

A disabled person is not required to contribute to the cost of a reasonable adjustment. However, if a disabled person has a particular piece of special or adapted equipment which he is prepared to use for work, this might make it reasonable for the employer to have to take some other step (as well as allowing use of the equipment).

An employer requires his employees to use company cars for all business travel. One employee's disability means she would have to use an adapted car or an alternative form of transport. If she has an adapted car of her own which she is willing to use on business, it might well be reasonable for the employer to have to allow this and pay her an allowance to cover the cost of doing so, even if it would not have been reasonable for him to have to provide an adapted company car, or to pay an allowance to cover alternative travel arrangements in the absence of an adapted car.

Other factors

4.32 Although the Act does not mention any further factors, others might be relevant depending on the circumstances. For example:

— effect on other employees

Employees' adverse reaction to an adjustment being made for the disabled employee which involves something they too would like (such as a special working arrangement) is unlikely to be significant.

— adjustments made for other disabled employees

An employer may choose to give a particular disabled employee, or group of disabled employees, an adjustment which goes beyond the duty—that is, which is more than it is reasonable for him to have to do. This would not mean he necessarily had to provide a similar adjustment for other employees with a similar disability.

— the extent to which the disabled person is willing to cooperate

An employee with a mobility impairment works in a team located on an upper floor, to which there is no access by lift. Getting there is very tiring for the employee, and the employer could easily make a more accessible location available for him (though the whole team could not be relocated). If that was the only adjustment which it would be reasonable for the employer to have to make but the employee refused to work there then the employer would not have to make any adjustment at all.

Could an employer have to make more than one adjustment?

4.33 Yes, if it is reasonable for the employer to have to make more than one.

A woman who is deafblind is given a new job with her employer in an unfamiliar part of the building. The employer (i) arranges facilities for her guide dog in the new area, (ii) arranges for her new instructions to be in Braille and (iii) suggests to visitors ways in which they can communicate with her.

Does an employer have to justify not making an adjustment?

4.34 *The Act says* that it is discrimination if an employer fails to take a step which it is reasonable for him to have to take, and he cannot justify that failure *(S5(2))*. However, if it is unreasonable (under *S6*) for an employer to have to make any, or a particular, adjustment, he would not then also have to justify (under *S5*) not doing so. Failure to comply with the duty of reasonable adjustment can only be justified if the reason for the failure is material to the circumstances of the particular case and substantial *(S5(4))*.

An employer might not make an adjustment which it was reasonable for him to have to make because of ignorance or wrong information about appropriate adjustments or about the availability of help with making an adjustment. He would then need to justify failing in his duty. It is unlikely that he could do so unless he had made a reasonable effort to obtain good information from a reputable source such as contacting the local Placing Assessment and Counselling Team or an appropriate disability organisation.

If either of two possible adjustments would remove a disadvantage, but the employer has cost or operational reasons for preferring one rather than the other, it is unlikely to be reasonable for him to have to make the one that is not preferred. If, however, the employee refuses to cooperate with the proposed adjustment the employer is likely to be justified in not providing it.

A disabled employee refuses to follow specific occupational medical advice provided on behalf of an employer about methods of working or managing his condition at work. If he has no good reason for this and his condition deteriorates as a result, the refusal may justify the employer's subsequent failure to make an adjustment for the worsened condition.

Building regulations, listed buildings, leases

How do building regulations affect reasonable adjustments?

4.35 A building or extension to a building may have been constructed in accordance with Part M of the building regulations (or the Scottish parallel, Part T of the Technical Standards) which is concerned with access and facilities for disabled people. *Regulations provide* in these circumstances that the employer does not have to alter any physical characteristic of the building or extension which still complies with the building regulations in force at the time the building works were carried out (Employment Regulations: see para. 1.6).

Where the building regulations in force at the time of a building's construction required that a door should be a particular width, the employer would not have to alter the width of the door later. However, he might have to alter other aspects of the door (*e.g.* the type of handle).

4.36 Employers can only rely upon this defence if the feature still satisfies the requirement of the building regulations that applied when the building or extension was constructed.

What about the need to obtain statutory consent for some building changes?

4.37 Employers might have to obtain statutory consent before making adjustments involving changes to premises. Such consents include planning permission, listed building consent, scheduled monument consent and fire regulations approval. The Act does not override the need to obtain such consents *(S59)*. Therefore an employer does not have to make an adjustment if it requires a statutory consent which has not been given.

4.38 The time it would take to obtain consent may make a particular adjustment impracticable and therefore one which it is not reasonable for the employer to have to make. However, the employer would then also need to consider whether it was reasonable to have to make a temporary adjustment—one that does not require consent—in the meantime.

4.39 Employers should explore ways of making reasonable adjustments which either do not require statutory consent or are likely to receive it. They may well find it useful to consult their local planning authority (in England and Wales) or planning authority (in Scotland).

> An employer needs statutory consent to widen an internal doorway in a listed building for a woman disabled in an accident who returned to work in a wheelchair. The employer considers using a different office but this is not practicable. In the circumstances the widening would be a reasonable adjustment. The employer knows from the local planning authority that consent is likely to be given in a few weeks. In the meantime the employer arranges for the woman to share an accessible office which is inconvenient for both employees, but does not prevent them doing their jobs and is tolerable for that limited period.

What happens where a lease says that certain changes to premises cannot be made?

4.40 Special provisions apply where a lease would otherwise prevent a reasonable adjustment involving an alteration to premises. *The Act modifies* the effect of the lease so far as necessary to enable the employer to make the alteration if the landlord consents, and to provide that the landlord must not withhold consent unreasonably but may attach reasonable conditions to the consent *(S16)*.

How will arrangements for getting the landlord's consent work?

4.41 *The Act says* that the employer must write to the landlord (called the "lessor" in the Act) asking for consent to make the alteration. If an employer fails to apply to the landlord for consent, anything in the lease which would prevent that alteration must be ignored in deciding whether it was reasonable for the employer to have to make that alteration *(Sch. 4 Para. 1)*. If the landlord consents, the employer can then carry out the alteration. If the landlord refuses consent the employer must notify the disabled person, but then has no further obligation (Employment Regulations: see para. 1.6). Where the landlord fails to reply within 21 days or a reasonable period after that he is deemed to have withheld his consent. In those circumstances the withholding of the consent will be unreasonable (see paras. 1.6 and 4.44).

4.42 If the landlord attaches a condition to the consent and it is reasonable for the employer to have to carry out the alteration on that basis, the employer must then carry out the alteration. If it would not be reasonable for the employer to have to carry out the alteration on that basis, the employer must notify the disabled person, but then has no further obligation.

When is it unreasonable for a landlord to withhold consent?

4.43 This will depend on the circumstances but a trivial or arbitrary reason would almost certainly be unreasonable. Many reasonable adjustments to premises will not harm a landlord's interests and so it would generally be unreasonable to withhold consent for them.

> A particular adjustment helps make a public building more accessible generally and is therefore likely to benefit the landlord. It would very probably be unreasonable for consent to be withheld in these circumstances.

4.44 *Regulations provide* that withholding consent will be unreasonable where:

— a landlord has failed to act within the time limits referred to in paragraph 4.41 above (*i.e.* 21 days of receipt of the employer's application or a reasonable period after that); or

— the lease says that consent will be given to alterations of that type or says that such consent will be given if it is sought in that way (Employment Regulations: see para. 1.6).

When is it reasonable for a landlord to withhold consent?

4.45 This will depend on the particular circumstances.

A particular adjustment is likely to result in a substantial permanent reduction in the value of the landlord's interest in the premises. The landlord would almost certainly be acting reasonably in withholding consent.

A particular adjustment would cause significant disruption or inconvenience to other tenants (for example, where the premises consist of multiple adjoining units). The landlord would be likely to be acting reasonably in withholding consent.

What conditions would it be reasonable for a landlord to make when giving consent?

4.46 This will depend on the particular circumstances. However, *Regulations provide* that it would be reasonable for the landlord to require the employer to meet any of the following conditions:

— obtain planning permission and other statutory consents;
— submit any plans to the landlord for approval (provided that the landlord then confirms that approval will not be withheld unreasonably);
— allow the landlord a reasonable opportunity to inspect the work when completed;
— reimburse the landlord's reasonable costs incurred in connection with the giving of his consent;
— reinstate the altered part of the premises to its former state when the lease expires but only if it would have been reasonable for the landlord to have refused consent in the first place (Employment Regulations: see para. 1.6).

What happens if the landlord has a "superior" landlord?

4.47 The employer's landlord may also hold a lease which prevents him from consenting to the alteration without the consent of the "superior" landlord. The statutory provisions have been modified by regulations to cover this. The employer's landlord will be acting reasonably by notifying the employer that consent will be given if the superior landlord agrees. The employer's landlord must then apply to the superior landlord to ask for agreement. The provisions in paragraphs 4.41–4.46, including the requirements not to withhold consent unreasonably and not to attach unreasonable conditions, then apply to the superior landlord (Disability Discrimination (Sub-leases and Sub-tenancies) Regulations 1996).

What if some agreement other than lease prevents the premises being altered?

4.48 An employer or landlord may be bound by the terms of an agreement or other legally binding obligation (for example, a mortgage or charge or restrictive convenant or, in Scotland, a feu disposition) under which the employer or landlord cannot alter the premises without someone else's consent. In these circumstances *Regulations provide* that it is always reasonable for the employer or landlord to have to take steps to obtain the necessary consent so that a reasonable adjustment can be made. Unless or until that consent is obtained the employer or landlord is not required to make the alteration in question. The step of seeking consent which it is always reasonable to have to take does not extend to having to apply to a court or tribunal (Employment Regulations: see para. 1.6). Whether it is reasonable for the employer or landlord to have to apply to a court or tribunal would depend on the circumstances of the case.

Agreements which breach the Act's provisions

Can a disabled person waive rights, or an employer's duties, under the Act?

4.49 *The Act says* that any term in a contract of employment or other agreement is "void" (*i.e.* not valid) to the extent that it would require a person to do anything that would breach any of the Act's employment provisions, or exclude or limit the operation of those provisions *(S9)*.

4.50 An employer should not include in an agreement any provision intended to avoid obligations under the Act, or to prevent someone from fulfilling obligations. An agreement should not, therefore, be used to try to justify less favourable treatment or deem an adjustment unreasonable. Moreover, even parts of agreements which have such an effect (even though unintended) are made void if they would restrict the working of the employment provisions in the Act. However, special arrangements cover leases and other agreements which might prevent a change to premises which could be an adjustment under the Act but where the possible restrictions to the Act's working were unintentional. These are described in paragraphs 4.40–4.48.

4.51 The Act also says that a contract term is void if it would prevent anyone from making a claim under the employment provisions in an industrial tribunal *(S9)*. Further information is given in Annex 3 about such agreements.

What about permits issued in accordance with the Agricultural Wages Acts?

4.52 Under the Agricultural Wages Act 1948 and the Agricultural Wages (Scotland) Act 1949 minimum wages, and terms and conditions, can be set for agricultural workers. Permits can be issued to individuals who are "incapacitated" for the purposes of those Acts and they can then be paid such lower minimum rates or be subject to such revised terms and conditions of employment that the permit specifies. *Regulations provide* that the treatment of a disabled person in accordance with such a permit would be taken to be justified (Employment Regulations: see para. 1.6). This would not prevent the employer from having to comply with the duty not to discriminate, including the duty of reasonable adjustment, for matters other than those covered by the permit.

Victimisation

What does the Act say about victimisation?

4.53 Victimisation is a special form of discrimination covered by the Act. *The Act makes* it unlawful for one person to treat another (the victim) less favourably than he would treat other people in the same circumstances because the "victim" has:
— brought, or given evidence or information in connection with, proceedings under the Act (whether or not proceedings are later withdrawn);
— done anything else under the Act; or
— alleged someone has contravened the Act (whether or not the allegation is later dropped);
or because the person believes or suspects that the victim has done or intends to do any of these things *(S55)*.

It is unlawful for an employer to victimise either disabled or non-disabled people.

A disabled employee complains of discrimination. It would be unlawful for the employer to subject non-disabled colleagues to any detriment (*e.g.* suspension) for telling the truth about the alleged discrimination at an industrial tribunal hearing or in any internal grievance procedures.

4.54 It is victimisation to treat a person less favourably because that person has made an allegation which was false and not made in good faith *(S55(b))*. (Harassment is covered in paragraphs 6.22–6.23.)

Setting up management systems to help avoid discrimination

What management systems might be set up to help avoid discrimination?

4.55 *The Act says* that employers are responsible for the actions done by their employees in the course of their employment. In legal proceedings against an employer based on actions of an employee, it is a defence that the employer took such steps as were reasonably practicable to prevent such actions. It is not a defence for the employer simply to show the action took place without his knowledge or approval. Employers who act through agents will also be liable for the actions of their agents done with the employer's express or implied authority *(S58)*.

> An employer makes it clear to a recruitment agency that the company will not take kindly to recruits with learning disabilities being put forward by the agency. The agency complies by not putting such candidates forward. Both the employer and the agency will be liable if such treatment cannot be justified in an individual case.

4.56 Employers should communicate to their employees and agents any policy they may have on disability matters, and any other policies which have elements relevant to disabled employees (such as health, absenteeism or equal opportunities). All staff should be made aware that it is unlawful to discriminate against disabled people, and be familiar with the policies and practices adopted by their employer to ensure compliance with the law. Employers should provide guidance on non-discriminatory practices for all employees, so they will be aware what they should do and how to deal with disabled colleagues and disabled applicants for vacancies in the organisation, and should ensure so far as possible that these policies and practices are implemented. Employers should also make it clear to their agents what is required of them with regard to their duties under the Act, and the extent of their authority.

4.57 *The Act says* that an employer is not under an obligation to make an adjustment if he does not know, and could not reasonably be expected to know, that a person has a disability which is likely to place the person at a substantial disadvantage *(S6(6))*. An employer must therefore do all he could reasonably be expected to do to find out whether this is the case.

> An employee has a disability which sometimes causes him to cry at work although the cause of this behaviour is not known to the employer. The employer's general approach on such matters is to tell staff to leave their personal problems at home and to make no allowance for such problems in the work arrangements. The employer disciplines the employee without giving him any opportunity to explain that the problem in fact arises from a disability. The employer would be unlikely to succeed in a claim that he could not reasonably be expected to have known of the disability or that it led to the behaviour for which the employee was disciplined.
>
> An employer has an annual appraisal system which specifically provides an opportunity to notify the employer in confidence if any employees are disabled and are put at a substantial disadvantage by the work arrangements or premises. This practice enables the employer to show that he could not reasonably be expected to know that an employee was put at such a disadvantage as a result of disability, if this was not obvious and was not brought to the employer's attention through the appraisal system.

4.58 In some cases a reasonable adjustment will not work without the co-operation of other employees. Employees may therefore have an important role in helping to ensure that a reasonable adjustment is carried out in practice.

> It is a reasonable adjustment for an employer to communicate in a particular way to an employee with autism (a disability which can make it difficult for someone to understand normal social interaction among people). As part of the reasonable adjustment it is the responsibility of that employer to seek the co-operation of other employees in communicating in that way.

4.59 It may be necessary to tell one or more of a disabled person's colleagues (in confidence) about a disability which is not obvious and/or whether any special assistance is required. This may be limited to the person's supervisor, or it may be necessary to involve other colleagues, depending on the nature of the disability and the reason they need to know about it.

> In order for a person with epilepsy to work safely in a particular factory, it may be necessary to advise fellow workers about the effects of the condition, and the methods for assisting with them.
>
> An office worker with cancer says that he does not want colleagues to know of his condition. As an adjustment he needs extra time away from work to receive treatment and to rest. Neither his colleagues nor the line manager needs to be told the precise reasons for the extra leave but the latter will need to know that the adjustment is required in order to carry it out effectively.

4.60 The extent to which an employer is entitled to let other staff know about an employee's disability will depend at least in part on the terms of employment. An employer could be held to be discriminating in revealing such information about a disabled employee if the employer would not reveal similar information about another person for an equally legitimate management purpose; or if the employer revealed such information without consulting the individual, whereas the employer's usual practice would be to talk to an employee before revealing personal information about him.

4.61 The Act does not prevent a disabled person keeping a disability confidential from an employer. But this is likely to mean that unless the employer could reasonably be expected to know about the person's disability anyway, the employer will not be under a duty to make a reasonable adjustment. If a disabled person expects an employer to make a reasonable adjustment, he will need to provide the employer—or, as the case may be, someone acting on the employer's behalf—with sufficient information to carry out that adjustment.

> An employee has symptomatic HIV. He prefers not to tell his employer of the condition. However, as the condition progresses, he finds it increasingly difficult to work the required number of hours in a week. Until he tells his employer of his condition—or the employer becomes or could reasonably be expected to be aware of it—he cannot require the employer to change his working hours to overcome the difficulty. However, once the employer is informed he may then have to make a reasonable adjustment.

4.62 If an employer's agent or employee (for example, an occupational health officer, a personnel officer or line manager) knows in that capacity of an employee's disability, then the employer cannot claim that he does not know of that person's disability, and that he is therefore excluded from the obligation to make a reasonable adjustment. This will be the case even if the disabled person specifically asked for such information to be kept confidential. Employers will therefore need to ensure that where information about disabled people may come through different channels, there is a means— suitably confidential—for bringing the information together, so the employer's duties under the Act are fulfilled.

> In a large company an occupational health officer is engaged by the employer to provide him with information about his employee's health. The officer becomes aware of an employee's disability, which the employee's line manager does not know about. The employer's working arrangements put the employee at a substantial disadvantage because of the effects of her disability and she claims that a reasonable adjustment should have been made. It will not be a defence for the employer to claim that he did not know of her disability. This is because the information gained by the officer on the employer's behalf is imputed to the employer. Even if the person did not want the line manager to know that she had a disability, the occupational health officer's knowledge means that the employer's duty under the Act applies. It might even be necessary for the line manager to implement reasonable adjustments without knowing precisely why he has to do so.

4.63 Information will not be imputed to the employer if it is gained by a person providing services to employees independently of the employer. This is the case even if the employer has arranged for those services to be provided.

An employer contracts with an agency to provide an independent counselling service to employees. The contract says that the counsellors are not acting on the employer's behalf while in the counselling role. Any information about a person's disability obtained by a counsellor during such counselling would not be imputed to the employer and so could not itself place a duty of reasonable adjustment on the employer.

What if someone says they have a disability and the employer is not convinced?

4.64 If a candidate asks for an adjustment to be made because of an impairment whose effects are not obvious, nothing in the Act or Regulations would prohibit the employer from asking for evidence that the impairment is one which gives rise to a disability as defined in the Act.

An applicant says she has a mental illness whose effects require her to take time off work on a frequent, but irregular, basis. If not satisfied that this is true, the employer would be entitled to ask for evidence that the woman has a mental illness which was likely to have the effects claimed and that it is clinically well recognised (as required by the Act).

Effects of other legislation

What about the effects of other legislation?

4.65 An employer is not required to make an adjustment—or do anything under the Act—that would result in a breach of statutory obligations *(S59)*.

If a particular adjustment would breach health and safety or fire legislation then an employer would not have to make it. However, the employer would still have to consider whether he was required to make any other adjustment which would not breach any legislation. For instance, if someone in a wheelchair could not use emergency evacuation arrangements such as a fire escape on a particular floor, it might be reasonable for the employer to have to relocate that person's job to an office where that problem did not arise.

An employer shortlisting applicants to fill a junior office post is considering whether to include a blind applicant who the employer believes might present a safety risk moving around the crowded office. A reasonable adjustment might be to provide mobility training to familiarise the applicant with the work area, so removing any risk there might otherwise be.

What about legislation which places restrictions on what employers can do to recruit disabled people?

4.66 The Disability Discrimination Act does not prevent posts being advertised as open only to disabled candidates. However, the requirement, for example, under Section 7 of the Local Government and Housing Act 1989 that every appointment to local authorities must be made on merit means that a post cannot be so advertised. Applications from disabled people can nevertheless be encouraged. However, this requirement to appoint "on merit" does not exclude the duty under the 1995 Act to make adjustments so a disabled person's "merit" must be assessed taking into account any such adjustments which would have to be made.

5. RECRUITMENT

Discrimination against applicants

How does the Act affect recruitment?

5.1 *The Act says* that it is unlawful for an employer to discriminate against a disabled person:

— in the arrangements made for determining who should be offered employment;
— in the terms on which the disabled person is offered employment; or
— by refusing to offer, or deliberately not offering, the disabled person employment *S4(1)*.

5.2 The word "arrangements" has a wide meaning. Employers should avoid discrimination in, for example, specifying the job, advertising the job, and the processes of selection, including the location and timing of interviews, assessment techniques, interviewing, and selection criteria.

Specifying the job

Does the Act affect how an employer should draw up a job specification?

5.3 Yes. The inclusion of unnecessary or marginal requirements in a job specification can lead to discrimination.

An employer stipulates that employees must be "energetic", when in fact the job in question is largely sedentary in nature. This requirement could unjustifiably exclude some people whose disabilities result in them getting tired more easily than others.

An employer specifies that a driving licence is required for a job which involves limited travelling. An applicant for the job has no driving licence because of the particular effects in his case of cerebral palsy. He is otherwise the best candidate for that job, he could easily and cheaply do the travelling involved other than by driving and it would be a reasonable adjustment for the employer to let him do so. It would be discriminatory to insist on the specification and reject his application solely because he had no driving licence.

5.4 Blanket exclusions (*i.e.* exclusions which do not take account of individual circumstances) may lead to discrimination.

An employer excludes people with epilepsy from all driving jobs. One of the jobs, in practice, only requires a standard licence and normal insurance cover. If, as a result, someone with epilepsy, who has such a licence and can obtain such cover, is turned down for the job then the employer will probably have discriminated unlawfully in excluding her from consideration.

An employer stipulates that candidates for a job must not have a history of mental illness, believing that such candidates will have poor attendance. The employer rejects an applicant solely because he has had a mental illness without checking the individual's probable attendance. Even if good attendance is genuinely essential for the job, this is not likely to be justified and is therefore very likely to be unlawful discrimination.

Can an employer stipulate essential health requirements?

5.5 Yes, but the employer may need to justify doing so, and to show that it would not be reasonable for him to have to waive them, in any individual case.

Can employers simply prefer a certain type of person?

5.6 Stating that a certain personal, medical or health-related characteristic is desirable may also lead to discrimination if the characteristic is not necessary for the performance of the job. Like a requirement, a preference may be decisive against an otherwise well-qualified disabled candidate and may have to be justified in an individual case.

An employer prefers all employees to have a certain level of educational qualification. A woman with a learning disability, which has prevented her from obtaining the preferred qualification, is turned down for a job because she does not have that qualification. If the qualification is not necessary in order to do the job and she is otherwise the best candidate, then the employer will have discriminated unlawfully against her.

Publicising the vacancy

What does the Act say about how an employer can advertise vacancies?

5.7 Where a job is advertised, and a disabled person who applies is refused or deliberately not offered it and complains to an industrial tribunal about disability discrimination, the Act requires the tribunal to assume (unless the employer can prove otherwise) that the reason the person did not get the job was related to his disability if the advertisement could reasonably be taken to indicate:

— that the success of a person's application for the job might depend to any extent on the absence of a disability such as the applicant's; or

— that the employer is unwilling to make an adjustment for a disabled person *(S11)*.

An employer puts in an advertisement for an office worker, "Sorry, but gaining access to our building can be difficult for some people". A man, who as a result of an accident some years previously can only walk with the aid of crutches but can do office work, applies for the job and is turned down. He complains to an industrial tribunal. Because of the wording of the advertisement, the tribunal would have to assume that he did not get the job for a reason relating to his disability unless the employer could prove otherwise.

What is an "advertisement" for the purposes of the Act?

5.8 *According to the Act* "advertisement" includes every form of advertisement or notice, whether to the public or not *(S11(3))*. This would include advertisements internal to a company or office.

Does an employer have to provide information about jobs in alternative formats?

5.9 In particular cases, this may be a reasonable adjustment.

A person whom the employer knows to be disabled asks to be given information about a job in a medium that is accessible to her (in large print, in braille, on tape or on computer disc). It is often likely to be a reasonable adjustment for the employer to comply, particularly if the employer's information systems, and the time available before the new employee is needed, mean it can easily be done.

Can an employer say that he would welcome applications from disabled people?

5.10 Yes. *The Act does not prevent* this and it would be a positive and public statement of the employer's policy.

Can an employer include a question on an application form asking whether someone is disabled?

5.11 Yes. *The Act does not prevent* employers including such a question on application forms. Employers can also ask whether the individual might need an adjustment and what it might be.

Selection

Does the duty of reasonable adjustment apply to applicants?

5.12 *The Act says* that the duty to make a reasonable adjustment does not apply where the employer does not know, and could not reasonably be expected to know, that the disabled person in question is or may be an applicant for the post, or, that a particular applicant has a disability which is likely to place him at a disadvantage *(S6(a))*.

Does an employer have to take special care when considering applications?

5.13 Yes. Employers and their staff or agents must not discriminate against disabled people in the way in which they deal with applications. They may also have to make reasonable adjustments.

Because of his disability, a candidate asks to submit an application in a particular medium, different from that specified for candidates in general (*e.g.* typewritten, by telephone, or on tape). It would normally be a reasonable adjustment for the employer to allow this.

Whom can an employer shortlist for interview?

5.14 If an employer knows that an applicant has a disability and is likely to be at a substantial disadvantage because of the employer's arrangements or premises, the employer should consider whether there is any reasonable adjustment which would bring the disabled person within the field of applicants to be considered even though he would not otherwise be within that field because of that disadvantage. If the employer could only make this judgement with more information it would be discriminatory for him not to put the disabled person on the shortlist for interview if that is how he would normally seek additional information about candidates.

What should an employer do when arranging interviews?

5.15 Employers should think ahead for interviews. Giving applicants the opportunity to indicate any relevant effects of a disability and to suggest adjustments to help overcome any disadvantage the disability may cause, could help the employer avoid discrimination in the interview and in considering the applicant, by clarifying whether any reasonable adjustments may be required.

5.16 Nevertheless, if a person, whom the employer previously did not know, and could not have known, to be disabled, arrives for interview and is placed at a substantial disadvantage because of the arrangements, the employer may still be under a duty to make a reasonable adjustment from the time that he first learns of the disability and the disadvantage. However, what the employer has to do in such circumstances might be less extensive than if advance notice had been given.

What changes might an employer have to make to arrangements for interviews?

5.17 There are many possible reasonable adjustments, depending on the circumstances.

A person has difficulty attending at a particular time because of a disability. It will very likely be reasonable for the employer to have to rearrange the time.

A hearing impaired candidate has substantial difficulties with the interview arrangements. The interviewer may simply need to ensure he faces the applicant and speaks clearly or is prepared to repeat questions. The interviewer should make sure that his face is well lit when talking to someone with a hearing or visual impairment. It will almost always be reasonable for an employer to have to provide such help with communication support if the interviewee would otherwise be at a substantial disadvantage.

An employer who pays expenses to candidates who come for interview could well have to pay additional expenses to meet any special requirements of a disabled person arising from any substantial disadvantage to which she would otherwise be put by the interview arrangements. This might include paying travelling expenses for a support worker or reasonable cost of travel by taxi, rather than by bus or train, if this is necessary because of the disability.

A job applicant does not tell an employer (who has no knowledge of her disability) in advance that she uses a wheelchair. On arriving for the interview she discovers that the room is not accessible. The employer did not know of the disability and so could not have been expected to make changes in advance. However, it would still be a reasonable adjustment for the employer to hold the interview in an alternative accessible room, if a suitable one was easily available at the time with no, or only an acceptable level of, disruption or additional cost.

Should an employer consider making changes to the way the interview is carried out?

5.18 Yes, although whether any change is needed—and, if so, what change—will depend on the circumstances.

It would almost always be reasonable to allow an applicant with a learning disability to bring a supportive person such as a friend or relative to assist when answering questions that are not part of tests.

It would normally be reasonable to allow a longer time for an interview to someone with a hearing impairment using a sign language interpreter to communicate.

Does an employer have to make changes to anticipate *any* disabled person applying for a job?

5.19 No. An employer is not required to make changes in anticipation of applications from disabled people in general. It is only if the employer knows or could be reasonably expected to know that a particular disabled person is, or may be, applying and is likely to be substantially disadvantaged by the employer's premises or arrangements, that the employer may have to make changes.

Should an employer ask about a disability?

5.20 The Act does not prohibit an employer from seeking information about a disability but an employer must not use it to discriminate against a disabled person. An employer should ask only about a disability if it is, or may be, relevant to the person's ability to do the job—after a reasonable adjustment, if necessary. Asking about the effects of a disability might be important in deciding what adjustments ought to be made. The employer should avoid discriminatory questions.

An applicant whose disability has left him using a wheelchair but healthy, is asked by an employer whether any extra leave might be required because of the condition. This is unlikely to be discriminatory because a need for extra time off work may be a substantial factor relevant to the person's ability to do the job. Therefore such a question would normally be justified. Similarly, a reasonable question about whether any changes may need to be made to the workplace to accommodate the use of the wheelchair would probably not be discriminatory.

Does the Act prevent employers carrying out aptitude or other tests in the recruitment process?

5.21 No, but routine testing of all candidates may still discriminate against particular individuals or substantially disadvantage them. If so, the employer would need to revise the tests—or the way the results of such tests are assessed—to take account of specific disabled candidates, except where the nature and form of the test were necessary to assess a matter relevant to the job. It may, for instance, be a reasonable adjustment to accept a lower "pass rate" for a person whose disability inhibits performance in such a test. The extent to which this is required would depend on how closely the test is related to the job in question and what adjustments the employer might have to make if the applicant were given the job.

An employer sets a numeracy test for prospective employees. A person with a learning disability takes the test and does not achieve the level the employer normally stipulates. If the job in fact entails very little numerical work and the candidate is otherwise well suited for the job it is likely to be a reasonable adjustment for the employer to waive the requirement.

An employer sets candidates a short oral test. An applicant is disabled by a bad stammer, but only under stress. It may be a reasonable adjustment to allow her more time to complete the tests, or to give the test in written form instead, though not if oral communication is relevant to the job and assessing this was the purpose of the test.

Can an employer specify qualifications?

5.22 An employer is entitled to specify that applicants for a job must have certain qualifications. However, if a disabled person is rejected for the job because he lacks a qualification, the employer will have to justify that rejection if the reason why the person is rejected (*i.e.* the lack of a qualification) is connected with his disability. Justification will involve showing that the qualification is relevant and significant in terms of the particular job and the particular applicant, and that there is no reasonable adjustment which would change this. In some circumstances it might be feasible to reassign those duties to which the qualification relates, or to waive the requirement for the qualification if this particular applicant has alternative evidence of the necessary level of competence.

An employer seeking someone to work in an administrative post specifies that candidates must have the relevant NVQ Level 4 qualification. If Level 4 fairly reflects the complex and varied nature and substantial personal responsibility of the work, and these aspects of the job cannot reasonably be altered, the employer will be able to justify rejecting a disabled applicant who has only been able to reach Level 3 because of his disability and who cannot show the relevant level of competence by other means.

An employer specifies that two GCSEs are required for a certain post. This is to show that a candidate has the general level of ability required. No particular subjects are specified. An applicant whose dyslexia prevented her from passing written examinations cannot meet this requirement, but the employer would be unable to justify rejecting her on this account alone if she could show she nevertheless had the skill and intelligence called for in the post.

Can an employer insist on a disabled person having a medical examination?

5.23 Yes. However, if an employer insists on a medical check for a disabled person and not others, without justification, he will probably be discriminating unlawfully. The fact that a person has a disability is unlikely in itself to justify singling out that person to have a health check, although such action might be justified in relation to some jobs.

An employer requires all candidates for employment to have a medical examination. That employer would normally be entitled to include a disabled person.

An applicant for a job has a disabling heart condition. The employer routinely issues a health questionnaire to job applicants, and requires all applicants who state they have a disability to undergo a medical examination. Under the Act, the employer would not be justified in requiring a medical examination whenever an applicant states he has a disability—for example, this would not normally be justified if the disability is clearly relevant neither to the job nor to the environment in which the job is done. However, the employer would probably be justified in asking the applicant with the disabling heart condition to have a medical examination restricted to assessing its implications for the particular job in its context. If, for example, the job required lifting and carrying but these abilities were limited by the condition, the employer would also have to consider whether it would be reasonable for him to have to make a change such as providing a mechanical means of lifting and/or carrying, or arranging for the few items above the person's limit to be dealt with by another person, whilst ensuring that any health and safety provisions were not breached.

How can an employer take account of medical evidence?

5.24 In most cases, having a disability does not adversely affect a person's general health. Medical evidence about a disability can justify an adverse employment decision (such as dismissing or not promoting). It will not generally do so if there is no effect on the person's ability to do the work (or any effect is less than substantial), however great the effects of the disability are in other ways. The condition or effects must be relevant to the employer's decision.

An applicant for a post on a short-term contract has a progressive condition which has some effects, but is likely to have substantial adverse effects only in the long term. The likelihood of these long-term effects would not itself be a justifiable reason for the employer to reject him.

An employer requires all candidates for a certain job to be able to work for at least two years to complete a particular work project. Medical evidence shows that a particular candidate is unlikely to be able to continue working for that long. It would be lawful to reject that candidate if the two-year requirement was justified in terms of the work, and if it would not be reasonable for the employer to have to waive it in the particular circumstances.

Advice from an occupational health expert simply that an employer was "unfit for work" would not mean that the employer's duty to make a reasonable adjustment was waived.

What will help an employer decide to select a particular disabled person?

5.25 The employer must take into account any adjustments that it is reasonable for him to have to make. Suggestions made by the candidate at any stage may assist in identifying these.

What if a disabled person just isn't the right person for the job?

5.26 An employer must not discriminate against a disabled candidate, but there is no requirement (aside from reasonable adjustment) to treat a disabled person more favourably than he treats or would treat others. An employer will have to assess an applicant's merits as they would be if any reasonable adjustments required under the Act had been made. If, after allowing for those adjustments, a disabled person would not be the best person for the job the employer would not have to recruit that person.

Terms and conditions of service

Are there restrictions on the terms and conditions an employer can offer a disabled person?

5.27 Terms and conditions of service should not discriminate against a disabled person. The employer should consider whether any reasonable adjustments need to be made to the terms and conditions which would otherwise apply.

An employer's terms and conditions state the hours an employee has to be in work. It might be a reasonable adjustment to change these hours for someone whose disability means that she has difficulty using public transport during rush hours.

Does that mean that an employer can never offer a disabled person a less favourable contract?

5.28 No. Such a contract may be justified if there is a material and substantial reason and there is no reasonable adjustment which can be made to remove that reason.

A person's disability means she has significantly lower output than other employees doing similar work, even after an adjustment. Her work is of neither lower nor higher quality than theirs. The employer would be justified in paying her less in proportion to the lower output if it affected the value of her work to the business.

Can employers still operate performance-related pay?

5.29 *Regulations provide* that this is justified so long as the scheme applies equally to all employees, or all of a particular class of employees. There would be no requirement to make a reasonable adjustment to an arrangement of this kind to ensure (for example) that a person's pay was topped up if a deteriorating condition happened to lead to lower performance (Employment Regulations: see para. 1.6). However, there would still be a duty to make a reasonable adjustment to any aspect of the premises or work arrangements if that would prevent the disability reducing the employee's performance.

6. EMPLOYMENT

Discrimination against employees

Does the Act cover all areas of employment?

6.1 Yes. *The Act says* that it is unlawful for an employer to discriminate against a disabled person whom he employs:
— in the terms of employment which he affords him;
— in the opportunities which he affords him for promotion, a transfer, training or receiving any other benefit;

— by refusing to afford him, or deliberately not affording him, any such opportunity; or
— by dismissing him, or subjecting him to any other detriment *(S4(2))*.

6.2 Therefore, an employer should not discriminate in relation to, for example: terms and conditions of service, arrangements made for induction, arrangements made for employees who become disabled (or who have a disability which worsens), opportunities for promotion, transfer, training or receiving any other benefit, or refusal of such opportunities, pensions, dismissal or any detriment.

Induction

What is the effect on induction procedures?

6.3 Employers must not discriminate in their induction procedures. The employer may have to make adjustments to ensure a disabled person is introduced into a new working environment in a clearly structured and supported way with, if necessary, an individually tailored induction programme *(S4(2) and S6(1))*.

An employer runs a one day induction course for a new recruits. A recruit with a learning disability is put at a substantial disadvantage by the way the course is normally run. The employer might have to make an alternative arrangement: for example running a separate, longer course for the person, or permitting someone to sit in on the normal course to provide support, assistance or encouragement.

Promotion and transfer

What are an employer's duties as far as promotion and transfer are concerned?

6.4 Employers must not discriminate in assessing a disabled person's suitability for promotion or transfer, in the practical arrangements necessary to enable the promotion or transfer to take place, in the operation of the appraisal, selection and promotion or transfer process, or in the new job itself—and may have to make a reasonable adjustment *(S4(2)(b) and (c) and S6(1))*.

A garage owner does not consider for promotion to assistant manager a clerk who has lost the use of her right arm, because he wrongly and unreasonably believes that her disability might prevent her performing competently in a managerial post. The reason used by the employer to deny the clerk promotion has meant that she was discriminated against.

An employer considering a number of people for a job on promotion is aware that one of the candidates for interview has a hearing impairment, but does not find out whether the person needs any special arrangements for the interview, for example a sign language interpreter. If the candidate requires such an adjustment, and it would be reasonable for the employer to have to make it, the employer would fail in his duty if he did not make that adjustment.

A civil engineer whose disability involves kidney dialysis treatment, is based in London and regularly visits hospital for the treatment. She wishes to transfer to a vacant post in her company's Scottish office. She meets all the requirements for the post, but her transfer is turned down on the ground that her need for treatment would mean that, away from the facilities in London, she would be absent from work for longer. The employer had made no attempt to discuss this with her or get medical advice. If the employer had done so, it would have been clear that similar treatment would be equally available in the new locality. In these circumstances, the employer probably could not show that relying on this reason was justified.

Someone disabled by a back injury is seeking promotion to supervisor. A minor duty involves assisting with the unloading of the weekly delivery van, which the person's back injury would prevent. In assessing her suitability for promotion, the employer should consider whether reallocating this duty to another person would be a reasonable adjustment.

What should an employer do to check that promotion and transfer arrangements do not discriminate?

6.5 The employer should review the arrangements to check that qualifications required are justified for the job to be done. He should also check that other arrangements, for example systems which determine other criteria for a particular job, do not exclude disabled people who may have been unable to meet those criteria because of their disability but would be capable of performing well in the job.

Training and other benefits provided by the employer

Does the Act apply to the provision of training?

6.6 Yes. Employers must not discriminate in selection for training and must make any necessary reasonable adjustments *(S4(2)(b) and (c) and S6(1))*.

An employer wrongly assumes that a disabled person will be unwilling or unable to undertake demanding training or attend a residential training course, instead of taking an informed decision. He may well not be able to justify a decision based on that assumption.

An employer may need to alter the time or the location of the training for someone with a mobility problem, make training manuals, slides or other visual media accessible to a visually impaired employee, perhaps by providing braille versions or having them read out, or ensure that an induction loop is available for someone with a hearing impairment.

An employer refuses to allow a disabled employee to be coached for a theory examination relating to practical work which the disability prevented the employee from doing. The employer would almost always be justified in refusing to allow the coaching because it was designed to equip employees for an area of work for which, because of the disability, the person could not be suited even by a reasonable adjustment.

What about other benefits provided by employers?

6.7 An employer must not discriminate in providing disabled people with opportunities for receiving benefits (which include "facilities" and "services") which are available to other employees *(S4(2)(b) and (c))*. The employer must make any necessary reasonable adjustment to the way the benefits are provided *(S6(1))* although this does not apply to benefits under occupational pension schemes or certain other employment related benefit schemes (paragraph 6.16).

Benefits might include canteens, meal vouchers, social clubs and other recreational activities, dedicated car parking spaces, discounts on products, bonuses, share options, hairdressing, clothes allowances, financial services, healthcare, medical assistance/insurance, transport to work, company car, education assistance, workplace nurseries, and rights to special leave.

If physical features of a company's social club would inhibit a disabled person's access it might be a reasonable adjustment for the employer to make suitable modifications.

An employer provides dedicated car parking spaces near to the workplace. It is likely to be reasonable for the employer to have to allocate one of these spaces to a disabled employee who has significant difficulty getting from the public car parks further away that he would otherwise have to use.

6.8 If an employer provides benefits to the public, or to a section of the public which includes the disabled employee, provision of those benefits will normally fall outside the duty not to discriminate in employment. Instead, the duty in the Act not to discriminate in providing goods, facilities and services will apply. However, the employment duty will apply if the benefit to employees is materially different (*e.g.* at a discount), is governed by the contract of employment, or relates to training *(S4(2) and (3))*.

A disabled employee of a supermarket chain who believes he has been discriminated against when buying goods as a customer at any branch of the supermarket would have no claim under the employment provisions. However, if that employee were using a discount card provided only to employees, then the employment provisions would apply if any less favourable treatment related to his use of the card.

Occupational pension schemes and insurance

What does the Act say about occupational pension schemes?

6.9 *The Act inserts* into every scheme a "non-discrimination" rule. The trustees or managers of the scheme are prohibited by that rule from doing—or omitting to do—anything to members or non-members of schemes that would be unlawful discrimination if done by an employer *(S17)*. References to employers in paragraphs 6.11–6.15 should therefore be read as if they also apply to trustees or managers when appropriate.

When is less favourable treatment justified?

6.10 Less favourable treatment for a reason relating to a disability can be justified only if the reason is material and substantial.

Trustees of a pension scheme would not be justified in excluding a woman simply because she had a visual impairment. That fact, in itself, would be no reason why she should not receive the same pension benefits as any other employee.

6.11 There are circumstances when a disabled person's health or health prognosis is such that the cost of providing benefits under a pension scheme is substantially greater than it would be for a person without the disability. In these circumstances *Regulations provide* that an employer is regarded as justified in treating a disabled person less favourably in applying the eligibility conditions for receiving the benefit. Employers should satisfy themselves, if necessary with actuarial advice and/or medical evidence, of the likelihood of there being a substantially greater cost (Employment Regulations: see para. 1.6).

When could the justification be used?

6.12 The justification would be available whenever the disabled person is considered for admission to the scheme. However, the justification cannot be applied to a disabled member, unless a term was imposed at the time of admission which allowed this.

Which benefits does this justification apply to?

6.13 The justification can apply to the following types of benefits provided by an occupational pension scheme: termination of service, retirement, old age or death, accident, injury, sickness or invalidity (Employment Regulations: see para. 1.6).

Would a minor degree of extra cost amount to a justification for less favourable treatment?

6.14 No. Only the likelihood of a substantial additional cost should be taken to be a justification. Substantial means something more than minor or trivial (Employment Regulations: see para. 1.6).

An employer receives medical advice that an individual with multiple sclerosis is likely to retire early on health grounds. The employer obtains actuarial advice that the cost of providing that early retirement benefit would be substantially greater than an employee without MS and so the individual is refused access to the scheme. This is justified.

What happens to an employee's rate of contributions if the employer is justified in refusing the employee access to some benefits but not others?

6.15 *Regulations provide* that if the employer sets a uniform rate of contribution the employer would be justified in applying it to a disabled person. A disabled person could therefore be required to pay the same rate of contributions as other employees, even if not eligible for some of the benefits (Employment Regulations: see para. 1.6).

Does the duty to make a reasonable adjustment apply?

6.16 No. The duty of reasonable adjustment does not apply to the provision of benefits under an occupational pension scheme or any other benefit payable in money or money's worth under a scheme or arrangement for the benefit of employees in respect of:
— termination of service;
— retirement, old age or death; or
— accident, injury, sickness or invalidity *(S6(11))*. (Although there is power to add other matters to this list by regulations, none have been added at the date of this Code).

Therefore, neither the employer nor the scheme's trustees or managers need to make any adjustment for a disabled person who, without that adjustment, will be justifiably denied access either to such a scheme or to a benefit under the scheme. Nor will they have to make an adjustment for someone receiving less benefit because they justifiably receive a lower rate of pay.

Does the Act cover the provision of insurance schemes for individual employees?

6.17 The Act also applies to provision of group insurance, such as permanent health insurance or life insurance, by an insurance company for employees under an arrangement with their employer. A disabled person in, or who applies or is considering applying to join, a group of employees covered by such an arrangement is protected from discrimination in the provision of the insurance services in the same way as if he were a member of the public seeking the services of that insurance company under the part of the Act relating to the provision of goods, facilities and services. However, the right of redress in this case would be exercised through an industrial tribunal (and not the courts) *(S18)*.

Does the Act cover the provision of insurance to an employer?

6.18 The employer may have to make reasonable adjustments to remove any disadvantage caused to a disabled person which arose from the arrangements made by the employer to provide himself with insurance cover. Such adjustments could include measures which would reduce any risk otherwise posed by the disabled person, so that the insurer would then provide cover, or seeking alternative cover. If cover could not be obtained at all at realistic cost it is most unlikely that the employer would have to bear the risk himself.

It comes to an employer's attention that someone who works for his antiques business has epilepsy. The employer is obliged to notify his insurance company who refuse to cover the employer against damage caused by the disabled person. To avoid dismissing the employee, it might be reasonable for the employer to have to bar the person from contact with valuable items, if this would mean the insurance company then provided cover.

Retention of disabled employees

6.19 An employer must not discriminate against an employee who becomes disabled, or has a disability which worsens *(S4(2))*. The issue of retention might also arise when an employee has a stable impairment but the nature of his employment changes.

6.20 If as a result of the disability an employer's arrangements or a physical feature of the employer's premises place the employee at a substantial disadvantage in doing his existing job, the employer must first consider any reasonable adjustment that would resolve the difficulty. The employer may also need to consult the disabled person at appropriate stages about what his needs are and what effect the disability might have on future employment, for example, where the employee has a progressive condition. The nature of the reasonable adjustments which an employer may have to consider will depend on the circumstances of the case.

It may be possible to modify a job to accommodate an employee's changed needs. This might be by rearranging working methods or giving another employee certain minor tasks the newly disabled person can no longer do, providing practical aids or adaptations to premises or equipment, or allowing the disabled person to work at different times or places from those with equivalent jobs (for instance, it may be that a change to part-time work might be appropriate for someone who needed to spend some time each work having medical treatment).

A newly disabled employee is likely to need time to readjust. For example, an employer might allow: a trial period to assess whether the employee is able to cope with the current job, or a new one; the employee initially to work from home; a gradual build-up to full time hours; or additional training for a person with learning disabilities who moves to another workplace.

It may be a reasonable adjustment for an employer to move a newly disabled person to a different post within the organisation if a suitable vacancy exists or is expected shortly.

Additional job coaching may be necessary to enable a disabled person to take on a new job.

In many cases where no reasonable adjustment would overcome a particular disability so as to enable the disabled person to continue with similar terms or conditions, it might be reasonable for the employer to have to offer a disabled employee a lower-paying job, applying the rate of pay that would apply to such a position under his usual pay practices.

If new technology (for instance a telephone or information technology system) puts a disabled person at a substantial disadvantage compared with non-disabled people, then the employer would be under a duty to make a reasonable adjustment. For example, some telephone systems may interfere with hearing aids for people with hearing impairments and the quality of the inductive coupler may need to be improved.

Termination of employment

6.21 Dismissal—including compulsory early retirement—of a disabled person for a reason relating to the disability would need to be justified and the reason for it would have to be one which could not be removed by any reasonable adjustment.

It would be justifiable to terminate the employment of an employee whose disability makes it impossible for him any longer to perform the main functions of his job, if an adjustment such as a move to a vacant post elsewhere in the business is not practicable or otherwise not reasonable for the employer to have to make.

It would be justifiable to terminate the employment of an employee with a worsening progressive condition if the increasing degree of adjustment necessary to accommodate the effects of the condition (shorter hours of work or falling productivity, say) became unreasonable for the employer to have to make.

An employer who needs to reduce the workforce would have to ensure that any scheme which was introduced for choosing candidates for redundancy did not discriminate against disabled people. Therefore, if a criterion for redundancy would apply to a disabled person for a reason relating to the disability, that criterion would have to be "material" and "substantial" and the employer would have to consider whether a reasonable adjustment would prevent the criterion applying to the disabled person after all.

Harassment

What does the Act say about harassment?

6.22 The Act does not refer to harassment as a separate issue. However, harassing a disabled person on account of a disability will almost always amount to a "detriment" under the Act. (Victimisation is covered in paragraphs 4.53–4.54.)

Are employers liable for harassment by their employees?

6.23 An employer is responsible for acts of harassment by employees in the course of their employment unless the employer took such steps as were reasonably practicable to prevent it. As a minimum first step harassment because of disability should be made a disciplinary matter and staff should be made aware that it will be taken seriously.

7. PARTICULAR PROVISIONS

Discrimination against contract workers

7.1 The Act deals specifically with work which is carried out by individuals ("contract workers") for a person (a "principal") who hires them under contract from their employer (generally an employment business)—referred to below as the "sending" employer.

What does the Act say about contract workers?

7.2 *The Act says* that it is unlawful for a principal to discriminate against a disabled person:
— in the terms on which the person is allowed to do the contract work;
— by not allowing the person to do, or continue to do, the contract work;
— in the way he affords the person access to, or by failing to afford him access to, benefits in relation to contract work; or
— by subjecting the person to any other detriment in relation to contract work *(S12(1))*.

7.3 *The Act and Regulations apply*, generally speaking, as if the principal were, or would be, the actual employer of the contract worker. Therefore, the same definition of "discrimination"—including the need to justify less favourable treatment—applies as for employers *(S12(3))*.

> The employer of a labourer, who some years ago was disabled by clinical depression but has since recovered, proposes to supply him to a contractor to work on a building site. Although his past disability is covered by the Act, the site manager refuses to accept him because of his medical history. Unless the contractor can show that the manager's action is justified, the contractor would be acting unlawfully.

What will be the effect of the duty to make adjustments for principals?

7.4 The duty to make a reasonable adjustment applies to a principal as to an employer *(S12(3))*.

7.5 In deciding whether any, and if so, what, adjustment would be reasonable for a principal to have to make, the period for which the contract worker will work for the principal is important. It might well be unreasonable for a principal to have to make certain adjustments if the worker will be with the principal for only a short time.

> An employment business enters into a contract with a firm of accountants to provide an assistant for two weeks to cover an unexpected absence. The employment business wishes to put forward a person who, because of his disability, finds it difficult to travel during the rush hour and would like his working hours to be modified accordingly. It might not be reasonable for the firm to have to agree given the short time in which to negotiate and implement the new hours.

Will the principal and the "sending" employer both have duties to make reasonable adjustments?

7.6 Both the "sending" employer and the principal may separately be under a duty of reasonable adjustment in the case of a contract worker who is disabled. If the "sending" employer's own premises or arrangements place the contract worker at a substantial disadvantage, then the "sending" employer may have a duty to make a reasonable adjustment *(S6(1))*. The "sending" employer may also have a duty to make a reasonable adjustment where a similar substantial disadvantage is likely to affect a contract worker as a result of the arrangements or premises of all or most of the principals to whom he might be supplied. The employer would not have to take separate steps in relation to each principal, but would have to make any reasonable adjustment within his power which would overcome the disadvantage wherever it might arise. The principal would not have to make any adjustment which the employer should make (Employment Regulations: see para. 1.6). However, subject to that the principal would be responsible only for any additional reasonable adjustment which is necessary solely because of the principal's own arrangements or premises *(S6(1)* applied by *S12(3))*. It would also usually be reasonable for a principal and a "sending" employer to have to cooperate with any steps taken by the other to assist a disabled contract worker.

> A travel agency hires a clerical worker from an employment business to fulfil a three month contract to file travel invoices during the busy summer holiday period. The contract worker is a wheelchair user, and is quite capable of doing the job if a few minor, temporary changes are made to the arrangement of furniture in the office. It would be reasonable for the travel agency to make this adjustment.

> A bank hires a blind word processor operator as a contract worker from an employment business. The employment business provides her with a specially adapted portable computer because she would otherwise be at a similar substantial disadvantage in doing the work wherever she does it. (In such circumstances the bank would not have to provide a specially adapted computer if the employment business did not.) The bank would have to cooperate by letting the contract worker use her computer whilst working for the bank if it is compatible with the bank's systems. If not, it could be a reasonable adjustment for the bank to make the computer compatible and for the employment business to allow that change to be made.

What about contract workers in small firms?

7.7 The Act applies to any employment business which has 20 or more employees (incuding people currently employed by it but hired out to principals). It also applies to any principal who has 20 or more workers (counting both the principal's own employees and any contract workers currently working for the principal). It does not apply to employment businesses or principals with fewer than 20 employees. Note the extended definition of "employment" in the Act (see paragraph 2.8).

> An employment business has 15 employees (including people currently hired out to others) and enters a contract to provide a worker in a shop. The shop employs 29 people. Neither the duty not to discriminate nor the duty to make a reasonable adjustment applies to the employment business, but both duties apply to the owner of the shop. However, the length of time the worker was contracted to work at the shop would be an important factor in assessing whether the shop-owner had to make any significant adjustment.

> A deaf individual is employed by an employment business that has 100 employees (including people currently hired out to others). He is hired regularly to do contract work and, as a reasonable adjustment, the business provides a portable induction loop for assignments. If he works for a principal with, say, 17 workers, (counting both employees and contract workers) that principal would not be required to cooperate with use of the induction loop. However, if the principal has 20 or more such workers the principal would be obliged to cooperate.

What about the Supported Placement Scheme (SPS)?

7.8 These arrangements also apply to the Employment Service's Supported Placement Scheme (SPS) for severely disabled people. The "contractor" under the scheme (usually a local authority or voluntary body) is the equivalent of the "sending" employer, and the "host employer" is the equivalent of the principal. A local authority can even be both the contractor and the host employer at the same time (as can a voluntary body) in which case the duty not to discriminate and the duty of reasonable adjustment would apply to it as to an employer.

Provisions applying to trade organisations

What does the Act say about trade organisations?

7.9 A trade organisation is defined as an organisation of workers or of employers, or any other organisation whose members carry on a particular profession or trade for the purposes of which the organisation exists *(S13(4))*. Therefore trade unions, employers' associations, and similar bodies like the Law Society and chartered professional institutions, for example, must comply with the legislation.

7.10 *The Act says* that it is unlawful for a trade organisation to discriminate against a disabled person:
— in the terms on which it is prepared to admit the person to membership; or
— by refusing to accept, or deliberately not accepting, an application for membership.

It is also unlawful for a trade organisation to discriminate against a disabled member of the organisation:
— in the way it affords the person access to any benefits or by refusing or deliberately omitting to afford access to them;
— by depriving the person of membership, or varying the terms of membership; or
— by subjecting the person to any other detriment *(S13)*.

Trade organisations should therefore check that they do not discriminate as regards, for example, training facilities, welfare or insurance schemes, invitations to attend events, processing of grievances, assistance to members in their employers' disciplinary or dismissal procedures.

7.11 *The Act defines* discrimination by a trade organisation in similar terms to the definition relating to discrimination by an employer. Therefore, the need to justify less favourable treatment for a reason relating to disability applies as in the case of an employer *(S14(3))*.

A trade organisation is arranging a trip to some of its members' workplaces but it decides to exclude a member in a wheelchair because too many of the sites are inaccessible to make participation worthwhile. This could well be justified. (Note, however, paragraph 7.12.)

Do trade organisations have a duty to make adjustments?

7.12 *The Act includes* a requirement on trade organisations to make reasonable adjustments *(S15)*. However, this duty will not be brought into force until after the other employment provisions, at a date which will be subject to consultation.

What about the actions of employees or representatives of trade organisations?

7.13 Individual employees or agents of trade organisations who have dealings with members or applicants are treated in the same way as individual employees or agents of employers who deal with job applicants or employees: the trade organisation is respnsible for their actions *(S58)*.

8. RESOLVING DISAGREEMENTS WITHIN THE EMPLOYING ORGANISATION

What does the Act say about resolving disagreements?

8.1 The Act does not require employers to resolve disputes within their organisations. However, it is in an employer's interests to resolve problems as they arise where possible. This should be in a non-discriminatory way to comply with the Act's general provisions.

8.2 One method might be the use of a grievance procedure. Grievance procedures provide an open and fair way for employees to make known their concerns and enable grievances to be resolved quickly before they become major difficulties. Use of the procedures can highlight areas where the employer's duty of reasonable adjustment may not have been observed, and can prevent misunderstandings in this area leading to tribunal complaints.

Do existing grievance and disciplinary procedures need changing?

8.3 Where grievance or disciplinary procedures are in place, the employer might wish to review, and where necessary adapt, them to ensure that they are flexible enough to be used by disabled employees. Where a formal grievance (or disciplinary) procedure operates, it must be open, or applied, to disabled employees on the same basis as to others. Employers will have to ensure that grievance (or disciplinary) procedures do not, in themselves, discriminate against disabled employees and may have to make reasonable adjustments to enable some disabled employees to use grievance procedures effectively or to ensure disciplinary procedures have the same impact on disabled employees as on others.

An employee with a learning disability has to attend an interview under the employer's disciplinary procedures. The employee would like his guardian or a friend to be present. The employer agrees to this but refuses to rearrange the interview to a time which is more convenient to the guardian or friend. The employer may be in breach of the duty to make a reasonable adjustment.

(See Annex 3 for information about industrial tribunals.)

ANNEX 1. WHAT IS MEANT BY DISABILITY

1. This Annex is included to aid understanding about who is covered by the Act and should provide sufficient information on the definition of disability to cover the large majority of cases. The definition of disability in the Act is designed to cover only people who would generally be considered to be disabled. A Government publication *Guidance on matters to be taken into account in determining questions relating to the definition of disability*, is also available.

When is a person disabled?

2. A person has a disability if he has a physical or mental impairment which has a substantial and long-term adverse effect on his ability to carry out normal day-to-day activities.

What about people who have recovered from a disability?

3. People who have had a disability within the definition are protected from discrimination even if they have since recovered.

What does "impairment" cover?

4. It covers physical or mental impairments; this includes sensory impairments, such as those affecting sight or hearing.

Are all mental impairments covered?

5. The term "mental impairment" is intended to cover a wide range of impairments relating to mental functioning, including what are often known as learning disabilities. However, the Act states that it does not include any impairment resulting from or consisting of a mental illness, unless that illness is a clinically well-recognised illness. A clinically well-recognised illness is one that is recognised by a respected body of medical opinion.

What is a "substantial" adverse effect?

6. A substantial adverse effect is something which is more than a minor or trivial effect. The requirement that an effect must be substantial reflects the general understanding of disability as a limitation going beyond the normal differences in ability which might exist among people.

What is a "long-term" effect?

7. A long-term effect of an impairment is one:
— which has lasted at least 12 months; or
— where the total period for which it lasts is likely to be at least 12 months; or
— which is likely to last for the rest of the life of the person affected.

8. Effects which are not long-term would therefore include loss of mobility due to a broken limb which is likely to heal within 12 months and the effects of temporary infections, from which a person would be likely to recover within 12 months.

What if the effects come and go over a period of time?

9. If an impairment has had a substantial adverse effect on normal day-to-day activities but that effect ceases, the substantial effect is treated as continuing if it is likely to recur; that is if it is more probable than not that the effect will *recur*. To take the example of a person with rheumatoid arthritis whose impairment has a substantial adverse effect, which then ceases to be substantial (*i.e.* the person has a period of remission). The effects are to be treated as if they are continuing, and are likely to continue beyond 12 months, *if*:
— the impairment remains; and
— at least one recurrence of the substantial effect is likely to take place 12 months or more after the initial occurrence.
This would then be a long-term effect.

What are "normal day-to-day activities"?

10. They are activities which are carried out by most people on a fairly regular and frequent basis. The term is not intended to include activities which are normal only for a particular person or group of people, such as playing a musical instrument, or a sport, to a provessional standard or performing a skilled or specialised task at work. However, someone who is affected in such a specialised way but is *also* affected in normal day-to-day activities, would be covered by this part of the definition. The test of whether an impairment affects normal day-to-day activities is whether it affects one of the broad categories of capacity listed in Schedule 1 to the Act. They are:
— mobility;
— manual dexterity;
— physical co-ordination;
— continence;
— ability to lift, carry or otherwise move everyday objects;
— speech, hearing or eyesight;
— memory or ability to concentrate, learn or understand; or
— perception of the risk of physical danger.

What about treatment?

11. Someone with an impairment may be receiving medical or other treatment which alleviates or removes the effects (though not the impairment). In such cases, the treatment is ignored and the impairment is taken to have the effect it would have had without such treatment. This does not apply if substantial adverse effects are not likely to recur even if the treatment stops (*i.e.* the impairment has been cured).

Does this include people who wear spectacles?

12. No. The sole exception to the rule about ignoring the effects of treatment is the wearing of spectacles or contact lenses. In this case, the effect while the person is wearing spectacles or contact lenses should be considered.

Are people who have disfigurements covered?

13. People with severe disfigurements are covered by the Act. They do not need to demonstrate that the impairment has a substantial adverse effect on their ability to carry out normal day-to-day activities.

What about people who know their condition is going to get worse over time?

14. Progressive conditions are conditions which are likely to change and develop over time. Examples given in the Act are cancer, multiple sclerosis, muscular dystrophy and HIV infection. Where a person has a progressive condition he will be covered by the Act from the moment the condition leads to an impairment which has *some* effect on ability to carry out normal day-to-day activities, even though not a *substantial* effect, if that impairment is likely eventually to have a substantial adverse effect on such ability.

What about people who are registered disabled?

15. Those registered as disabled under the Disabled Persons (Employment) Act 1944 both on 12 January 1995 and 2 December 1996 will be treated as being disabled under the Disability Discrimination Act 1995 for three years from the latter date. At all times from 2 December 1996 onwards they will be covered by the Acts as people who have had a disability. This does not preclude them from being covered as having a current disability any time after the three year period has finished. Whether they are or not will depend on whether they—like anyone else—meet the definition of disability in the Act.

Are people with genetic conditions covered?

16. If a genetic condition has no effect on ability to carry out normal day-to-day activities, the person is not covered. Diagnosis does not in itself bring someone within the definition. If the condition is progressive, then the rule about progressive conditions applies.

Are any conditions specifically excluded from the coverage of the Act?

17. Yes. Certain conditions are to be regarded as not amounting to impairments for the purposes of the Act. These are:
— addiction to or dependency on alcohol, nicotine, or any other substance (other than as a result of the substance being medically prescribed);
— seasonal allergic rhinitis (*e.g.* hayfever), except where it aggravates the effect of another condition;
— tendency to set fires;
— tendency to steal;
— tendency to physical or sexual abuse of other persons;
— exhibitionism;
— voyeurism.
Also, disfigurements which consist of a tattoo (which has not been removed), non-medical body piercing, or something attached through such piercing, are to be treated as not having a substantial adverse effect on the person's ability to carry out normal day-to-day activities (Definition Regulations: see para. 1.6).

ANNEX 2. HOW TO GET FURTHER INFORMATION, HELP AND ADVICE

1. A range of leaflets about various aspects of the Act is available. To obtain copies, all 0345 622 633 (local rate), or textphone 0345 622 644. Copies of the leaflets are also available in braille and audio cassette.

2. Statutory Guidance on the definition of disability is produced separately. This can be obtained from HMSO bookshops—see back cover of this Code. This Guidance should prove helpful where it is not clear whether or not a person has or has had a disability.

3. There is a wide range of practical help and advice available to assist employers in the recruitment and employment of people, including disabled people, for example from Jobcentres, Careers Service offices, Training and Enterprise Councils (in England and Wales) and Local Enterprise Companies (in Scotland). Addresses and telephone numbers are available in local telephone directories.

4. Where necessary, specialist help and advice for disabled people and for employers who might, or do, employ disabled people is available from the Employment Service through its local Placing, Assessment and Counselling Teams (PACTs). PACTs can help with issues related to employing disabled people, but cannot advise on an employer's specific legal obligations.

5. PACTs may be able to provide help with special aids, equipment and other measures to overcome the effects of disability in the working environment.

6. The addresses and telephone numbers of PACTs are listed in local telephone directories under "Employment Service", or can be obtained from the nearest Jobcentre.

7. Many specialist organisations for disabled people also offer a range of employment help and advice. The Employment Service publish a booklet called *Sources of Information an Advice (Ref. PGP6)* which lists many of the specialist organisations offering help to employers on employment and disability issues. The booklet can be obtained from PACTs.

8. The Advisory, Conciliation and Arbitration Service (ACAS) can help employers and individuals with factual information on the legislation and assistance related to its effects on industrial relations practices and procedures. The address and telephone numbers of ACAS offices are listed in local telephone directories under "ACAS".

9. Employers working in historic buildings, or other heritage properties, may also wish to obtain a copy of *Easy Access to Historic Properties* from English Heritage at 23 Savile Row, London W1X 1AB. Tel: 0171 973 3434.

10. Disability can take a very large number of forms and the action an employer may be required to take will depend to a very large extent on the particular circumstances of the case. Any advice and information employers receive should be considered in that light. In some circumstances employers may wish to consider whether they should seek legal advice.

ANNEX 3. COMPLAINTS UNDER THE EMPLOYMENT PROVISIONS

What does the Act say about making complaints?

1. *The Act says* that a person who believes that an employer has unlawfully discriminated or failed to make a reasonable adjustment, or that a person has aided an employer to do such an act, may present a complaint to an industrial tribunal *(S8(1))*.

What does the Act say about conciliation?

2. When a formal complaint has been made to an industrial tribunal *the Act places a duty* on the Advisory, Conciliation and Arbitration Service's

(ACAS) conciliation officers to try to promote settlement of the dispute without a tribunal hearing *(Sch. 3, Para. 1)*. ACAS can also assist in this way without a formal application to a tribunal being made.

What does the Act say about obtaining a remedy for unlawful discrimination?

3. *The Act says* that a disabled person who believes someone has unlawfully discriminated against him or failed to make a reasonable adjustment, in breach of the employment provisions of the Act or Regulations, may present a complaint to an industrial tribunal *(S8(1))*.

4. If the tribunal upholds the complaint it may:
— declare the rights of the disabled person(the complainant), and the other person (the respondent) in relation to the complaint;
— order the other person to pay the complainant compensation; and
— recommend that, within a specified time, the other person take reasonable action to prevent or reduce the adverse effect in question *(S8(2))*.

5. *The Act allows* compensation for injury to feelings to be awarded whether or not other compensation is awarded *(S8(4))*.

6. *The Act says* that if a respondent fails, without reasonable justification, to comply with an industrial tribunal's recommendation, the tribunal may:
— increase the amount of compensation to be paid; or
— order the respondent to pay compensation if it did not make such an order earlier *(S8(5))*.

Who can be taken to an Industrial Tribunal?

7. The tribunal complaints procedure applies to anyone who, it is claimed, has discriminated in the employment field—employers (and their employees and agents for whose acts they are responsible), trade organisations, people who hire contract workers and people who aid any of these to discriminate.

Complaints involving landlords

8. If a reasonable adjustment requiring the consent of the employer's landlord (or a superior landlord) is not made, for whatever reason, the disabled person may bring a complaint against the employer in an industrial tribunal. Either the disabled person or the employer may ask the tribunal to make the landlord a party to the proceedings. If the industrial tribunal finds that the landlord acted unreasonably in withholding consent, or gave consent but attached an unreasonable condition, it can make any appropriate declaration, order that the alteration may be made, or award compensation against the landlord *(S27 and Sch. 4 Para. 2)*.

Complaining about pension schemes

9. A disabled person who considers that the trustees or managers of a pension scheme have discriminated against him may complain through the pensions dispute resolution mechanism. Information about the scheme should give details about this. If necessary, a complaint may be made to the Pensions Ombudsman.

10. From April 1997, all occupational pension schemes will be required to set up and operate procedures for resolving disputes between individual pension scheme members and the trustees or managers.

11. The Occupational Pensions Advisory Service (OPAS) can provide an advice and conciliation service for members of the public who have problems with their occupational pension. OPAS can be contacted at 11 Belgrave Road, London SW1U 1RB. Tel: 0171 233 8080.

12. A disabled person who considers that an employer has discriminated against him in providing access to a pension scheme can complain to an individual tribunal following the same process for other complaints against employers.

What is the "Questionnaire Procedure"?

13. *The Act provides for* a procedure (the questionnaire procedure) to assist a person who believes that discrimination has occurred, to decide whether or not to start proceedings and, if the person does, to formulate and present a case in the most effective manner *(S56)*. Questionnaire forms will be obtainable from Jobcentres.

Can compromise agreements be an alternative to making tribunal complaints?

14. *The Act says* that, in general, the terms of an agreement (such as a contract of employment) cannot prevent a disabled person from complaining to an industrial tribunal, or force a complaint to be stopped *(S9)*. However, *the Act also says* that in some circumstances a disabled person can make an arrangement not to make a complaint or to stop one *(S9)*.

15. These circumstances are if:
— an ACAS conciliation officer has acted under the Act on the matter; *or* the following conditions apply:
— the disabled person must have received independent legal advice from a qualified lawyer about the terms and effects of the agreement, particularly its effect on his ability to complain to a tribunal;
— the adviser must have an insurance policy covering any loss arising from the advice; and
— the agreement must be in writing, relate to the complaint, identify the adviser and say that these conditions are satisfied.

16. It may be in the interests of some disabled people to make such "compromise" agreements instead of pursuing complaints to industrial tribunal hearings, but care should be taken to ensure that the above conditions are met.

How is a complaint made to an Industrial Tribunal?

17. Complaints to an industrial tribunal can be made on an application form (IT1). Forms are obtainable from Jobcentres. Completed applications should be returned to the Industrial Tribunals Central Office. The address is on the form.

18. Applications to an industrial tribunal must be made within three months of the time when the incident being complained of occurred. The time limit will not normally be extended to allow for the time it might take to try to settle the dispute within the organisation *e.g.* by way of internal grievance procedures (see paragraphs 8.1–8.3). A tribunal may, however, consider a complaint which is out of time, if it considers, in all the circumstances of the case, that it is just and equitable to do so *(Sch. 3, Para. 3)*.

What does the Act say about reporting restrictions?

19. *The Act empowers* a tribunal to make "restricted reporting orders" if it considers that evidence of a personal nature is likely to be heard by the tribunal. Such orders prohibit the publication, for example in a newspaper, of any matter likely to lead members of the public to identify the complainant or any other person mentioned in the order, until the tribunal's decision is promulgated.

APPENDIX 2

CODE OF PRACTICE

Rights of Access

Goods, Facilities, Services and Premises

Issued by the Secretary of State for Social Security pursuant to s.51(2) of the Disability Discrimination Act 1995.

GENERAL NOTE

This Code of Practice is issued under s. 51(2) of the 1995 Act. It does not itself impose legal obligations, nor is it an authoritative statement of the law, but it is admissible in evidence in any proceedings under the Act before an industrial tribunal or court, and it must be taken into account in any such proceedings where it appears to the tribunal or court to be relevant: see the note to s. 51 of the 1995 Act.

The Code deals only with those duties coming into force on December 2, 1996 (*i.e.* the duty not to refuse a service, the duty not to provide a service of a worse standard or in a worse manner, the duty not to provide a service on less favourable terms, and the duties which apply to those selling, letting or managing premises); it does not cover the duties which require service providers to make adjustments to the way in which services are provided (*e.g.* the duty to change policies, practice and procedures, to provide auxiliary aids and services, or to remove physical barriers), which are to come into force at a later date.

Chapter 1 recommends that service providers think about their attitude towards disabled people and the way in which they and their staff deal with customers, and suggests some actions that might be taken, *e.g.* informing staff that it is unlawful to discriminate against disabled customers, establishing a policy towards disabled customers and communicating it to staff, providing disability awareness training and having a complaints mechanism.

Chapter 2 describes who is and who is not affected by the Act, and explains the meaning of discrimination. Paragraph 2.6 confirms that the Act does not apply to services which are not generally available to the public (*e.g.* those provided by private clubs), or to the manufacture or design of products. Paragraph 2.14 explains that less favourable treatment is not necessarily the same as bad treatment, so that it is not discriminatory if all customers are given the same poor standard of service, and para. 2.15 states that treating a disabled person less favourably for a reason which relates to his or her disability cannot be justified on the basis that anyone who behaves in a like manner is treated in the same way, unless the treatment can be justified.

Chapters 3 and 4 describe the duties in relation to goods, facilities and services, and in relation to premises, which come into force on December 2, 1996. Paragraph 3.4 confirms that discrimination is unlawful whatever the intention, even if a service provider believes that he or she is helping the disabled person, and para. 3.6 advises that using abusive behaviour towards disabled customers is very likely to be used as evidence that they have been provided with a worse standard of service. Paragraph 3.7 confirms that the duty not to refuse a service, or to provide a worse standard of service, or to provide a service on worse terms, does not require a service provider to change the service which he or she provides in order to overcome the effects of a disability, nor does it require that special products be stocked for disabled customers; those duties are to come into force at a later date. Positive action in favour of disabled people (*e.g.* providing services or premises on more favourable terms) is not prohibited by the Act (paras. 3.9 and 4.15).

Chapter 5 describes the circumstances in which less favourable treatment of a disabled person may be justified. Paragraph 5.6 warns that spurious health and safety reasons should not be used as an excuse to place unnecessary restrictions on disabled people; and para. 5.9 recommends that it should be assumed that a disabled person has the capacity to enter into a contract unless there is clear evidence to the contrary (see also the Services and Premises Regulations 1996, S.I. 1996 No. 1836, reg. 8). A service provider may be able to justify refusing to serve a disabled person if the service provider would otherwise be unable to provide that service to other customers, but para. 5.13 states that this cannot be used to justify refusal of a service where other customers would merely be inconvenienced or delayed; the same point is made in para. 5.17 in relation to the benefits or facilities associated with premises.

Chapter 6 describes other actions which are unlawful under the provisions on access to goods, facilities, services and premises, and explains the circumstances in which employers may be held liable for the actions of their employees. Chapter 7 explains what happens if discrimination is alleged.

1. INTRODUCTION

Purpose of Code

1.1 The Disability Discrimination Act 1995 (the Act) brings in new measures to prevent discrimination against disabled people. Part III of the Act is based on the principle that disabled people should not be treated less favourably, simply because of their disability, by those *providing goods, facilities or services to the public* or by those *selling, letting or managing premises.* If you are in either of these categories, you must comply with the duties set out in the Act, which are described and explained in this Code of Practice (the Code).

1.2 The Code gives practical advice on how to comply with the new duties. The Code will also help disabled people to understand the law. The Code is issued by the Secretary of State on the basis of proposals prepared by the National Disability Council. It applies to England, Scotland and Wales and comes into effect on 2 December 1996. A separate Code applies to Northern Ireland.

Status of Code

1.3 The Code does not impose legal obligations. Nor is it an authoritative statement of the law—that is a matter for the courts. However, the Code can be used in evidence in any legal proceedings under the Act. Courts must take into account any part of the Code that appears to them relevant to any question arising. If you follow the advice in the Code, you may avoid an adverse judgement by the court in any proceedings taken against you.

Using the Code

1.4 *Chapter two* describes who is and who is not affected by the Act, and explains the meaning of discrimination. You will need to read this chapter to have a proper understanding of the Code. Provision of goods, facilities and services is covered in *chapter three.* If you are selling or letting premises you will need to read *chapter four.* There are some exceptions to the duties set out in chapters three and four—these are covered in *chapter five. Chapter six* describes other actions which are unlawful under the access to goods, facilities, services and premises provisions of the Act. *Chapter seven* explains what happens if discrimination is alleged.

1.5 The Code should not be read narrowly. Each section should be viewed as part of an overall explanation of the Act.

1.6 Examples of how the Act is likely to work in practice are given in boxes. The examples are given *for illustrative purposes* only and should not be treated as a complete or authoritative statement of the law. References to the Act are shown in {} (for example {S1(1)} means Section 1(1) of the Act).

General Approach

1.7 Discrimination may stem from lack of awareness about disability. It may also be the result of making assumptions. For example, you might assume that a disabled person would not benefit from a service or that you could not cope with serving him or her. When in doubt, ask the disabled person.

1.8 You will need to think about your *attitude towards disabled people* and the way you and your staff deal with customers. For example, you should consider:

— informing all staff dealing with customers that it is unlawful to discriminate against disabled people;
— establishing a policy towards disabled customers which is communicated to all staff;

> — providing disability awareness training for all staff serving customers and monitoring its implementation; and
> — having an appropriate complaints mechanism.

Further Information

1.9 Copies of the Act, and any regulations made under it, are available from HMSO. A separate code, covering the rights of disabled employees, is also available from the same source. Further information on the Act is available from Disability on the Agenda (telephone 0345 622 633, textphone 0345 622 644). Organisations providing information or advice to business, and advice agencies, may also be able to help.

2. WHO IS AFFECTED BY THE ACT?

What does the Act mean by "disabled people"?

2.1 An adult or child is disabled if he or she has a physical or mental impairment which has an affect which is:
> — substantial (not just trivial or minor);
> — adverse; and
> — long term (lasting or expected to last for at least a year)

on his or her ability to carry out normal day-to-day activities {S1(1)}. Physical or mental impairment includes a sensory impairment.

2.2 People who have had a disability within the definition are protected from discrimination even if they have since recovered.

2.3 The appendix to the Code gives some more detail about who is covered.

Providing goods, facilities and services—who is affected?

2.4 In the Act the provision of services includes the provision of goods and facilities. Subject to the exclusions set out in paragraph 2.9, the Act affects anyone concerned with the provision of services to the public, whether in the public, private or voluntary sectors. It does not matter if the service in question is provided free (such as access to a public park) or in return for payment (for example, a meal in a restaurant).

2.5 Unlike the Act's employment provisions, there is no exemption for small employers.

2.6 Services not generally available to the public, such as those provided by private clubs, are not covered. Nor does the Act cover the manufacture or design of products. Where clubs or manufacturers do provide services to the public—for example, a company selling the goods it produces by mail order or a private golf club hiring out its facilities for a wedding reception—the Act applies to those services.

2.7 Among the services covered are those provided by local councils, hotels, banks, solicitors, advice agencies, pubs, theatres, hairdressers, any kind of shop, telesales businesses, places of worship, courts and doctors {S19 (3)}. All those involved in providing the service are affected—from the most senior person to the most junior employee, whether full or part-time, permanent or temporary.

Premises—who is affected?

2.8 Subject to the exemptions set out in paragraphs 2.10 and 2.11, the Act also covers anyone involved in the sale, letting and management of all types of premises, for example, land, houses, flats and business premises. Local councils, housing associations, private landlords, estate agencies, accommodation agencies, property developers, managing agents and private owner-occupiers could be affected.

What is not affected?

2.9 The only services which are excluded are:
— *education,* and some services which are very closely related to it— such as the youth service (whether provided by a local education authority or the voluntary sector), some examination and assessment services and facilities for research students. Any other services which are provided on school, college or university premises (for example, where a Parent Teachers' Association organises a fund-raising event) are subject to the duties described in the Code. (Part IV of the Act requires schools, colleges and universities to provide information on access).
— *transport vehicles,* although the transport infrastructure, for example, bus stations and airports, is covered (Part V of the Act allows the Government to set access standards for buses, trains, trams and taxis).

2.10 You are exempt from the measures that apply to selling, letting and managing premises if you, or a near relative of yours:
— live on the premises; and
— share accommodation, other than storage accommodation or a means of access, with others who are not members of your household.

This applies only if the premises in question are small which means:
— only you and your household live in the accommodation you occupy, and there is accommodation, let on a separate tenancy or similar agreement, for normally no more than two other households; *or*
— you do not normally let accommodation in your own home to more than six people {S23}.

2.11 In addition, you are exempt from the measures that apply to selling and letting premises if you are an owner-occupier and you do not use an estate agent or advertise publicly {S22(2)}.

What is "discrimination"?

2.12 It is unlawful for you to discriminate against a disabled person in the circumstances described in chapter 3 and chapter 4 {S19(1) & S21(1)}. The Act says discrimination occurs when:
— for a reason which relates to a disabled person's disability,
— you treat him or her less favourably than you treat or would treat others to whom that reason does not or would not apply, and
— you cannot show this treatment was justified {S20(1) & S24(1)}.

A waiter asks a disabled customer to leave the restaurant because she has difficulty eating as a result of her disability. He serves other customers who have no difficulty eating. The waiter has therefore treated her *less favourably* than other customers. The treatment was for *a reason related to her disability*—her difficulty when eating. And the reason for her less favourable treatment did *not apply to the other customers.*

If the waiter could not justify the less favourable treatment, he would have discriminated unlawfully.

2.13 The disabled person does not have to point to others who *were* treated more favourably than he or she was. It is still "less favourable" treatment if others *would have been* treated better.

2.14 Less favourable treatment is not necessarily the same as bad treatment. Treatment must be less favourable by comparison with others (including other disabled people). If, for example, all customers were given the same poor standard of service and a disabled customer was treated no worse than others, no less favourable treatment would have occurred.

2.15 Treating a disabled person less favourably cannot be justified on the basis that anyone who behaves in a like manner is treated in the same way. In the above example, the waiter could not justify refusing to serve the disabled customer on the grounds that he would also have refused to serve anyone who was eating messily, for example, a child. Less favourable treatment of a disabled person is unlawful if it is for a reason which relates to his or her disability *and* it cannot be justified in one of the specified circumstances explained in more detail in chapter 5.

2.16 The Act cannot be used as an excuse for disruptive or anti-social behaviour. For example, if a publican refuses to serve a disabled person because he or she is abusive or drunk, the treatment would not be for a reason which related to the disabled person's disability. It would therefore be lawful to treat him or her in the same way as any other customer who was drunk. For such treatment to be caught by the Act, there must be a direct connection between the disabled person's disability and his or her less favourable treatment.

3. DUTIES UNDER THE ACT—Goods, Facilities & Services

What does the Act say?

3.1 *The Act says* it is unlawful for you to discriminate against a disabled person:
— in refusing to provide or deliberately not providing any service which you provide, or are prepared to provide, to members of the public (paragraphs 3.3 to 3.5) {S19(1)(a)};
— in the standard of service you provide or the manner in which you provide it (paragraphs 3.6 to 3.7) {S19(1)(c)}; or
— in the terms on which you provide a service (paragraph 3.8) {S19(1)(d)}.

3.2 Discrimination is unlawful if it is for a reason relating to a person's disability (discussed in more detail in paragraphs 2.12 to 2.16) and you cannot justify your actions. There are only limited circumstances in which you may be able to justify treating a disabled person less favourably (see chapter 5). The rest of this chapter should be read in this light.

What is the duty not to refuse service?

3.3 It is unlawful for you to refuse to serve, or deliberately not provide a service to, a disabled person for any reason related to his or her disability {S19(1)(a)}.

> A group of deaf people is refused entry to a night club because the doorman thinks that communication using sign language might be seen as threatening. *This is against the law.*

3.4 Discrimination is unlawful whatever the intention. Even where you think you are helping the disabled person, but are nonetheless refusing to serve them, you may still be breaking the law. For example, you cannot refuse to serve disabled customers on the grounds that another service provider caters better for their needs.

> A sweet shop refuses to serve a deaf child because the owner of a nearby sweet shop can communicate using British Sign Language and is therefore able to offer a better service. *This is against the law.*

3.5 Spurious reasons cannot be used to justify refusing to serve a disabled person.

> A hotel pretends that all rooms are taken in order to refuse a booking from a mentally ill customer. *This is against the law.*

What is the duty not to provide a worse standard or manner of service?

3.6 It is against the law for you to offer a disabled person a lower level of service than the service you offer to other people {S19(1)(c)}. It is also against the law to adopt a worse manner in serving disabled people. Abusive behaviour towards disabled customers, especially the use of insulting language about their disability, is very likely to be used as evidence that they have been provided with a worse standard of service.

> A restaurant tells a severely disfigured person he must sit at a table out of sight of other customers, despite other tables being free. *This is against the law.*

3.7 This duty does not mean that you have to change the service you provide to overcome the effects of the disability. Nor do you have to stock special products for disabled people. In due course, however, the later duties in the Act might require you to make adjustments to the way you provide your services to disabled customers (see inside front cover).

> A shop selling telephones does not stock telephones with keyboards and screens for deaf customers. *This is within the law.*

What is the duty not to provide a service on worse terms?

3.8 It is unlawful for you to provide a service to a disabled person on terms which are worse than the terms offered to other people {S19(1)(d)}. This includes charging more for a service or imposing extra restrictions.

> A travel agent asks a person who is deaf and blind for a larger deposit than she requires from others because she assumes without good reason that the customer will be more likely to cancel his holiday. *This is against the law.*

Can you treat disabled people more favourably?

3.9 The Act does not prohibit positive action in favour of disabled people. You can therefore provide services on more favourable terms to a disabled person.

> A theatre manager offers a better seat to a blind person to allow room for her guide dog. *This is within the law.*

4. DUTIES UNDER THE ACT—Premises

What does the Act say?

4.1 It is unlawful for you to discriminate against a disabled person:
— in the terms on which you offer to dispose of premises to him or her (paragraph 4.10) {S22(1)(a)};
— by refusing to dispose of premises to him or her (paragraph 4.11) {S22(1)(b)}; or
— in the way you treat him or her in relation to a list of people needing premises (paragraph 4.12) {S22(1)(c)}.

4.2 The Act also says that if you manage premises it is unlawful for you to discriminate against a disabled person:
— in the way that you allow him or her to make use of any benefits or facilities (paragraph 4.13) {S22(3)(a)};
— by refusing or deliberately omitting to allow him or her to make use of any benefits or facilities (paragraph 4.13) {S22(3)(b)}; or
— by evicting him or her or subjecting him or her to any other detriment (paragraph 4.14) {S22(3)(c)}.

4.3 If your consent is required to dispose of premises to a tenant, you must not discriminate against a disabled person by withholding it. This applies to tenancies that were created both before and after the passing of the Act {S22(4)}.

4.4 However, you do not have to make adjustments to the premises to make them more suitable for a disabled person.

4.5 Some landlords and owner-occupiers are exempt from these duties (see paragraphs 2.10–2.11).

4.6 Discrimination is unlawful if it is for a reason relating to a person's disability (discussed in more detail in paragraphs 2.12 to 2.16) and you cannot justify your actions. There are only limited circumstances in which you may be able to justify treating a disabled person less favourably (see chapter 5). The rest of this chapter should be read in this light.

What is "disposing of premises"?

4.7 Disposing of premises includes selling and letting premises. Premises includes land and buildings, for example, houses, flats and business premises. Disposing of premises does not cover the hire of premises or rooms booked in hotels and guest houses. These are covered by the provisions relating to services (see chapter 3).

What is "managing premises"?

4.8 The term "managing premises" could include actions by accommodation agencies, housekeepers and estate agents who, for example, may collect the rent or provide access to particular benefits or facilities.

What are "benefits and facilities"?

4.9 Examples of benefits and facilities include laundry facilities, access to a garden and parking facilities.

What is the duty not to sell or let premises on worse terms?

4.10 It is unlawful for you to discriminate against a disabled person in the terms on which premises are sold or let {S22(1)(a)}.
A landlord asks a mentally ill person for a deposit when others have to pay none. *This is against the law.*

What is the duty not to refuse to sell or let premises?

4.11 It is against the law for you to refuse to sell or let premises to a disabled person {S22(1)(b)}.
Without any supporting evidence, a landlord refuses to let a flat to a person who has fully recovered from cancer because he believes her former disability might recur and would prevent her from keeping up the rent payments. *This is against the law.*

Are housing lists affected?

4.12 It is unlawful for you to treat a disabled person less favourably when maintaining housing lists {S22(1)(c)}.
A housing association keeps all disabled people at the bottom of its waiting list. *This is against the law.*

Using benefits and facilities

4.13 It is against the law for you to discriminate in the way in which a disabled tenant is allowed to make use of the benefits or facilities of premises, such as shared recreational areas {S22(3)(a)}. It is also against the law for you to prevent him or her from using them {S22(3)(b)}.
A landlord prevents a person with a severe facial disfigurement from using the swimming pool in a block of flats. *This is against the law.*

Eviction and other detriments

4.14 It is against the law for you to evict a disabled person simply because of his or her disability or otherwise place him or her at a disadvantage, such as harassment {S22(3)(c)}.
A landlord charges a person with a learning disability more than he charges other tenants for repairs to his flat. *This is against the law.*

Can you treat disabled people more favourably?

4.15 The Act does not prohibit positive action in favour of disabled people. You can therefore offer premises on better terms.

A local authority gives priority to disabled people ahead of other people on their waiting list for housing. *This is within the law.*

5. WHEN LESS FAVOURABLE TREATMENT CAN BE JUSTIFIED UNDER THE ACT

Introduction

5.1 This chapter sets out the limited circumstances in which you may be able to justify less favourable treatment of a disabled person for a reason which relates to his or her disability. No other form of justification is available. You should read this chapter in conjunction with the explanation of the meaning of discrimination (paragraphs 2.12 to 2.16).

5.2 You may be able to justify treating a disabled person less favourably *only if you believed that one or more of the conditions below applied and it was reasonable in all the circumstances of the case for you to have held that opinion.* You do not have to be an expert on disability but you are expected to take account of all the circumstances, including the information available to you, at the time.

A swimming pool attendant refuses to allow a child who uses a wheelchair to use the swimming pool because he believes the child is unable to swim. In the absence of further information, *this may be within the law.*

Despite being told subsequently by the child's mother that the child is a competent swimmer, the attendant persists in refusing him admission. *This is likely to be against the law.*

5.3 If a disabled person can show that he or she has been treated less favourably, you will have to prove that your actions were justified.

5.4 *Some of the conditions specified below (for example, those relating to health or safety) apply both to service providers and to those involved in disposing of premises. Others apply to one group alone. The heading for each section makes clear to whom it applies.*

Health or safety—services and premises

5.5 The Act does not require you to do anything which would endanger the health or safety of any person, including that of the disabled person {S20(4)(a) & S24(3)(a)}.

A driving instructor refuses to give lessons to a person with such severely impaired vision that he fails the eyesight test, even with glasses. *This is within the law.*

A landlord refuses to let a third floor flat to a disabled person living alone who is clearly unable to negotiate the stairs in safety or use the fire escape or other escape routes in an emergency. *This is within the law.*

5.6 Spurious health and safety reasons will provide no defence. For example, fire regulations should not be used as an excuse to place *unnecessary* restrictions on disabled people. It is for the management of the establishment concerned, in conjunction with the licensing authority, to make any special provision needed.

Although there are adequate means of escape, a cinema manager turns away a wheelchair user because he assumes, without checking, that she could be in danger in the event of a fire. *This is against the law.*

Despite knowing that there is no health risk, a landlord refuses to let a flat to someone with AIDS on the grounds that other tenants might be put at risk. *This is against the law.*

5.7 Every opportunity should be taken, as far as practicable, to enable disabled people to use cinemas, theatres, leisure centres and other entertainment venues. Equally, disabled people should not be prevented from living where they choose through unfounded concerns for safety.

Incapacity to contract—services and premises

5.8 The Act does not require you to contract with a disabled person who is incapable of entering into a legally enforceable agreement or of giving an informed consent {S20(4)(b) & S24(3)(b)}. If a disabled person is unable to understand a particular transaction due to mental incapacity, you may refuse to enter into a contract.

A landlord refuses to let a flat to a person with a severe learning disability who does not understand that rent would have to be paid. *This is within the law.*

5.9 Your refusal must be reasonable. A person may be able to understand less complicated transactions, but have difficulty with more complex ones. Unless there is clear evidence to the contrary, you should assume that a disabled person is able to enter into any contract.

Staff in a bakery refuse to sell a loaf of bread to a person with a severe learning disability because they claim she does not understand the nature of the agreement even though her order is clear and she is able to pay. *This is against the law.*

5.10 Regulations will prevent a service provider from justifying less favourable treatment of a disabled person on the grounds of incapacity to contract in a situation where another person is legally acting on his or her behalf (for example, under a power of attorney).

A salesman refuses to rent a television to someone simply because she is legally acting on behalf of someone who is mentally ill. *This is against the law.*

Providing the service—services

5.11 You may be able to justify refusing to serve a disabled person if this is necessary to serve other customers {S20(4)(c)}.

A tour guide refuses to allow an unaccompanied wheelchair user on a tour of old city walls because he has well-founded reasons to believe that the extra help he has to give her would prevent the party from completing the tour. *This is within the law.*

5.12 Similarly, you may be able to justify providing a lower standard of service or on worse terms if this is necessary to serve the disabled person or other customers {S20(4)(d)}.

A hotel restricts a wheelchair user to rooms on the ground floor because rooms on other floors are not accessible. This restriction of his choice of rooms is necessary in order to provide the service to him. *This is within the law.*

5.13 These conditions will justify less favourable treatment only where not treating the disabled person less favourably would effectively prevent other customers or the disabled person from using the service. They cannot be used to justify refusal simply because other people would be inconvenienced or delayed. The distinction is between people who have paid for a service and cannot receive it at all and those who are merely being delayed. It is more unlikely, for example, that you could justify asking a disabled person to go to the back of the queue so as not to delay other customers waiting to be served.

A clerk in a post office refuses to serve a deaf person because the extra time taken means that other customers have to queue for longer. *This is against the law.*

Greater expense—services

5.14 In general, it is unlawful for you to charge a disabled person more for a service than you charge anyone else, *except* where *additional costs* are incurred in providing a special service to the disabled person's particular requirements {S20(4)(e)}. Charging more can be justified only where the service is individually tailored to the needs of the customer and the disabled person's particular requirements increase costs due to greater materials or work.

A furniture shop charges more for an orthopaedic bed, made to the disabled person's specification, but does not charge more for a standard bed. *This is within the law.*

Necessary to provide the benefits or facilities—premises

5.15 You may be able to justify restricting access to benefits or facilities associated with premises if this is necessary to allow access to others or to the disabled person {S24(3)(c)}.

A landlord refuses to allow a mentally ill tenant to use the shared laundry facilities because he frequently breaks the washing machine. *This is within the law.*

5.16 Similarly, you may be able to justify denying access to benefits or facilities if this is necessary to allow access to others {S24(3)(d)}.

A landlord requires a disabled tenant to park her car at the side of the building as otherwise it would block the main entrance for other tenants. *This is within the law.*

5.17 These conditions will justify less favourable treatment only where not treating the disabled tenant less favourably would effectively prevent other tenants, or the disabled person, from using the benefit of facility. They cannot be used to justify less favourable treatment simply because other tenants would be inconvenienced or delayed.

A landlord refuses to allow a mentally ill tenant to use the shared kitchen because he sometimes takes a little longer and so delays other tenants. *This is against the law.*

What about the effects of other legislation?

5.18 The Act does not:
— make unlawful anything done to comply with other legislation (if you are required to do something under another law this takes precedence over anything required by the Act);
— make unlawful any act done to safeguard national security {S59}.

Special rules for insurance

5.19 Regulations will make special rules for insurance which recognise the need for insurers to be able to distinguish between individuals on the basis of the risks against which they seek to insure. Insurers will be able to justify less favourable treatment only if that treatment is based on actuarial or other statistical data or other information on which it is reasonable to rely. If a disabled person establishes in a court that less favourable treatment has occurred, it will be up to the insurer to prove that there is an additional risk associated with the disabled person which arises from his or her disability.

An insurance company charges a higher premium to a deaf person for car insurance although it has no evidence of an increased risk. *This is against the law.*

Special rules for guarantees and warranties

5.20 Many retailers go beyond their statutory duties by replacing goods if they wear out or break within a specified period of time. Generally speaking, they do this if the goods have been subjected to only an average amount of wear and tear. However, there are situations in which a person's disability might result in higher than average wear and tear. Regulations will exempt service providers from replacing goods in the latter circumstances.

A person with mobility problems buys a pair of shoes but wears out the left shoe after a few months because his left foot has to bear most of his weight. The retailer refuses to provide a new pair of shoes because the old pair has undergone abnormal wear and tear. *This is within the law.*

6. OTHER UNLAWFUL ACTIONS

Victimisation

6.1 It is unlawful for you to victimise (to pick on or treat less favourably) any person, *whether disabled or not*, who has:
— brought legal proceedings under the Act;
— given evidence or information in connection with such proceedings;
— done anything else under the Act; or
— alleged that the Act has been broken;

or because you believe that he or she has done or intends to do any of the above {S55}.

6.2 It is not victimisation to treat a person less favourably because that person has made an allegation which was false and not made in good faith.

Aiding unlawful actions

6.3 It is unlawful for you to aid anyone to discriminate against a disabled person, unless you are relying on a statement that the action is allowed under the Act and it is reasonable for you to rely on that statement. However, anyone who knowingly or recklessly makes a false statement of this kind is committing an offence {S57}.

> A receptionist in a small hairdresser's, following his employer's instructions, refuses to book an appointment for a person with cerebral palsy. His employer has told him that small firms are exempt from Part III of the Act, despite knowing that this exemption applies only to the employment provisions in Part II. *The employee is within the law but the employer is not.*

Liability of employers for their employees' actions

6.4 Each of your employees is individually responsible for complying with the law. However, if one of your employees breaks the law in the course of his or her employment, action could also be taken against you even if you were unaware or did not approve of what he or she had done {S58(1)}. However, in a case where one of your employees breaks the law, you may have a defence if you can prove that you took such steps as were reasonably practicable to prevent him or her from discriminating {S58(5)}. Examples of the type of steps which might be reasonably practicable are set out in paragraph 1.8.

> A sales assistant refuses to serve a disabled person, despite the employer having provided relevant and recent training, instructing staff to serve disabled people and checking regularly that they are complying. *The employer is likely to be within the law but the employee is not.*

6.5 If someone you authorise to act on your behalf—for example an agent—breaks the law, action could also be taken against you {S58(2)}. This applies whether the authority was express or implied and whether it was given before or after the unlawful act. You may, however, have a defence if you can show that your agent was not acting with your authority.

Terms of agreements

6.6 Any term in an agreement, such as a lease, is void if its effect is to:
— require someone to do something which would be unlawful under Part III of the Act (the part relating to services and premises);
— exclude or limit the operation of Part III; or
— prevent someone making a claim under Part III {S26}.

> A landlord's lease includes a term forbidding the tenant from subletting to people with learning disabilities. *This term is not legally binding.*

7. DISPUTES AND PENALTIES

What happens if there is a dispute?

7.1 If you unlawfully discriminate against a disabled person he or she may seek to discuss the problem with you in order to resolve it. He or she may also seek assistance from an organisation representing his or her interests. Similarly, you might wish to seek advice from a business or service providers' organisation.

7.2 The Government will establish a service to provide advice and assistance to the many general or specialist advisers who are already operating. This will ensure that those providing advice on the Act will have access to specialist knowledge of its provisions and a pool of experience in dealing with cases of particular difficulty.

What happens if a dispute cannot be resolved?

7.3 If you cannot resolve a dispute in this way, a disabled person would be able to take you to court and, if successful, could receive compensation for any financial loss or injury to his or her feelings. A disabled person may also be able to seek an injunction or, in Scotland, interdict, against you to prevent the repeat of any discriminatory act {S25}.

Making false statements

7.4 If you are found guilty of making a false statement of the kind described in paragraph 6.3 you will be liable to a fine up to level 5 on the standard scale (£5,000 as of May 1996) {S57(5)}.

APPENDIX—WHAT IS MEANT BY DISABILITY

This Appendix does not form part of the Code. It is included to aid understanding about who is covered by the Act and should provide sufficient information on the definition of disability to cover the large majority of cases. The definition of disability in the Act is designed to cover only people who would generally be considered to be disabled. A Government publication "Guidance on matters to be taken into account in determining questions relating to the definition of disability", is also available.

When is a person disabled?

A person has a disability if he has a physical or mental impairment which has a substantial and long-term adverse effect on his ability to carry out normal day-to-day activities.

What about people who have recovered from a disability?

People who have had a disability within the definition are protected from discrimination even if they have since recovered.

What does "impairment" cover?

It covers physical or mental impairments; this includes sensory impairments, such as those affecting sight or hearing.

Are all mental impairments covered?

The term "mental impairment" is intended to cover a wide range of impairments relating to mental functioning, including what are often known as learning disabilities. However, the Act states that it does not include any impairment resulting from or consisting of a mental illness, unless that illness is a clinically well-recognised illness. A clinically well-recognised illness is one that is recognised by a respected body of medical opinion.

What is a "substantial" adverse effect?

A substantial adverse effect is something which is more than a minor or trivial effect. The requirement that an effect must be substantial reflects the gen- individual tribunal following the same process for other complaints against employers.

What is a "long-term" effect?

A long-term effect of an impairment is one:
— which has lasted at least 12 months; or
— where the total period for which it lasts is likely to be at least 12 months; or
— which is likely to last for the rest of the life of the person affected.
Effects which are not long-term would therefore include loss of mobility due to a broken limb which is likely to heal within 12 months and the effects of temporary infections, from which a person would be likely to recover within 12 months.

What if the effects come and go over a period of time?

If an impairment has had a substantial adverse effect on normal day-to-day activities but that effect ceases, the substantial effect is treated as continuing if it is likely to *recur*; that is, if it is more probable than not that the effect will recur. Take the example of a person with rheumatoid arthritis whose impairment has a substantial adverse effect, which then ceases to be substantial (*i.e.* the person has a period of remission). The effects are to be treated as if they are continuing, and are likely to continue beyond 12 months, *if*:
— the impairment remains; and
— at least one recurrence of the substantial effect is likely to take place 12 months or more after the initial occurrence.
This would then be a long-term effect.

What are "normal day-to-day activities"?

They are activities which are carried out by most people on a fairly regular and frequent basis. The term is not intended to include activities which are normal only for a particular person or group of people, such as playing a musical instrument, or a sport, to a professional standard or performing a skilled or specialised task at work. However, someone who is affected in such a specialised way but is *also* affected in normal day-to-day activities would be covered by this part of the definition. The test of whether an impairment affects normal day-to-day activities is whether it affects one of the broad categories of capacity listed in Schedule 1 to the Act. They are:
— mobility;
— manual dexterity;
— physical co-ordination;
— continence;
— ability to lift, carry or otherwise move everyday objects;
— speech, hearing or eyesight;
— memory or ability to concentrate, learn or understand; or
— perception of the risk of physical danger.

What about treatment?

Someone with an impairment may be receiving medical or other treatment which alleviates or removes the effects (though not the impairment). In such cases, the treatment is ignored and the impairment is taken to have the effect it would have had without such treatment. This does not apply if substantial adverse effects are not likely to recur even if the treatment stops (*i.e.* the impairment has been cured).

Does this include people who wear spectacles?

No. The sole exception to the rule about ignoring the effects of treatment is the wearing of spectacles or contact lenses. In this case, the effect while the person is wearing spectacles or contact lenses should be considered.

Are people who have disfigurements covered?

People with severe disfigurements are covered by the Act. They do not need to demonstrate that the impairment has a substantial adverse effect on their ability to carry out normal day-to-day activities.

What about people who know their condition is going to get worse over time?

Progressive conditions are conditions which are likely to change and develop over time. Exemples given in the Act are cancer, multiple sclerosis, muscular dystrophy and HIV infection. Where a person has a progressive condition he will be covered by the Act from the moment the condition leads to an impairment which has *some* effect on ability to carry out normal day-to-day activities, even though not a *substantial* effect, if that impairment is likely eventually to have a substantial adverse effect on such ability.

What about people who are registered disabled?

Those registered as disabled under the Disabled Persons (Employment) Act 1944 both on 12 January 1995 and 2 December 1996 will be treated as being disabled under the Disability Discrimination Act 1995 for three years from the latter date. At all times from 2 December 1996 onwards they will be covered by the Act as people who have had a disability. This does not preclude them from being covered as having a current disability any time after the three year period has finished. Whether they are or not will depend on whether they—like anyone else—meet the definition of disability in the Act.

Are people with genetic conditions covered?

If a genetic condition has no effect on ability to carry out normal day-to-day activities, the person is not covered. Diagnosis does not in itself being someone within the definition. If the condition is progressive, then the rule about progressive conditions applies.

Are any conditions specifically excluded from the coverage of the Act?

Yes. Certain conditions are to be regarded as not amounting to impairments for the purposes of the Act. These are:
— addiction to or dependency on alcohol, nicotine, or any other substance (other than as a result of the substance being medically prescribed);
— seasonal allergic rhinitis (*e.g.* hayfever), except where it aggravates the effect of another condition;
— tendency to set fires;
— tendency to steal;
— tendency to physical or sexual abuse of other persons;
— exhibitionism;
— voyeurism.

Also, disfigurements which consist of a tattoo (which has not been removed), non-medical body piercing, or something attached through such piercing, are to be treated as not having a substantial adverse effect on the person's ability to carry out normal day-to-day activities.

THE DISABILITY DISCRIMINATION ACT 1995

The Disability Discrimination Act introduces new laws and measures aimed at ending the discrimination which many disabled people face. Over time, the Act will give disabled people new rights in the areas of:
— employment
— access to goods, facilities and services

— buying or renting land or property.

In addition the Act:

— requires schools, colleges and universities to provide information for disabled people

— allows the Government to set minimum standards so that disabled people can use public transport easily

— sets up the National Disability Council (in Northern Ireland, the Northern Ireland Disability Council) to advise the Government on discrimination against disabled people.

There is a separate Code of Practice containing guidance on the elimination of discrimination against disabled people in the field of employment. This can be obtained from HMSO bookshops.

NORTHERN IRELAND

The Act (as modified by Schedule 8) also applies in Northern Ireland. A Code of Practice reflecting those modifications is published in Northern Ireland.

APPENDIX 3

THE DISABILITY DISCRIMINATION ACT, 1995

[Guidance on matters to be taken into account in determining questions relating to the definition of disability.]

GENERAL NOTE

This guidance is issued under s. 3 of the 1995 Act. It does not impose any legal obligations, nor is it an authoritative statement of the law, but it must be taken into account where relevant by any court or tribunal which is determining whether a person's impairment has a substantial and long-term adverse effect on his or her ability to carry out normal day-to-day activities: see the note to s. 3 of the 1995 Act.

Much of the document simply describes the provisions contained in the 1995 Act and the associated Definition Regulations (the Disability Discrimination (Meaning of Disability) Regulations 1996, S.I. 1996 No. 1455), but it also provides an explanation of the relevant provisions, and gives some useful examples, particularly on whether the effect of an impairment is substantial and/or long-term. The Introduction to the guidance emphasises that in the vast majority of cases there is unlikely to be any doubt whether or not a person has or has had a disability, but that the guidance is intended to prove helpful in cases where it is not clear (para. 1).

Part II of the guidance is divided into three main sections: "substantial", "long-term" and "normal day-to-day activities".

Substantial. The guidance confirms that a "substantial" effect is one which is more than "minor" or "trivial" (para. A1), and suggests that in determining whether the effect of an impairment is substantial, account should be taken of the time taken to carry out the activity (para. A2) and the way in which it is carried out (para. A3); account should also be taken of the cumulative effects of an impairment on a range of normal day-to-day activities (para. A4), and of the cumulative effects of more than one impairment (para. A6).

In assessing the effects of an impairment, the guidance states that account should be taken of how far a person can reasonably be expected to modify their behaviour to prevent or reduce the effects of the impairment (para. A7), but if it is possible that such a "coping strategy" might break down, so that the effects of the impairment might recur, that possibility must be taken into account when assessing the effects of the impairment (para. A8). If, however, a particular coping strategy is followed on the medical advice, it may have to be disregarded altogether (para. A9); this is because the Act provides (in Sched. 1, para. 6(1)) that where measures are being taken to treat or correct an impairment (*e.g.* by medication or use of a prosthesis or other aid), the impairment must be treated as having the effect it would have without those measures, even if the measures result in the impairment being completely under control or not at all apparent (para. A12). Note however the specific exclusion in Sched. 6, para. 6(2), for sight impairments which are correctable by spectacles or contact lenses.

Long-term. The guidance states that it is not necessary for the effect of an impairment to be the same throughout the relevant period, provided it continues to have, or is likely to have, the required effect throughout the period (para. B2). Where an impairment has recurring effects, the Act states that the substantial effect of the impairment will be treated as continuing if the effect is "likely to recur" (Sched. 1, para. 2(2)). The guidance states that likelihood of recurrence should be considered taking into account all the circumstances, including any coping strategies which a person might reasonably be expected to adopt to prevent a recurrence, such as avoiding substances to which he or she is allergic, although when assessing the likelihood of a recurrence the possibility that such a coping strategy might break down must also be taken into account (para. B5). Account should also be taken of the likelihood of the impairment being cured by medical or other treatment, so that it would be unlikely to recur even if there were no further treatment; if however the treatment merely controls the impairment rather than curing it, so that the impairment would be likely to recur if the treatment were stopped, the treatment must be ignored and the effect must be regarded as likely to recur (para. B6). The guidance states that an event is likely to happen "if it is more probable than not that it will happen" (para. B7).

Normal day-to-day activities. The guidance confirms that "normal day-to-day activities" are those which are normal for most people and carried out by most people on a daily or frequent or fairly regular basis (para. C2); the term "normal day-to-day activities" does not include work of any particular form, "because no particular form of work is 'normal' for most people" (para. C3). In addition to the direct effects of an impairment, account should be taken of any indirect effects which an impairment might have on normal day-to-day activities, *e.g.* where a person has been advised on medical grounds to act in a way which affects that person's ability to carry out a normal day-to-day activity, or where a person, although capable of performing those activities, suffers pain or fatigue in doing so (para. C6).

Paragraphs C14 to C21 give a series of examples of what it would, and what it would not, be reasonable to regard as substantial adverse effects on the normal day-to-day activities listed in Sched. 1, para. 4.

STATUS AND PURPOSE OF THE GUIDANCE

This guidance is issued by the Secretary of State under section 3 of the Disability Discrimination Act 1995. It concerns the definition of disability in the Act. Section 3 of the Act enables the Secretary of State to issue guidance about matters to be taken into account in determining whether an impairment has a **substantial adverse effect** on a person's ability to carry out normal day-to-day activities and/or whether an impairment has a **long-term effect**. The guidance may give examples.

This guidance does not impose any legal obligations in itself, nor is it an authoritative statement of the law. However, section 3(3) of the Act requires that an industrial tribunal or a court, which is determining for any purpose of the Act whether a person's impairment has a substantial and long-term adverse effect on his or her ability to carry out normal day-to-day activities, must take into account any of this guidance which appears to it to be relevant.

PART I INTRODUCTION

Using the guidance

1. Although this guidance is primarily designed for courts and tribunals, it is likely to be of value to a range of people and organisations. *In the vast majority of cases there is unlikely to be any doubt whether or not a person has or has had a disability, but this guidance should prove helpful in cases where it is not clear.*

2. The definition of disability has a number of elements. The guidance covers each of these elements in turn. Each section contains an explanation of the relevant provisions of the Act which supplement the basic definition; guidance and examples are provided where relevant. Those using this guidance for the first time may wish to read it all, as each part of the guidance builds upon the part(s) preceding it.

3. Part II of the guidance relates to matters to be taken into account when considering whether an effect is substantial and/or long term. Most of the examples are to be found here, and particularly in *Section C*. Because the purpose of this guidance is to help in the cases where there is doubt, examples of cases where there will not be any doubt are not included.

4. Throughout the guidance descriptions of the provisions in the legislation are immediately preceded by bold italic text. They are immediately followed by a reference to the relevant provision of the Act or Regulations. References to sections of the Act are marked *"S"*; references to schedules are marked *"Sch."*; and references to paragraphs in schedules are marked *"Para."*. References in footnotes to "Definition Regulations" mean The Disability Discrimination (Meaning of Disability) Regulations 1996.

Main elements of the definition of disability

5. *The Act defines* "disabled person" as a person with "*a physical or mental impairment which has a substantial and long-term adverse effect on his ability to carry out normal day-to-day activities*" *(S1)*.

6. This means that:
— the person must have an *impairment*, that is either physical or mental (see paragraphs 10–15 below);
— the impairment must have adverse effects which are *substantial* (see **Section A**);
— the substantial effects must be *long-term* (see **Section B**); and
— the long-term substantial effects must be *adverse* effects on *normal day-to-day activities* (see **Section C**).

This definition is subject to the provisions in Schedule 1 *(Sch. 1)*.

Inclusion of people who have had a disability in the past

7. *The Act says* that Part I of the Act (definition), Part II (employment) and Part III (goods, facilities, services and premises) also apply in relation to a person who has had a disability as defined in paragraphs 5 and 6 above. For this purpose, those Parts of the Act are subject to the provisions in Schedule 2 to the Act *(S2, Sch. 2)*.

Exclusions from the definition

8. Certain conditions are not to be regarded as impairments for the purposes of the Act. These are:
- addiction to or dependency on alcohol, nicotine, or any other substance (other than in consequence of the substance being medically prescribed);
- the condition known as seasonal allergic rhinitis (*e.g.* hayfever), except where it aggravates the effect of another condition;
- tendency to set fires;
- tendency to steal;
- tendency to physical or sexual abuse of other persons;
- exhibitionism;
- voyeurism.

Also, disfigurements which consist of a tattoo (which has not been removed), non-medical body piercing, or something attached through such piercing, are to be treated as not having a substantial adverse effect on the person's ability to carry out normal day-to-day activities (Definition Regulations).

Registered disabled people

9. The introduction of the employment provisions in the Act coincides with the abolition of the Quota scheme which operated under the Disabled Persons (Employment) Act 1944. *The Disability Discrimination Act says* that anyone who was registered as a disabled person under the Disabled Persons (Employment) Act 1944 and whose name appeared on the register both on 12 January 1995 and on 2 December 1996 (the date the employment provisions come into force) is to be treated as having a disability for the purposes of the Disability Discrimination Act during the period of three years starting on 2 December 1996. This applies regardless of whether the person otherwise meets the definition of "disabled person" during that period. Those who are treated by this provision as being disabled for the three-year period are also to be treated after this period has ended as having had a disability in the past *(Sch. 1, Para. 7)*.

Impairment

10. The definition requires that the effects which a person may experience arise from a physical or mental impairment. In many cases there will be no dispute whether a person has an impairment. Any disagreement is more likely to be about whether the effects of the impairment are sufficient to fall within the definition. Even so, it may sometimes be necessary to decide whether a person has an impairment so as to be able to deal with the issues about its effects.

11. It is not necessary to consider how an impairment was caused, even if the cause is a consequence of a condition which is excluded. For example, liver disease as a result of alcohol dependency would count as an impairment.

12. *Physical or mental impairment* includes sensory impairments, such as those affecting sight or hearing.

13. *Mental impairment* includes a wide range of impairments relating to mental functioning, including what are often known as learning disabilities (formerly known as "mental handicap"). However, *the Act states* that it does not include any impairment resulting from or consisting of a mental illness unless that illness is a clinically well-recognised illness *(Sch. 1, Para. 1)*.

14. A *clinically well-recognised illness* is a mental illness which is recognised by a respected body of medical opinion. It is very likely that this would include those specifically mentioned in publications such as the World Health Organisation's International Classification of Diseases.

15. *The Act states* that mental impairment does not have the special meaning used in the Mental Health Act 1983 or the Mental Health (Scotland) Act 1984, although this does not preclude a mental impairment within the meaning of that legislation from coming within the definition in the Disability Discrimination Act *(S68)*.

PART II GUIDANCE ON MATTERS TO BE TAKEN INTO ACCOUNT IN DETERMINING QUESTIONS RELATING TO THE DEFINITION OF DISABILITY

A Substantial

Meaning of "substantial" adverse effect

A1. The requirement that an adverse effect be substantial reflects the general understanding of "disability" as a limitation going beyond the normal differences in ability which may exist among people. A "substantial" effect is more than would be produced by the sort of physical or mental conditions experienced by many people which have only minor effects. A "substantial" effect is one which is more than "minor" or "trivial".

The time taken to carry out an activity

A2. The time taken by a person with an impairment to carry out a normal day-to-day activity should be considered when assessing whether the effect of that impairment is substantial. It should be compared with the time that might be expected if the person did not have the impairment.

The way in which an activity is carried out

A3. Another factor to be considered when assessing whether the effect of an impairment is substantial is the way in which a person with that impairment carries out a normal day-to-day activity. The comparison should be with the way the person might be expected to carry out the activity if he or she did not have the impairment.

Cumulative effects of an impairment

A4. *The Act provides* that an impairment is to be taken to affect the ability of a person to carry out normal day-to-day activities only if it affects that person in one (or more) of the respects listed in paragraph C4 *(Sch. 1, Para. 4)*. An impairment might not have a substantial adverse effect on a person in any one of these respects, but its effects in more than one of these respects taken together could result in a substantial adverse effect on the person's ability to carry out normal day-to-day activities.

A5. For example, although the great majority of people with cerebral palsy will experience a number of substantial effects, someone with mild cerebral palsy may experience minor effects in a number of the respects listed in paragraph C4 which together could create a substantial adverse effects on a range of normal day-to-day activities; fatigue may hinder walking, visual perception may be poor, co-ordination and balance may cause some difficulties. Similarly, a person whose impairment causes breathing difficulties may experience minor effects in a number of respects but which overall have a substantial adverse effect on their ability to carry out normal day-to-day activities. For some people, mental illness may have a clear effect in one of the respects in C4. However, for others, depending on the extent of the condition, there may be effects in a number of different respects which, taken together, substantially adversely affect their ability to carry out normal day-to-day activities.

A6. A person may have more than one impairment, any one of which alone would not have a substantial effect. In such a case, account should be taken of whether the impairments together have a substantial effect overall on the person's ability to carry out normal day-to-day activities. For example a minor impairment which affects physical co-ordination and an irreversible but minor injury to a leg which affects mobility, taken together, might have a substantial effect on the person's ability to carry out certain normal day-to-day activities.

Effects of behaviour

A7. Account should be taken of how far a person can reasonably be expected to modify behaviour to prevent or reduce the effects of an impairment on normal day-to-day activities. If a person can behave in such a way that the impairment ceases to have a substantial adverse effect on his or her ability to carry out normal day-to-day activities the person would no longer meet the definition of disability.

A8. In some cases people have such "coping" strategies which cease to work in certain circumstances (for example, where someone who stutters or has dyslexia is placed under stress). If it is possible that a person's ability to manage the effects of an impairment will break down so that effects will sometimes still occur, this possibility must be taken into account when assessing the effects of the impairment.

A9. If a disabled person is advised by a medical practitioner to behave in a certain way in order to reduce the impact of the disability, that might count as treatment to be disregarded (see paragraph A11 below).

Effects of environment

A10. Whether adverse effects are substantial may depend on environmental conditions which may vary; for example, the temperature, humidity, the time of day or night, how tired the person is or how much stress he or she is under may have an impact on the effects. When assessing whether adverse effects are substantial, the extent to which such environmental factors are likely to have an impact should also therefore be considered.

Effects of treatment

A11. *The Act provides* that where an impairment is being *treated or corrected* the impairment is to be treated as having the effect it would have without the measures in question *(Sch. 1, Para. 6(1))*. *The Act states* that the treatment or correction measures to be disregarded for these purposes include medical treatment and the use of a prosthesis or other aid *(Sch. 1, Para. 6(2)2)*.

A12. This applies even if the measures result in the effects being completely under control or not at all apparent.

A13. For example, if a person with a hearing impairment wears a hearing aid the question whether his or her impairment has a substantial adverse effect is to be decided by reference to what the hearing level would be without the hearing aid. And in the case of someone with diabetes, whether or not the effect is substantial should be decided by reference to what the condition would be if he or she was not taking medication.

A14. However, *the Act states* that this provision does not apply to sight impairments to the extent that they are capable of correction by spectacles or contact lenses. In other words the only effects on ability to carry out normal day-to-day activities to be considered are those which remain when spectacles or contact lenses are used (or would remain if they were used). This does not include the use of devices to correct sight which are not spectacles or contact lenses *(Sch. 1, Para. 6(3))*.

Progressive conditions

A15. A progressive condition is one which is likely to change and develop over time. *The Act gives* the following examples of progressive conditions: cancer, multiple sclerosis, muscular dystrophy, HIV infection. *The Act provides* for a person with such a condition to be regarded as having an impairment which has a substantial adverse effect on his or her ability to carry out normal day-to-day activities before it actually does so. Where a person has a progressive condition, he or she will be treated as having an impairment which has a *substantial* adverse effect from the moment any impairment resulting from that condition first has *some* effect on ability to carry out normal day-to-day activities. The effect need not be continuous and need not be substantial. For this rule to operate medical diagnosis of the condition is not by itself enough *(Sch. 1, Para. 8)*.

Severe disfigurements

A16. *The Act provides* that where an impairment consists of a severe disfigurement, it is to be treated as having a substantial adverse effect on the person's ability to carry out normal day-to-day activities. There is no need to demonstrate such an effect *(Sch. 1, Para. 3)*. *Regulations provide* that a disfigurement which consists of a tattoo (which has not been removed) is not to be considered as a severe disfigurement. Also excluded is a piercing of the body for decorative purposes including anything attached through the piercing (Definition Regulations).

A17. Examples of disfigurements include scars, birthmarks, limb or postural deformation or diseases of the skin. Assessing severity will be mainly a matter of the degree of the disfigurement. However, it may be necessary to take account of where the feature in question is (*e.g.* on the back as opposed to the face).

B Long term

Meaning of long-term effects

B1. *The Act states* that, for the purpose of deciding whether a person is disabled, a long-term effect of an impairment is one:
— which has lasted at least twelve months; or
— where the total period for which it lasts, from the time of the first onset, is likely to be at least twelve months; or
— which is likely to last for the rest of the life of the person affected *(Sch. 1, Para. 2)*.
For the purpose of deciding whether a person has had a disability in the past, a long-term effect of an impairment is one which lasted at least 12 months *(Sch. 2, Para. 5)*.

B2. It is not necessary for the effect to be the same throughout the relevant period. It may change, as where activities which are initially very difficult become possible to a much greater extent. The main adverse effect might even disappear—or it might disappear temporarily—while one or other effects on ability to carry out normal day-to-day activities continue or develop. Provided the impairment continues to have, or is likely to have, such an effect throughout the period, there is a long-term effect.

Recurring effects

B3. *The Act states* that if an impairment has had a substantial adverse effect on a person's ability to carry out normal day-to-day activities but that effect ceases, the substantial effect is treated as continuing if it is likely to recur; that is, it is more likely than not that the effect will recur. (In deciding whether a person has had a disability in the past, the question is whether a substantial adverse effect has in fact recurred.) Conditions which recur only sporadically or for short periods (*e.g.* epilepsy) can still qualify. *(Sch. 1 Para. 2(2), Sch. 2, Para. 5). Regulations specifically exclude* seasonal allergic rhinitis (*e.g.* hayfever) from this category, except where it aggravates the effects of an existing condition (Definition Regulations).

B4. For example, a person with rheumatoid arthritis may experience effects from the first occurrence for a few weeks and then have a period of remission. But, if the effects are likely to recur, they are to be treated as if they were continuing. If the effects are likely to recur beyond twelve months after the first occurrence, they are to be treated as long-term.

B5. Likelihood of recurrence should be considered taking all the circumstances of the case into account. This should include what the person could reasonably be expected to do to prevent the recurrence; for example, the person might reasonably be expected to take action which prevents the impairment from having such effects (*e.g.* avoiding substances to which he or she is allergic). This may be unreasonably difficult with some substances. In addition, it is possible that the way in which a person can control or cope with the effects of a condition may not always be successful because, for example, a routine is not followed or the person is in an unfamiliar environment. If there is an increased likelihood that the control will break down, it will be more likely that there will be a recurrence. That possibility should be taken into account when assessing the likelihood of a recurrence.

Effects of treatment

B6. If medical or other treatment is likely to cure an impairment, so that recurrence of its effects would then be unlikely even if there were no further treatment, this should be taken into consideration when looking at the likelihood of recurrence of those effects. However, as **Section A** describes, if the treatment simply delays or prevents a recurrence, and a recurrence would be likely if the treatment stopped, then the treatment is to be ignored and the effect is to be regarded as likely to recur.

Meaning of "likely"

B7. It is *likely* that an event will happen if it is more probable than not that it will happen.

B8. In assessing the likelihood of an effect lasting for any period, account should be taken of the total period for which the effect exists. This includes any time before the point when the discriminatory behaviour occurred as well as time afterwards. Account should also be taken of both the typical length of such an effect on an individual, and any relevant factors specific to this individual (for example, general state of health, age).

Assessing whether a past disability was long-term

B9. *The Act provides that* a person who has had a disability within the definition is protected from discrimination even if he or she has since recovered or the effects have become less than substantial. In deciding whether a past condition was a disability, its effects count as long-term if they lasted twelve months or more after the first occurrence, or if a recurrence happened or continued until more than twelve months after the first occurrence *(S2, Sch. 2, Para. 5).*

C Normal day-to-day activities

Meaning of "normal day-to-day activities"

C1. *The Act states* that an impairment must have a long-term substantial adverse effect on normal day-to-day activities *(S1)*.

C2. The term "normal day-to-day activities" is not intended to include activities which are normal only for a particular person or group of people. Therefore in deciding whether an activity is a "normal day-to-day activity" account should be taken of how far it is normal for most people and carried out by most people on a daily or frequent and fairly regular basis.

C3. The term "normal day-to-day activities" does not, for example, include work of any particular form, because no particular form of work is "normal" for most people. In any individual case, the activities carried out might be highly specialised. The same is true of playing a particular game, taking part in a particular hobby, playing a musical instrument, playing sport, or performing a highly skilled task. Impairments which affect only such an activity and have no effect on "normal day-to-day activities" are not covered. The examples included in this section give an indication of what are to be taken as normal day-to-day activities.

C4. *The Act states* that an impairment is only to be treated as affecting the person's ability to carry out *normal day-to-day activities* if it affects one of the following:
— mobility;
— manual dexterity;
— physical co-ordination;
— continence;
— ability to lift, carry or otherwise move everyday objects;
— speech, hearing or eyesight;
— memory or ability to concentrate, learn or understand; or
— perception of the risk of physical danger *(Sch. 1, Para. 4)*.

C5. In many cases an impairment will adversely affect the person's ability to carry out a range of normal day-to-day activities and it will be obvious that the overall adverse effect is substantial or the effect on at least one normal day-to-day activity is substantial. In such a case it is unnecessary to consider precisely how the person is affected in each of the respects listed in paragraph C4. For example, a person with a clinically well-recognised mental illness may experience an adverse effect on concentration which prevents the person from remembering why he or she is going somewhere; the person would not also have to demonstrate that there was an effect on, say, speech. A person with an impairment which has an adverse effect on sight might be unable to go shopping unassisted; he or she would not also have to demonstrate that there was an effect on, say, mobility.

C6. Many impairments will, by their nature, adversely affect a person directly in one of the respects listed in C4. An impairment may also indirectly affect a person in one or more of these respects, and this should be taken into account when assessing whether the impairment falls within the definition. For example:
— medical advice: where a person has been professionally advised to change, limit or refrain from a normal day-to-day activity on account of an impairment or only do it in a certain way or under certain conditions;
— pain or fatigue: where an impairment causes pain or fatigue in performing normal day-to-day activities, so the person may have the capacity to do something but suffer pain in doing so; or the impairment might make the activity more than usually fatiguing so that the person might not be able to repeat the task over a sustained period of time.

C7. Where a person has a mental illness such as depression account should be taken of whether, although that person has the physical ability to perform a task, he or she is, in practice, unable to sustain an activity over a reasonable period.

C8. Effects of impairments may not be apparent in babies and young children because they are too young to have developed the ability to act in the respects listed in C4. *Regulations provide* that where an impairment to a child under six years old does not have an effect in any of the respects in C4, it is to be treated as having a substantial and long-term adverse effect on the ability of that child to carry out normal day-to-day activities where it would normally have a substantial and long-term adverse effect on the ability of a person aged six years or over to carry out normal day-to-day activities (Definition Regulations).

C9. In deciding whether an effect on the ability to carry out a normal day-to-day activity is a substantial adverse effect, account should be taken of factors such as those mentioned under each heading below. The headings are exhaustive—the person must be affected in one of these respects. The lists of examples are not exhaustive; they are only meant to be illustrative. The assumption is made in each example that there is an adverse effect on the person's ability to carry out normal day-to-day activities. A person only counts as disabled if the substantial effect is adverse.

C10. The examples below of what it would, and what it would not, be reasonable to regard as substantial adverse effects are indicators and not tests. They do not mean that if a person can do an activity instead then he or she does not experience any substantial adverse effects; the person may be inhibited in other actitivies, and this instead may indicate a substantial effect.

C11. In reading examples of effects which it would not be reasonable to regard as substantial, the effect described should be thought of as if it were the only effect of the impairment. That is, if the effect listed in the example were the only effect it would not be reasonable to regard it as substantial in itself.

C12. Examples of effects which are obviously within the definition are not included below. So for example, inability to dress oneself, inability to stand up, severe dyslexia or a severe speech impairment would clearly be covered by the definition and are not included among the examples below. The purpose of these lists is to provide help in cases where there may be doubt as to whether the effects on normal day-to-day activities are substantial.

C13. The examples below describe the effect which would occur when the various factors described in Parts A and B above have been allowed for. This includes, for example, the effects of a person making such modifications of behaviour as might reasonably be expected, or of disregarding the impact of medical or other treatment.

Mobility

C14. This covers moving or changing position in a wide sense. Account should be taken of the extent to which, because of either a physical or a mental condition, a person is inhibited in getting around unaided or using a normal means of transport, in leaving home with or without assistance, in walking a short distance, climbing stairs, travelling in a car or completing a journey on public transport, sitting, standing, bending, or reaching, or getting around in an unfamiliar place.

Examples

It *would be reasonable* to regard as having a substantial adverse effect:
- inability to travel a short journey as a passenger in a vehicle;
- inability to walk other than at a slow pace or with unsteady or jerky movements;

— difficulty in going up or down steps, stairs or gradients;
— inability to use one or more forms of public transport;
— inability to go out of doors unaccompanied.

It *would not be reasonable* to regard as having a substantial adverse effect:
— difficulty walking unaided a distance of about 1.5 kilometres or a mile without discomfort or having to stop—the distance in question would obviously vary according to the age of the person concerned and the type of terrain;
— inability to travel in a car for a journey lasting more than two hours without discomfort.

Manual dexterity

C15. This covers the ability to use hands and fingers with precision. Account should be taken of the extent to which a person can manipulate the fingers on each hand or co-ordinate the use of both hands together to do a task. This includes the ability to do things like pick up or manipulate small objects, operate a range of equipment manually, or communicate through writing or typing on standard machinery. Loss of function in the dominant hand would be expected to have a greater effect than equivalent loss in the non-dominant hand.

Examples

It *would be reasonable* to regard as having a substantial adverse effect:
— loss of function in one or both hands such that the person cannot use the hand or hands;
— inability to handle a knife and fork at the same time;
— ability to press the buttons on keyboards or keypads but only much more slowly than is normal for most people.

It *would not be reasonable* to regard as having a substantial adverse effect:
— inability to undertake activities requiring delicate hand movements, such as threading a small needle;
— inability to reach typing speeds standardised for secretarial work;
— inability to pick up a single small item, such as a pin.

Physical co-ordination

C16. This covers balanced and effective interaction of body movement, including hand and eye co-ordination. In the case of a child, it is necessary to take account of the level of achievement which would be normal for a person of the particular age. In any case, account should be taken of the ability to carry out "composite" activities such as walking and using hands at the same time.

Examples

It *would be reasonable* to regard as having a substantial adverse effect:
— ability to pour liquid into another vessel only with unusual slowness or concentration;
— inability to place food into one's own mouth with fork/spoon without unusual concentration or assistance.

It *would not be reasonable* to regard as having a substantial adverse effect:
— mere clumsiness;
— inability to catch a tennis ball.

Continence

C17. This covers the ability to control urination and/or defecation. Account should be taken of the frequency and extent of the loss of control and the age of the individual.

Examples

It *would be reasonable* to regard as having a substantial adverse effect:
— even infrequent loss of control of the bowels;
— loss of control of the bladder while asleep at least once a month;
— frequent minor faecal incontinence or frequent minor leakage from the bladder.

It *would not be reasonable* to regard as having a substantial adverse effect:
— infrequent loss of control of the bladder while asleep;
— infrequent minor leakage from the bladder.

Ability to lift, carry or otherwise move everyday objects

C18. Account should be taken of a person's ability to repeat such functions or, for example, to bear weights over a reasonable period of time. Everyday objects might include such items as books, a kettle or water, bags of shopping, a briefcase, an overnight bag, a chair or other piece of light furniture.

Examples

It *would be reasonable* to regard as having a substantial adverse effect:
— inability to pick up objects of moderate weight with one hand;
— inability to carry a moderately loaded tray steadily.

It *would not be reasonable* to regard as having a substantial adverse effect:
— inability to carry heavy luggage without assistance;
— inability to move heavy objects without a mechanical aid.

Speech, hearing or eyesight

C19. This covers the ability to speak, hear or see and includes face-to-face, telephone and written communication.

(i) Speech

Account should be taken of how far a person is able to speak clearly at a normal pace and rhythm and to understand someone else speaking normally in the person's native language. It is necessary to consider any effects on speech patterns or which impede the acquisition or processing of one's native language, for example by someone who has had a stroke.

Examples

It *would be reasonable* to regard as having a substantial adverse effect:
— inability to give clear basic instructions orally to colleagues or providers of a service;
— inability to ask specific questions to clarify instructions;
— taking significantly longer than average to say things.

It *would not be reasonable* to regard as having a substantial adverse effect:
— inability to articulate fluently due to a minor stutter, lisp or speech impediment;
— inability to speak in front of an audience;
— having a strong regional or foreign accent;
— inability to converse in a language which is not the speaker's native language.

(ii) Hearing

If a person uses a hearing aid or similar device, what needs to be considered is the effect that would be experienced if the person were not using the hearing aid or device. Account should be taken of effects where the level of background noise is within such a range and of such a type that most people would be able to hear adequately.

Examples

It *would be reasonable* to regard as having a substantial adverse effect:
— inability to hold a conversation with someone talking in a normal voice in a moderately noisy environment;
— inability to hear and understand another person speaking clearly over the voice telephone.

It *would not be reasonable* to regard as having a substantial adverse effect:
— inability to hold a conversation in a very noisy place, such as a factory floor;
— inability to sing in tune.

(iii) Eyesight

If a person's sight is corrected by spectacles or contact lenses, or could be corrected by them, what needs to be considered is the effect remaining while they are wearing such spectacles or lenses, in light of a level and type normally acceptable to most people for normal day-to-day activities.

Examples

It *would be reasonable* to regard as having a substantial adverse effect:
— inability to see to pass the eyesight test for a standard driving test;
— inability to recognise by sight a known person across a moderately-sized room;
— total inability to distinguish colours;
— inability to read ordinary newsprint;
— inability to walk safely without bumping into things.

It *would not be reasonable* to regard as having a substantial adverse effect:
— inability to read very small or indistinct print without the aid of a magnifying glass;
— inability to distinguish a known person across a substantial distance (*e.g.* playing field);
— inability to distinguish between red and green.

Memory or ability to concentrate, learn or understand

C20. Account should be taken of the person's ability to remember, organise his or her thoughts, plan a course of action and carry it out, take in new knowledge, or understand spoken or written instructions. This includes considering whether the person learns to do things significantly more slowly than is normal. Account should be taken of whether the person has persistent and significant difficulty in reading text in standard English or straightforward numbers.

Examples

It *would be reasonable* to regard as having a substantial adverse effect:
— intermittent loss of consciousness and associated confused behaviour;
— persistent inability to remember the names of familiar people such as family or friends;
— inability to adapt after a reasonable period to minor change in work routine;
— inability to write a cheque without assistance;
— considerable difficulty in following a short sequence such as a simple recipe or a brief list of domestic tasks.

It *would not be reasonable* to regard as having a substantial adverse effect:
— occasionally forgetting the name of a familiar person, such as a colleague;
— inability to concentrate on a task requiring application over several hours;

— inability to fill in a long, detailed, technical document without assistance;
— inability to read at faster than normal speed;
— minor problems with writing or spelling.

Perception of the risk of physical danger

C21. This includes both the underestimation and overestimation of physical danger, including danger to well-being. Account should be taken, for example, of whether the person is inclined to neglect basis functions such as eating, drinking, sleeping, keeping warm or personal hygiene; reckless behaviour which puts the person or others at risk; or excessive avoidance behaviour without a good cause.

Examples

It *would be reasonable* to regard as having a substantial adverse effect:
— inability to operate safely properly-maintained equipment;
— persistent inability to cross a road safely;
— inability to nourish oneself (assuming nourishment is available);
— inability to tell by touch that an object is very hot or cold.
It *would not be reasonable* to regard as having a substantial adverse effect:
— fear of significant heights;
— underestimating the risk associated with dangerous hobbies, such as mountain climbing;
— underestimating risks—other than obvious ones—in unfamiliar workplaces.

APPENDIX 4

DISABLED PERSONS

THE DISABILITY DISCRIMINATION (SUB-LEASES AND SUB-TENANCIES) REGULATIONS 1996

(S.I. 1996 No. 1333)

Made	-	-	-	-	-	*17th May 1996*
Laid before Parliament						*17th May 1996*
Coming into force						*7th June 1996*

GENERAL NOTE

These Regulations (the "Sub-leases and Sub-tenancies Regulations") are made under s. 16 and Sched. 4 of the 1995 Act; they provide that where an occupier of premises occupies those premises under a sub-lease or sub-tenancy, any consent to an alteration of those premises must be sought from the occupier's immediate landlord rather than from the superior landlord. The occupier's immediate landlord will be deemed to have withheld his consent to an alteration unless he notifies the occupier that consent will be given if the superior landlord agrees, and he applies to the superior landlord seeking consent to the alteration: see the Employment Regulations 1996, S.I. 1996 No. 1456, reg. 11(2)(b). Where the immediate landlord makes an application to the superior landlord, the provisions in s. 16 of the Act, including the requirements not to withhold consent unreasonably and not to attach unreasonable conditions to the consent, then apply to the superior landlord (reg. 4, inserting a new s. 16(2A)).

In exercise of the powers conferred on the Secretary of State by section 16(3) of and paragraph 4 of Schedule 4 to the Disability Discrimination Act 1955 (c. 50. For the meaning of "prescribed" and "regulations" see section 68(1). Apart from the cited provisions, section 16 and Schedule 4 are not yet in force) the Secretary of State for Education and Employment hereby makes the following Regulations:

Citation and commencement

1.—(1) These Regulations may be cited as the Disability Discrimination (Sub-leases and Sub-tenancies) Regulations 1996 and shall come into force on 7th June 1996.

Interpretation

2. In these Regulations "the Act" means the Disability Discrimination Act 1995.

Definition of sub-lease and sub-tenancy

3. For the purposes of section 16 of the Act "sub-lease" means any sub-term created out of or deriving from a leasehold interest and "sub-tenancy" means any tenancy created out of or deriving from a superior tenancy.

Modification of section 16 and paragraph 1 of Schedule 4

4. Where the occupier occupies premises under a sub-lease or sub-tenancy the following modifications and additions shall have effect—

   (a) (subject to paragraph (b) below), section 16 of and paragraph 1 of Schedule 4 to the Act are modified so that for references to "lessor" there are substituted references to the lessor who is the occupier's immediate landlord;

   (b) the following subsection is added to follow section 16(2) of the Act:

"(2A) Except to the extent to which it expressly so provides, any superior lease under which the premises are held shall have effect in relation to the lessor and lessee who are parties to that lease as if it provided—

50–185

    (i) for the lessee to have to make a written application to the lessor for consent to the alteration;

   (ii) if such an application is made, for the lessor not to withhold his consent unreasonably; and

  (iii) for the lessor to be entitled to make his consent subject to reasonable conditions.";

 (c) paragraphs 2 and 3 of Schedule 4 to the Act are modified so that references to "lessor" include any superior landlord.

Henley
Minister of State,
Department for Education and Employment

17th May 1996

EXPLANATORY NOTE

(This note is not part of the Order)

These Regulations modify and supplement the provisions of section 16 of and Schedule 4 to the Disability Discrimination Act 1995 in relation to cases where premises are occupied under a sub-lease or sub-tenancy. Section 16 and paragraph 1 of Schedule 4 are modified so that "lessor" refers to the occupier's immediate landlord. The effect of this is that any consent to alterations has to be sought from the immediate landlord rather than a superior landlord.

Section 16 is also supplemented to cover the position with regard to the obligations of lessors and lessees under superior leases and tenancies.

Schedule 4 paragraph 2 (joining lessors in industrial tribunal proceedings) and paragraph 3 (regulation making power) are modified so that references to the lessor include any superior landlord.

The Regulations define sub-lease and sub-tenancy for the purposes of section 16.

APPENDIX 5

DISABLED PERSONS

THE DISABILITY DISCRIMINATION (MEANING OF DISABILITY) REGULATIONS 1996

(S.I. 1996 No. 1455)

Made - - - - -	*4th June 1996*
Laid before Parliament	*6th June 1996*
Coming into force	*30th July 1996*

GENERAL NOTE

These Regulations (the "Definition Regulations") are made under Sched. 1 of the 1995 Act; they exclude certain conditions from the scope of the definition of disability, and make provision for babies and young children.

Regulations 3 and 4 provide that the following conditions are not to be regarded as impairments for the purposes of the Act: addiction to or dependency on alcohol, nicotine or any other substance not medically prescribed; a tendency to set fires (pyromania); a tendency to steal (kleptomania); a tendency to physical or sexual abuse of others; exhibitionism; voyeurism; and seasonal allergic rhinitis (hayfever), unless it aggravates the effect of another condition.

Regulation 5 provides that disfigurements which consist of a tattoo or non-medical body piercing are to be treated as not having a substantial adverse effect on the ability of a person to carry out normal day-to-day activities.

Regulation 6 provides that where a child under the age of six has an impairment which does not have an effect on normal day-to-day activities on account of the child's age, the impairment will be treated as having a substantial and long-term adverse effect where it would normally have such an effect on the ability of a person aged six years or over to carry out normal day-to-day activities.

In exercise of the powers conferred on the Secretary of State by paragraphs 1(2), 2(4), 3(2) and (3), 4(2)(a) and 5(a) of Schedule 1 to the Disability Discrimination Act 1995 (c. 50. For the meaning of "prescribed" and of "regulations" see section 68), the Secretary of State for Social Security hereby makes the following Regulations:

Citation and commencement

1. These Regulations may be cited as the Disability Discrimination (Meaning of Disability) Regulations 1996 and shall come into force on 30th July 1996.

Interpretation

2. In these Regulations—
"the Act" means the Disability Discrimination Act 1995; and
"addiction" includes a dependency.

Addictions

3.—(1) Subject to paragraph (2) below, addiction to alcohol, nicotine or any other substance is to be treated as not amounting to an impairment for the purposes of the Act.

(2) Paragraph (1) above does not apply to addiction which was originally the result of administration of medically prescribed drugs or other medical treatment.

Other conditions not to be treated as impairments

4.—(1) For the purposes of the Act the following conditions are to be treated as not amounting to impairments:
(a) a tendency to set fires,

(b) a tendency to steal,
(c) a tendency to physical or sexual abuse of other persons,
(d) exhibitionism, and
(e) voyeurism.

(2) Subject to paragraph (3) below for the purposes of the Act the condition known as seasonal allergic rhinitis shall be treated as not amounting to an impairment.

(3) Paragraph (2) above shall not prevent that condition from being taken into account for the purposes of the Act where it aggravates the effect of another condition.

Tattoos and piercings

5. For the purposes of paragraph 3 of Schedule 1 to the Act a severe disfigurement is not to be treated as having a substantial adverse effect on the ability of the person concerned to carry out normal day-to-day activities if it consists of—
(a) a tattoo (which has not been removed), or
(b) a piercing of the body for decorative or other non-medical purposes, including any object attached through the piercing for such purposes.

Babies and Young Children

6. For the purposes of the Act where a child under six years of age has an impairment which does not have an effect falling within paragraph 4(1) of Schedule 1 to the Act that impairment is to be taken to have a substantial and long-term adverse effect on the ability of that child to carry out normal day-to-day activities where it would normally have a substantial and long-term adverse effect on the ability of a person aged 6 years or over to carry out normal day-to-day activities.

Alistair Burt
Minister of State,
4th June 1996   Department of Social Security

EXPLANATORY NOTE

(This note is not part of the Regulations)

Section 1 of the Disability Discrimination Act 1995 provides that, subject to Schedule 1, a person has a disability if he has a physical or mental impairment which has a substantial and long-term adverse effect on his ability to carry out normal day-to-day activities.

These Regulations (made under Schedule 1) have the effect of excluding from the scope of the definition:
(a) addictions (other than those medically caused) (regulation 3),
(b) certain personality disorders (regulation 4(1)) and
(c) hayfever and similar conditions (regulation 4(2)).

Regulation 5 excludes tattoos and piercings. These might otherwise amount to severe disfigurements falling within paragraph 3 of Schedule 1.

The effect of regulation 6 is that a child under six is treated as if he were six or over for the purposes of determining the effect of his disability.

APPENDIX 6

DISABLED PERSONS

THE DISABILITY DISCRIMINATION (EMPLOYMENT) REGULATIONS 1996

(S.I. 1996 No. 1456)

Made - - - - -	*6th June 1996*
Laid before Parliament	*6th June 1996*
Coming into force	*2nd December 1996*

GENERAL NOTE

These Regulations (the "Employment Regulations") are made under Pt. II of the 1995 Act; they provide for a number of circumstances where the less favourable treatment of a disabled employee, or a failure to make adjustments to premises, is deemed to be justified.

Regulation 3 provides that where the employer operates a performance-related pay scheme, less favourable treatment of a disabled person which results from such a scheme may be justified, provided the scheme applies equally to all of the employer's employees, or to a class of employees which includes the disabled person.

Regulation 4 provides that an employer is justified in treating a disabled person less favourably in applying the eligibility conditions for benefits under an occupational pension scheme where, on account of the disabled person's disability, the cost of providing such a benefit is likely to be substantially greater than it would be for a person without the disability. Regulation 5 provides that if the employer imposes a uniform rate of contribution to an occupation pension scheme, the employer is justified in applying it to a disabled person, even if that person is not eligible to receive the same level of benefits under the scheme as an employee who is not disabled.

Regulation 8 provides that where a building was constructed in accordance with the requirements of Pt. M of the Building Regulations concerning access and facilities for disabled people, the duty to make reasonable adjustments to a physical feature of the employer's premises does not apply to any physical characteristic of the building which was adopted in order to meet those requirements, and which still complies with the requirements which were in force at the time the building works were carried out.

Regulation 9 defines physical features of premises for the purposes of the duty to make reasonable adjustments.

Regulations 11 to 15 deal with the position where the employer's premises are held under a lease or tenancy. Regulation 11 provides that a landlord will be deemed to have withheld his consent to an alteration to leased premises where he fails to reply within 21 days (or a further reasonable period) to a written application for consent to make the alteration; for the position where the employer occupies the premises under a sub-lease or sub-tenancy, see the note to the Sub-Leases and Sub-Tenancies Regulations 1996, S.I. 1996 No. 1333. Regulations 12 and 13 provide that the withholding of consent to an alteration by a landlord will be deemed to be reasonable or unreasonable in certain specified circumstances; and reg. 14 specifies certain conditions which it would be reasonable for a landlord to impose when giving his consent to alterations, *e.g.* requiring the employer to obtain planning permission, to submit plans to the landlord for approval, to allow the landlord a reasonable opportunity to inspect the work, etc.

In exercise of the powers conferred on the Secretary of State by sections 5(6) and (7), 6(8)(a), (c) to (g) and (10), 12(3) of and paragraph 3(a) and (b) of Schedule 4 to the Disability Discrimination Act 1995 (c. 50. For the meaning of "prescribed" and of "regulations" see section 68. Paragraph 3 of Schedule 4 is modified (where premises are occupied under a sublease or subtenancy) by S.I. 1996/1333) the Secretary of State for Education and Employment hereby makes the following Regulations:

Citation and commencement

1. These Regulations may be cited as the Disability Discrimination (Employment) Regulations 1996 and shall come into force on 2nd December 1996.

Interpretation

2. In these Regulations—
"the Act" means the Disability Discrimination Act 1995;
"binding obligation" means a legally binding obligation (not contained in a lease) in relation to the premises whether arising from an agreement or otherwise;
"building" means an erection or structure of any kind;
"building regulations" has the meaning given by section 122 of the Building Act 1984 (c. 55);
"lease" has the meaning assigned by section 16(3) of the Act;
"pay" means remuneration of any kind including any benefit;
"performance" includes performance as assessed by reference to any measure, whether relative or absolute, of output, efficiency or effectiveness in an employment;
"section 6 duty" means any duty imposed by or under section 6 of the Act;
"Technical Standards" means the technical standards for compliance with the Building Standards (Scotland) Regulations 1990 (S.I. 1990/2179) issued by the Scottish Office in 1990 and as amended by the substitute pages issued by the Scottish Office in and dated July 1993 and July 1994 (these amendments to the Technical Standards were given effect to by S.I. 1993/1457 and S.I. 1994/1266).

Pay

3.—(1) For the purposes of section 5 of the Act, treatment is to be taken to be justified if it results from applying to the disabled person a term or practice—
(a) under which the amount of a person's pay is wholly or partly dependent on that person's performance; and
(b) which is applied to all of the employer's employees or to all of a class of his employees which includes the disabled person but which is not defined by reference to any disability.

(2) Arrangements consisting of the application to a disabled person of a term or practice of the kind referred to in paragraph (1) above are not to be taken to place that disabled person at a substantial disadvantage of the kind mentioned in section 6(1) of the Act.

(3) Nothing in this regulation affects the operation of section 6 of the Act in relation to any arrangements or physical features of premises which, by placing a disabled person at a substantial disadvantage, cause reduced performance by him.

Occupational pension schemes

4.—(1) For the purposes of section 5(1) of the Act less favourable treatment of a disabled person is to be taken to be justified in the circumstances described in paragraph (2) below if it results from applying the eligibility conditions set for receiving any benefit referred to in paragraph (3) below or from determining the amount of any such benefit.

(2) The circumstances are that by reason of the disabled person's disability (including any clinical prognosis flowing from the disability) the cost of providing any benefit referred to in paragraph (3) below is likely to be substantially greater than it would be for a comparable person without that disability.

(3) The benefits are those provided under an occupational pension scheme in respect of any of the following:
(a) termination of service;
(b) retirement, old age or death; or
(c) accident, injury, sickness or invalidity.

Uniform rates of contributions

5. For the purposes of section 5 of the Act, treatment is always to be taken to be justified if an employer requires from a disabled person the same rate of contribution to an occupational pension scheme as he requires from his other employees (or from any class of his employees which includes the disabled person but which is not defined by reference to any disability), notwithstanding that the disabled person is not eligible under that scheme, for a reason related to his disability, to receive a benefit or to receive a benefit at the same rate as a comparable person to whom that reason does not apply.

Agricultural wages

6. For the purposes of section 5 of the Act—
- (a) treatment of a disabled person is to be taken to be justified to the extent that the treatment relates to a matter within the terms and conditions of a permit granted to that person under section 5 of the Agricultural Wages Act 1948 (c. 47) or section 5 of the Agricultural Wages (Scotland) Act 1949 (c. 30) (permits to incapacitated persons) and accords with those terms and conditions, and
- (b) failure to take a step otherwise required to comply with a section 6 duty is to be taken to be justified if that step would relate to a matter within the terms and conditions of the permit referred to in (a) above but would exceed the requirements of those terms and conditions.

Contract Work

7.—(1) Paragraph (2) below applies for the purposes of section 6 of the Act (and that section as applied by section 12(3) of the Act) where a contract worker is likely to be placed at a similar substantial disadvantage by arrangements made by or on behalf of, or premises occupied by, all or most of the principals to whom he is or might be supplied.

(2) It is reasonable for the employer to have to take such steps as are within his power as it would be reasonable for him to have to take if the arrangements were made by him or on his behalf or, as the case may be, the premises were occupied by him.

(3) For the purposes of section 6 of the Act (and that section as applied by section 12(3) of the Act) it is not reasonable for any principal to whom a contract worker is supplied to have to take any step which it is reasonable for the employer to have to take pursuant to paragraph (2) above or otherwise.

Building Regulations

8.—(1) This regulation applies only to a physical characteristic included within building works which—
- (a) was adopted with a view to meeting the requirements for the time being of—
    - (i) (in England and Wales) Part M of the building regulations (the Regulations currently in force are the Building Regulations 1991 (S.I. 1991/2768). Schedule 1 contains Part M. Part M was originally introduced by the Building (Disabled People) Regulations 1987 (S.I. 1987/1445)), and
    - (ii) (in Scotland) Part T of the Technical Standards,
    with regard to access and facilities for disabled people, and
- (b) met those requirements at the time the building works were carried out and continues substantially to meet those requirements which applied at the time the building works were carried out.

(2) For the purposes of section 6(1) of the Act it is never reasonable for an employer to have to take steps in relation to a disabled person to the extent

that this would involve altering any physical characteristic to which this regulation applies.

Physical features

9. For the purposes of section 6(1) of the Act the following are to be treated as physical features (whether permanent or temporary)—

(a) any feature arising from the design or construction of a building on the premises;

(b) any feature on the premises of any approach to, exit from or access to such a building;

(c) any fixtures, fittings, furnishings, furniture, equipment or materials in or on the premises;

(d) any other physical element or quality of any land comprised in the premises.

Consent to an adjustment

10.—(1) For the purposes of section 6(1) of the Act where under any binding obligation the employer is required to obtain the consent of any person to any alteration of the premises occupied by him it is always reasonable for the employer to have to take steps to obtain that consent and it is never reasonable for the employer to have to make that alteration before that consent is obtained.

(2) The steps referred to in paragraph (1) above shall not be taken to include an application to a court or tribunal.

Lessor withholding consent

11.—(1) For the purposes of section 16 of and Part I of Schedule 4 to the Act a lessor is to be taken to have withheld his consent to an alteration where he has received a written application by or on behalf of the occupier for consent to make the alteration and has failed to meet the requirements specified in paragraph (2) below.

(2) The requirements are that the lessor within a period of 21 days (beginning with the day on which he receives the application referred to in paragraph (1) above) or such longer period as is reasonable—

(a) replies consenting to or refusing the application, or

(b) (i) replies consenting to the application subject to obtaining the consent of another person required under a superior lease or pursuant to a binding obligation, and

(ii) seeks that consent.

(3) A lessor who fails to meet the requirements in paragraph (2) above but who subsequently meets those requirements (except as to time)—

(a) shall be taken to have withheld his consent from the date of such failure, and

(b) shall be taken not to have withheld his consent from the time he met those requirements (except as to time).

(4) For the purposes of this regulation, a lessor is to be treated as not having sought another person's consent unless he has applied in writing to that person, indicating—

(i) that the lessor's consent to the alteration has been applied for in order to comply with a section 6 duty, and

(ii) that he has given his consent conditionally upon obtaining the other person's consent.

Lessor withholding consent unreasonably

12. For the purposes of section 16 of and Part I of Schedule 4 to the Act, a lessor is to be taken to have withheld his consent unreasonably where—

(a) the lease provides that consent shall or will be given to an alteration of the kind in question; or

(b) the lease provides that consent shall or will be given to an alteration of the kind in question if the consent is sought in a particular way and the consent has been sought in that way; or

(c) the lessor is to be taken to have withheld his consent by virtue of regulation 11 above.

Lessor withholding consent reasonably

13.—(1) For the purposes of section 16 of and Part I of Schedule 4 to the Act a lessor is to be taken to have acted reasonably in withholding his consent where—

(a) there is a binding obligation requiring the consent of any person to the alteration;

(b) he has taken steps to seek that consent; and

(c) that consent has not been given or has been given subject to a condition making it reasonable for him to withhold his consent.

(2) For the purposes of section 16 of and Part I of Schedule 4 to the Act a lessor is to be taken to have acted reasonably in withholding his consent where—

(a) he is bound by an agreement which allows him to consent to the alteration in question subject to a condition that he makes a payment, and

(b) that condition does not permit the lessor to make his own consent subject to a condition that the occupier reimburse him the payment.

Lessor's consent subject to conditions

14.—(1) For the purposes of section 16 of and Part I of Schedule 4 to the Act a condition subject to which a lessor has given his consent is to be taken to be reasonable in all circumstances if it is any of the following (or a condition to similar effect)—

(a) that the occupier must obtain any necessary planning permission and any other consent or permission required by or under any enactment;

(b) that the occupier must submit any plans or specifications for the alteration to the lessor for approval (provided that the condition binds the lessor not to withhold approval unreasonably) and that the work is carried out in accordance with such plans or specifications;

(c) that the lessor must be permitted a reasonable opportunity to inspect the work when completed; and

(d) that the occupier must repay to the lessor the costs reasonably incurred in connection with the giving of his consent.

(2) For the purposes of section 16 of and Part I of Schedule 4 to the Act in a case where it would be reasonable for the lessor to withhold consent, a condition that upon expiry of the lease the occupier (or any assignee or successor) must reinstate any relevant part of the premises which is to be altered to its state before the alteration was made is to be taken as reasonable.

Steps contrary to the terms of the lease

15. For the purposes of section 6 of the Act it is not reasonable for an employer to have to take a step in relation to premises occupied by him which would otherwise be required in order to comply with a section 6 duty and which is contrary to the terms of any lease under which he occupies those premises if—

(a) he has applied to the lessor in writing to take the step,
(b) he has indicated in writing that he proposes to take the step, subject to that consent, in order to comply with a section 6 duty,
(c) the lessor has withheld that consent, and
(d) the occupier has informed the disabled person that he has applied for the consent of the lessor and that the lessor has withheld it.

Henley
Minister of State,
6th June 1996   Department for Education and Employment

EXPLANATORY NOTE

(This note is not part of the Regulations)

These Regulations (made under the Disability Discrimination Act 1995) provide, among other things, for circumstances where treatment of a disabled employee (or a failure to make an adjustment to premises) is justified. These include:
(a) where pay is linked to performance (regulation 3);
(b) where there are uniform rates of contribution to an occupational pension scheme regardless of the benefits received (regulation 4);
(c) where building works complied with (and continue to comply with) the building regulations in relation to access and facilities for disabled people at the time the works were carried out (regulation 8).
Regulations 11 to 15 deal with the position where the employer's premises are held under a lease or tenancy.

APPENDIX 7

DISABLED PERSONS

THE DISABILITY DISCRIMINATION (SERVICES AND PREMISES)
REGULATIONS 1996

(S.I. 1996 No. 1836)

Made	-	-	-	-	-	15th July 1996
Laid before Parliament						*18th July 1996*
Coming into force						*2nd December 1996*

GENERAL NOTE

These Regulations (the "Services and Premises Regulations") are made under Pt. III of the 1995 Act; they provide for a number of circumstances where less favourable treatment of a disabled person in relation to the provision of services is deemed to be justified.

Regulation 2 provides that less favourable treatment of a disabled person in relation to the provision of insurance is justified if it is based on actuarial, statistical, medical or other information which is relevant to the assessment of the risk to be insured, and on which it is reasonable to rely; regs. 3 and 4 contain transitional provisions for existing insurance policies, and for policies which are derived from a general master policy.

Regulation 5 provides that less favourable treatment of a disabled person by a service provider in refusing to honour a guarantee to refund the price of unsatisfactory services, or to replace or repair unsatisfactory goods, will be justified if the item in respect of which the guarantee was provided has been damaged beyond the level at which the guarantee would normally be honoured, and the reason for the damage is related to the disabled person's disability; similar provision is made with regard to the refund of deposits provided by a disabled person in respect of the provision of goods or facilities (reg. 6) and the right to occupy premises (reg. 7).

Regulation 8 provides that s. 20(4)(b) of the 1995 Act, which provides that less favourable treatment of a disabled person may be justified if the disabled person is incapable of entering into an enforceable agreement or giving informed consent, will not apply where another person is legally acting on his or her behalf (*e.g.* under a power of attorney, or under the Mental Health Act 1983 (c. 20)).

Regulation 9 excludes from ss. 19 to 21 of the 1995 Act certain youth and community services provided by local education authorities or voluntary organisations, the provision of facilities for research, and some examination and assessment services.

The Secretary of State for Social Security, in exercise of the powers conferred by sections 19(5)(c), 20(7) and (8), 24(5), 67(2) and (3) and 68(1) of the Disability Discrimination Act 1995 (c. 50; section 68(1) is an interpretation provision and is cited for the definitions of "prescribed" and "regulations"), and of all other powers enabling him in that behalf, hereby makes the following Regulations:

Citation, commencement and interpretation

1.—(1) These Regulations may be cited as the Disability Discrimination (Services and Premises) Regulations 1996 and shall come into force on 2nd December 1996.

(2) In these Regulations—

"the Act" means the Disability Discrimination Act 1995;

"incepted" refers to the time when the liability to risk of an insurer under a policy of insurance commenced;

"insurance business" has the same meaning as in the Insurance Companies Act 1982 (c. 50);

"insurer" means an insurance company as defined in section 96 of the Insurance Companies Act 1982.

(3) In these Regulations, unless the context otherwise requires, a reference—

(a) to a numbered regulation is to the regulation in these Regulations bearing that number;

(b) in a regulation to a numbered paragraph is to the paragraph in that regulation bearing that number;

(c) in a paragraph to a lettered or numbered sub-paragraph is to the sub-paragraph in that paragraph bearing that letter or number.

Circumstances in which less favourable treatment is justified: insurance

2.—(1) Where, for a reason which relates to the disabled person's disability, a provider of services treats a disabled person less favourably than he treats or would treat others to whom that reason does not or would not apply, that treatment shall be taken to be justified for the purposes of section 20 of the Act in the circumstances specified in paragraph (2).

(2) The circumstances referred to in paragraph (1) are that the less favourable treatment is—

(a) in connection with insurance business carried on by the provider of services;

(b) based upon information (for example, actuarial or statistical data or a medical report) which is relevant to the assessment of the risk to be insured and is from a source on which it is reasonable to rely; and

(c) reasonable having regard to the information relied upon and any other relevant factors.

Existing policies of insurance: transitional provisions

3.—(1) Subject to paragraph (2), and except where regulation 4 applies, where, for a reason which relates to the disabled person's disability, a provider of services treats a disabled person less favourably than he treats or would treat others to whom that reason does not or would not apply, that treatment shall be taken to be justified for the purposes of section 20 of the Act if the treatment is in connection with insurance business carried on by the provider of services and relates to an existing policy.

(2) Subject to paragraph (3), where an existing policy is due to be renewed, or the terms of such a policy are due to be reviewed, on or after 2nd December 1996, any less favourable treatment which occurs on or after the date that the review or renewal is due shall not be taken to be justified under paragraph (1).

(3) A review of an existing policy which is part of, or incidental to, a general reassessment by the provider of services of the pricing structure for a group of policies shall not be treated as a review for the purposes of paragraph (2).

(4) In this regulation "an existing policy" means a policy of insurance which incepted before 2nd December 1996.

Cover documents and master policies: transitional provisions

4.—(1) Subject to paragraphs (2) and (3), where, for a reason which relates to the disabled person's disability, a provider of services treats a disabled person less favourably than he treats or would treat others to whom that reason does not or would not apply, that treatment shall be taken to be justified for the purposes of section 20 of the Act if the treatment is in connection with insurance business carried on by the provider of services and—

(a) results in a refusal to issue a cover document to or in respect of the disabled person, and the refusal occurs before 2nd December 1997; or

(b) relates to a cover document which incepted before 2nd December 1997.

(2) Paragraph (1) does not apply in a case where—

(a) the relevant master policy was entered into or renewed on or after 2nd December 1996; or

(b) the terms of the relevant master policy were reviewed on or after 2nd December 1996, and for this purpose "the relevant master policy" means the master policy under which the cover document was issued, or under which a cover document would have been issued but for the refusal to issue it.

(3) Where a cover document is due to be renewed, or the terms of a cover document are due to be reviewed, on or after 2nd December 1997, any less favourable treatment which occurs on or after the date that the review or renewal is due shall not be taken to be justified under paragraph (1).

(4) In this regulation—

"cover document" means a certificate or policy issued under a master policy;

"master policy" means a contract between an insurer and another person under which that person is entitled to issue certificates or policies to individuals, and which details the terms on which that person may do so.

Circumstances in which less favourable treatment is justified: guarantees

5.—(1) Where, for a reason which relates to the disabled person's disability, a provider of services (the provision of "services" for these purposes includes the provision of any goods or facilities; see section 19(2)(a) of the Act) ("the provider") treats a disabled person less favourably than he treats or would treat others to whom that reason does not or would not apply, that treatment shall be taken to be justified for the purposes of section 20 of the Act in the circumstances specified in paragraph (2).

(2) The circumstances referred to in paragraph (1) are that—

  (a) the provider provides a guarantee (whether or not legally enforceable) that—

    (i) the purchase price of services that he has provided will be refunded if the services are not of satisfactory quality; or

    (ii) services in the form of goods that he has provided will be replaced or repaired if those goods are not of satisfactory quality; and

  (b) the provider refuses to provide a replacement, repair or refund under the guarantee because damage has occurred for a reason which relates to the disabled person's disability, and the damage is above the level at which the provider would normally provide a replacement, repair or refund under the guarantee; and

  (c) it is reasonable in all the circumstances of the case for the provider to refuse to provide a replacement, repair or refund under the guarantee.

(3) In this regulation "guarantee" includes any document having the effect referred to in paragraph (2)(a) whether or not that document is described as a guarantee by the provider.

Circumstances in which less favourable treatment is justified: deposits in respect of goods and facilities

6.—(1) Where, for a reason which relates to the disabled person's disability, a provider of services ("the provider") treats a disabled person less favourably than he treats or would treat others to whom that reason does not or would not apply, that treatment shall be taken to be justified for the purposes of section 20 of the Act in the circumstances specified in paragraph (2).

(2) The circumstances referred to in paragraph (1) are that—

  (a) when goods or facilities are provided, the disabled person is required to provide a deposit which is refundable if the goods or facilities are undamaged; and

  (b) the provider refuses to refund some or all of the deposit because damage has occurred to the goods or facilities for a reason which relates to the disabled person's disability, and the damage is above the level at which the provider would normally refund the deposit in full; and

(c) it is reasonable in all the circumstances of the case for the provider to refuse to refund the deposit in full.

Circumstances in which less favourable treatment is justified: deposits in respect of premises

7.—(1) Where, for a reason which relates to the disabled person's disability, a person with power to dispose of any premises ("the provider") treats a disabled person less favourably than he treats or would treat others to whom that reason does not or would not apply, that treatment shall be taken to be justified for the purposes of section 24 of the Act in the circumstances specified in paragraph (2).

(2) The circumstances referred to in paragraph (1) are that—

(a) the provider grants a disabled person a right to occupy premises (whether by means of a formal tenancy agreement or otherwise);

(b) in respect of that occupation the disabled person is required to provide a deposit which is refundable at the end of the occupation provided that the premises and contents are not damaged;

(c) the provider refuses to refund some or all of the deposit because the premises or contents have been damaged for a reason which relates to the disabled person's disability, and the damage is above the level at which the provider would normally refund the deposit in full; and

(d) it is reasonable in all the circumstances of the case for the provider to refuse to refund the deposit in full.

Mental incapacity

8. Section 20(4)(b) of the Act (treatment justified where disabled person is incapable of entering into an enforceable agreement or giving informed consent) shall not apply where a disabled person is acting through another person by virtue of—

(a) a power of attorney; or

(b) functions conferred by or under Part VII of the Mental Health Act 1983 (c. 20); or

(c) powers exercisable in Scotland in relation to the disabled person's property or affairs in consequence of the appointment of a curator bonis, tutor or judicial factor.

Exemption from sections 19 to 21 of the Act for certain educational services

9.—(1) Sections 19 to 21 of the Act shall not apply to the following services (insofar as they do not fall within section 19(5)(a) of the Act)—

(a) services provided by a local education authority in carrying out their functions under section 41 or 53 of the Education Act 1944 (c. 31; section 41 was substituted by section 11 of the Further and Higher Education Act 1992 (c. 13); section 53 was amended by Part I of Schedule 1 to the Education (Miscellaneous Provisions) Act 1948 (c. 40), Schedule 7 to the Education Act 1980 (c. 20) and paragraph 54 of Schedule 12 to the Education Reform Act 1988 (c. 40)), or by an education authority in carrying out their functions under section 1(3) of the Education (Scotland) Act 1980 (c. 44);

(b) the provision by a voluntary organisation of social, cultural and recreational activities and facilities for physical education and training, where such activities are designed to promote the personal or educational development of persons taking part in them;

(c) the provision of facilities for research (including the supervision of or guidance of research) at any relevant establishment;

(d) the assessment at a relevant establishment—
  (i) of pupils or students in connection with education provided to them by the establishment or by another relevant establishment; or
  (ii) of pupils or students to whom education has not been provided by the establishment where the assessment is undertaken as part of an assessment referred to in head (i) above.
(2) In this regulation "relevant establishment" means—
  (a) an establishment which is funded by a body mentioned in paragraphs (a) to (k) of section 19(6) of the Act or by a Minister of the Crown; or
  (b) an establishment referred to in section 19(5)(a)(ii) of the Act.

Signed by authority of the Secretary of State for Social Security.

Alistair Burt
Minister of State,
15th July 1996   Department of Social Security

EXPLANATORY NOTE

(This note is not part of the Regulations)

These regulations are made under the Disability Discrimination Act 1995, which makes it unlawful to discriminate against disabled persons. Sections 19 and 20 of the Act concern discrimination in relation to the provision of services, including the provision of goods and facilities, to the public. Section 20(1) of the Act states that a person who provides services discriminates against a disabled person if, for a reason relating to the disabled person's disability, he treats him less favourably than he treats others, and he cannot show that the treatment is justified. Section 20 contains powers to make regulations concerning circumstances when treatment shall be taken to be justified, and so will not constitute discrimination for the purposes of the Act.

These regulations make provision for treatment to be justified in specified circumstances. Firstly treatment is justified in relation to the provision of insurance, if it is based on certain factors and it is reasonable to rely on those factors (regulation 2). Transitional provision is also made for existing insurance policies; any treatment in relation to a policy which existed before these regulations came into force is automatically taken to be justified until such date as the policy is due to be reviewed or renewed (regulation 3). Further special transitional provision is made for insurance policies which are derived from a general master policy (regulation 4).

Secondly treatment is justified in relation to the provision of guarantees and deposits; a service provider will be justified in refusing to honour a guarantee or refund a deposit if the item in respect of which the guarantee or deposit was provided has been damaged beyond the level at which the guarantee would normally be honoured, or the deposit refunded, and the reason for the damage is related to the disabled person's disability (regulations 5 and 6).

The regulations also provide that sections 19 to 21 of the Act do not apply to certain youth and community services provided by education authorities or voluntary organisations, to the provision of facilities for research in certain circumstances or to some examination and assessment services (regulation 9).

Sections 22 to 24 of the Act concern discrimination in relation to premises. Section 24 makes similar provision to section 20 in relation to the definition of "discrimination" and the justification of treatment. The regulations provide that treatment may be justified where a landlord refuses to refund a deposit to a disabled person if the property that was occupied by the disabled person has been damaged beyond the level at which the deposit would normally be refunded, and the reason for the damage is related to the disabled person's disability (regulation 7).

The regulations also provide that the condition in section 20(4)(b) of the Act, which may allow treatment to be justified if the disabled person is incapable of entering into an agreement, will not apply where the disabled person is acting through an attorney or a person similarly acting on his behalf (regulation 8).

An assessment of the compliance costs for business has been made and a copy placed in the libraries of both Houses of Parliament. Copies can be obtained by post from the Disability Unit, the Department of Social Security, Room 6/13 The Adelphi, 1–11 John Adam Street, London WC2N 6HT.

INDEX

References are to the relevant section or Schedule of the Act or the page number of the Appendices. References to the commentary to the section or Schedule are denoted by the letter 'N'. Thus the reference s.35N is to the commentary to section 35 of the Act.

[1]